Strategic Management
An Introduction

Strategic Management
An Introduction

Ronald Rosen

PITMAN PUBLISHING
128 Long Acre, London WC2E 9AN

A Division of Pearson Professional Limited

First published in Great Britain in 1995

ISBN 0 273 61250 6

British Library Cataloguing in Publication Data

A CIP catalogue record for this book can be obtained from the British Library

10 9 8 7 6 5 4 3 2 1

Typeset by WestKey Ltd, Falmouth, Cornwall
Printed and bound in Great Britain by Clays Ltd, St Ives plc

The Publishers' policy is to use paper manufactured from sustainable forests.

CONTENTS

Preface vii

1 What is strategic management? **1**
Positioning • Strategy formulation

2 Influences on strategic management **11**
Environmental influences • Internal influences

3 What business are we in? **21**
The mission • Objectives • How are the mission and objectives determined? • Stakeholder analysis

4 The environment **33**
Monitoring the environment • Industry analysis • Life-cycles • Market-place analysis • The power of customers • The power of suppliers • Porter's five-force model • The macro-environment • PEST analysis

5 Analysing the organisation **46**
Analysing the organisation as a whole • The organisation in relation to its objectives • The organisation in relation to the environment

6 Structure **59**
The simple structure • The functional structure • The divisional structure • The multidivisional structure • The matrix structure • The holding company • The ad-hocracy or innovative organisation • The position of power

7 Culture and management style **69**
Culture • Classifications of culture • Management style • Organisational life-cycle • Business ethics

8 Strategic options **76**
Urgency and importance • The SWOT analysis • Creativity • Ansoff's product/market matrix

9 Money matters **87**
Profit • Costs • The experience curve • Costs and market share • PIMS • Differentiation • Porter's generic strategies • Interactions • Price • Sources of funds

10 Criteria for strategic choice **98**
Evaluation

11 Planning, implementation and control **106**
The relationship between planning, implementation and control • The influence of structure • Styles of control • The influence of culture • Implementation • Resistance to change • Planning Processes • Control processes • Means of control

12 The turbulent environment **118**
Environmental predictability • Environmental complexity • Environmental novelty • Predictability • Complexity • Novelty • Cross-impact analysis • Strategic issue management • Crisis management

13 Strategic planning **130**

14 Strategic planning worksheets **138**

Glossary 180

Index 188

PREFACE

The Managerial Revolution by James Burnham was published some 50 years ago and the author's thesis was: 'The control of the world is passing into the hands of the managers . . . The future governing class will not be the possessors of wealth, but the possessors of technical or administrative skill'. By this he was referring not merely to the boards of directors of multinationals, but to lesser managers as well.

The need to educate the second group – future administrators – in *strategic management* has long been recognised, but it is only relatively recently that employers, educators and students themselves have fully appreciated that such an understanding is just as important for the 'possessors of technical skill' such as students of engineering, hotel and catering, computer studies, science, languages, and professional studies. However, the needs of these students, their interests and the role of such a module within their courses are different from those of a business or management student. Furthermore, the time available is usually much shorter, and these factors should be reflected in the objectives, content and style of the module and the text they use.

Not dissimilar, are the needs of those MBA students faced with an advanced strategic management module, but who have not previously encountered the topic, and who, perhaps, come from a professional or technical background. This frequently presents problems, not only for the students but also in course design, when fellow students possess, for example, a BA (Business Studies), a DMS or have had an initiatory course.

An elementary book aimed at a lower level, or one which is primarily intended for practising managers whose needs and background are very different, or attempting to use the main course text are all unsatisfactory approaches. Even worse would be an introductory text that attempted to include, in condensed form, most of the important topics contained in a mega-page door-stopper. It is to fill that gap that this book was written. The aim is to meet the needs of both groups of students by providing a text with relatively short chapters which are easy to read, follow, absorb, and which maintain interest.

The book is in three sections; the first provides comprehensive coverage of relatively few classic theories, principles, models and concepts in order to ensure a thorough understanding of these fundamentals. MBA students will be studying the topic in greater depth, the others may not have the time (and possibly, because it is a peripheral topic, not the inclination) to assimilate what, at this level, could – brutally – be seen as academic and redundant clutter which obscures the essentials. On the other hand, it does present a full picture of the complexity of the processes of strategic management, the business environment and the interactions of forces within them. The text, although concentrating upon basics, does not oversimplify reality and recommended texts for pursuing topics in greater detail are provided at the ends of chapters.

Numerous, but brief, examples are included in order to illustrate specific points. The aim of this work is to provide an understanding of the context of the students' future career, the forces and processes acting in the workplace, on organisations and in their environment; it is *about* strategic management rather than *for* budding strategic managers.

Although many real-life examples have been incorporated, case studies have not been included; lecturers who incorporate case study analysis in the module will usually have their preferred cases appropriate to the nature of the students and the course.

When case studies are used on courses, the very comprehensive and largely self-contained Chapters 13 and 14 on strategic planning contain 15 pro forma worksheets and provide step-by-step guidance where necessary. These make no concessions to simplification and are equally suitable for case study analysis on more advanced or subsequent courses.

This separation of detailed strategic analysis from the main text on strategic management achieves greater overall clarity, reflecting the distinction both in theory and in practice between strategic management and business or strategic planning which is lacking in many texts.

One of the needs of a new student is to become familiar with the vocabulary of strategic management, which is extensive. To facilitate this, the book concludes with a Glossary which also lists several terms not dealt with in the text itself. (This will be of particular value to students whose first language is not English.)

Lecturers will also note certain terms which are used in a popular sense, but which also have a particular significance either in the context of strategic management or another subject. This provides the opportunity to refer to, revise, develop or ignore the underlying concept at their discretion.

The author is very much aware that what others may consider as important topics are omitted entirely or mentioned only in passing, but is nevertheless unrepentant in view of the aims of the book. As students – and particularly as lecturers – we have had the experience of great areas of study being completely forgotten within a matter of weeks. By limiting the scope of this book and concentrating on essentials, there is hope that if the managerial revolution finally comes, the 'future governing class' may retain some memories of it and, as a result, become better managers than their predecessors.

CHAPTER 1

What is strategic management?

Psycho-history dealt not with man but with man-masses . . . It could forecast reactions to stimuli with something of the accuracy that a lesser science could bring to the forecast of a rebound billiard ball.
Isaac Asimov, *Foundation and Empire*, prologue, Panther Books (1964)

Hari Seldon, in Asimov's classic science fiction trilogy 'plotted the social and economic trends of the time, sighted along the curves'. He predicted, 30 000 years into the future, and planned an Empire – strategic planning on a grand scale. Not bad for a solo strategic planner.

Asimov, a highly respected scientist, wrote at a time when the scientific approach appeared to hold out great promise, not merely in helping us to understand the world about us, but in providing solutions to its problems. This was reflected in the emphasis on strategic planning as the basis of management education and in the actual management of many organisations.

The adoption of planning at this organisational level paralleled that of planning the work of employees – scientific management – which developed at the turn of the century – although the lessons of mistakes made then, and since, were not learned. Over 80 years ago, an official American Senate subcommittee issued a devastating report on scientific management, commenting: 'So long, therefore, as industry continues to be the complex and diversified thing that it is, so long as it is in flux, developing continuously new products, new modes, new machinery and processes, and as long as productive concerns are required in order to survive, to adapt themselves quickly to fluctuating market demands, this element of economy will without doubt . . . retard the uniform development of ideals and technique in this connection. With such possibilities in view, neither in the present nor in the near future is there any reasonable ground for the sweeping . . . claims of scientific management . . .'

Since then, experience of strategic planning has exposed the weaknesses of managing an organisation largely on the basis of a rigid plan that is in turn based on forecasts of the future which, to a greater or lesser extent, must nearly always be wrong. Furthermore, the approach was frequently based on top-down, rational, objective, logical, *hard systems* thinking – often undertaken by corporate planners rather than by managers themselves and this tended to neglect uncomfortable *fuzzy factors*, particularly social and behavioural aspects that could not be quantified but which were often central to the problem, while complex problems were oversimplified in order to enable them to be coped with.

There was, for a time, a similar reaction to strategic planning as had occurred with scientific management. The pendulum has now swung back, and its important, but not dominant role, is now recognised – after all, it might be thought, what is the alternative? Well, there is one, and its implications are considered later. What is now seen as essential to the success of an organisation, in times that are at least as turbulent as when that report was written, is not a crystal ball and a computer model but an understanding of the complexity and requirements of management *at all levels*.

What then is strategic management if it is not basically strategic planning? The answer can be put very simply:

Running an organisation as a whole

This implies that the day-to-day management of an organisation – which usually occupies so much of a manager's time – is as essential to strategic success as weighty decisions concerning future strategy made in the board-room, and as relevant to a sole trader as to, say, running a national railway system. It may not matter very much, from the railway's point of view, that a particular train was dirty and late, unless an important and influential passenger was travelling on it, but what if trains are frequently dirty and late, losing business as a result? There could be many causes ranging from sloppy supervision at the lowest levels of management to lack of investment by the board; the loss of business could range from trivial to disastrous. Lord Weinstock, the Managing Director of GEC said 'Profit is something you get because you are doing things well'; there *is* no clear distinction between day-to-day management and strategic management.

Nevertheless, to ensure that, day after day, trains are clean and arrive on time, track and rolling stock must be maintained according to a schedule laid down months ahead; main-line termini must be designed years before they are built; the time-scale for modernising the system as a whole will be measured in decades; contingency plans must be prepared for events that may never occur, and these activities must be integrated and controlled overall, possibly within the context of independent privatised companies.

Many of these activities involve planning, and plans are made in anticipation of future circumstances that must be forecast. They are implemented – and frequently prevented from being implemented – by people who must be managed, i.e. recruited, controlled, motivated, trained, paid, etc. They are made in the context of policies, for example, the extent to which uneconomic branch-line services should be subsidised by other services. Plans are made with objectives in mind, such as to make a profit, to serve the community, to provide employment and to fulfil commercial or other commitments. These objectives will often conflict and must, somehow, be balanced against each other.

Although planning, and in particular strategic planning – deciding the overall and long-term direction of an organisation – is central to the traditional view of strategic management and, while this book reflects that importance, strategic management involves much more than making plans. Strategic management draws on and applies a multitude of competencies, techniques and knowledge at all levels of the organisation relating to both short-term and long-term issues, but it is particularly, although not exclusively, concerned with:

The future impact on the organisation of current decisions by managers at all levels

This implies that decisions concerning the current situation should be made with an eye to the future.

The new-product director of Bass the brewery firm said, 'We have to take a long-term view of recouping new product development costs on a five to ten year horizon. If we stopped developing new products because of the recession we would have a hole in our portfolio in two years' time.'[1]

Similarly, when considering the economics of building a nuclear reprocessor, the costs and problems of decommissioning it decades later should be allowed for.

The focus of strategic management is on:

What an organisation is trying to achieve in the long run

and

When it should be achieved – i.e. the organisation's *objectives*

For example, one objective of a grocery manufacturer might be to achieve a turnover of £50 million within five years. Equally important, however, is:

How they propose to achieve them – i.e. the organisation's *strategy*

Thus, the grocery manufacturer's strategy might be to achieve the turnover objective by increasing sales through supermarket chains. This, perhaps, suggests a clear distinction between *means* – the strategy, and *ends* – the objectives, which does not exist; one may blend into the other, and the means often become the ends. Consider the apparently simple concept of market share. In the example above, the means – the strategy – used by the firm to achieve their turnover objective is to concentrate on supermarkets. They might set a target of 80 per cent of supermarkets stocking their product which they calculate will achieve their turnover objective. This target would therefore be both a means and an end. However, in the grocery trade, where supermarkets dominate the market but may stock only the two or three leading brands of a product, high market share is crucial if a firm's brand is to maintain its presence on the shelves. The cost of protecting market share by, for example, promotional activity such as advertising could be very high and eat into profit margins.

Brook Bond, who were losing market share, revamped the packaging of Red Mountain instant coffee in order 'to give a more quirky personality, less pompous and more friendly than Nescafe', and relaunched with a new advertising campaign in order to avoid being dropped by supermarkets.[2]

In some markets, particularly where the product life-cycle is short, and continuous research and development (R&D) is vital for survival, high market share may be essential to provide the sales revenue to fund new product development. In this case revenue may even be a more important objective than short-term profit if the firm is to survive.

R&D investment in the manufacture of leading-edge microchips is expected to rise from a level of 13 per cent in 1993 to 70 per cent of sales by the year 2000, while the cost of entering the market has been put at $1 billion. This means that, to be viable, a firm must have annual sales of at least $2 billion, demanding very high market share.[3]

High market share may be an objective itself; unless they can be brand leaders some firms are not interested in entering – or may leave – an otherwise attractive market, although there are usually additional underlying reasons associated with volume and market share.

In 1994 Allied Lyons, who dominate the tea market, sold their instant coffee businesses (they had only 11 per cent market share) to Kraft, who had about 24 per cent and who already owned Maxwell House, Cafe Häg and Kenco. They also disposed of their roast and ground coffee brands in order to concentrate on tea. (However, in 1995, the parent company that owned Allied Lyons sold it because of their own corporate objectives.)

At about the same time, HJ Heinz acquired Farley's Rusks because, said the managing director, 'It would help Heinz towards its goal of being a significant player in baby feeding in Europe.'

Nevertheless, high market share and revenue, although important, are not the primary objectives in the profit sector; profit, and in particular, return on investment (ROI), must be the ultimate objective, at any rate for investors (senior managers, however, who would otherwise lose their jobs, might see survival of the firm as their ultimate objective, which illustrates the point that different people will have different objectives for an organisation).

In 1994, Toshiba withdrew from the microwave oven market despite being the third biggest brand and having doubled market share in two years. This was because profit margins would not sustain further sales. The reallocation of resources enabled them to focus on the audiovisual sector and re-enter the satellite receiver market, both of which were ready for high-priced, higher-profit models.

POSITIONING

Different needs lead to different strategies and to different criteria for judging success. These are frequently reflected in the 'positioning' of the organisation's products or services. Positioning refers to the way management would like these to be seen by the outside world and internally. It reflects the organisational culture and the focus of its strategy – its marketing mix – for example, value for money, innovation, high quality, reliability, helpfulness and, in particular, the image it attempts to project in order to differentiate itself, or its products, from competitors.

If what you offer is no different from, or better than, your competitors, why should a customer come to you?

Positioning or repositioning can, however, be a costly component of overall strategy:

When Safeway appointed a new Marketing Director, his remit was to 'rebuild its image and give the chain a brand identity to help stand out from rivals Tesco and Sainsbury.' The advertising budget for this was £7 million.[4]

Abbey National increased its 1995 advertising budget by more than 40 per cent to £40 million 'As part of its ongoing attempt to reposition itself.'[5]

The early 1990s theme of Woolworth's positioning was 'everyday low pricing', focused on the slogan 'street value', an evocative expression with a strong image. The cost of just one 'right up your street' advertising campaign to project this image was £20 million.

A firm positions or repositions itself in relation to its particular target market; if this changes, so too must its positioning:

When Babycham changed its target market from teenagers to 'a fun brand for confident, independent women', it reformulated the product, bottle, symbol and, of course, advertising.[6]

Identification of the appropriate target market and their needs and wants is crucial to a firm's success:

In 1994, Cathay Pacific airline realised that, although most of their business came from Asia, the advertising was using Western images. They therefore repositioned themselves to stress their Asian heritage.

The previous image may, however, be so strong that the strategy fails:

Bovril, after decades of being positioned as a warming, sustaining hot drink, attempted to reposition itself as a low-calorie drink for younger women. The attempt was unsuccessful; the firm said: 'The return to the brand's traditional values is in harmony with the times, and encapsulates what consumers believe about the product.'

STRATEGY FORMULATION

Objectives and strategy may change; they may be deliberately altered as time passes, or they may just evolve with time. This may be in response to environmental changes, but is often because the organisation itself has changed; as they grow or gain experience, organisations may undertake activities that were previously beyond their capabilities or outside their previous field of activities. Strategies may therefore develop in a number of ways.

Planned strategies

It might be thought that the most common way of developing a strategy is as a carefully planned decision, worked out in some detail, that results in a deliberate strategy. This 'scientific approach' is the implied basis of many texts on strategic management.

Phileas Fogg was a highly successful and innovative but relatively small snack brand that was confined to London and the South, being virtually unknown in the rest of the country. The company was acquired by United Biscuits who also own the national snack brand KP. The resources and experience of the two brands enabled Phileas Fogg to plan to go national, and a sixfold increase in distribution was targeted – a strategy of market development.

A proposed strategy may result from a very thorough analysis of the situation and be very carefully planned, it may also, nevertheless, be implemented incrementally rather than with a big bang. This is particularly suitable when the environment is changing and the strategy may need to be adapted progressively or when the firm is entering a new area and feels the need to learn by experience.

BhS, as a deliberate and planned strategy, moved upmarket to compete more directly with Marks & Spencer. This, however, left some outlets in locations that were too down-market for the new image. BhS therefore used these premises gradually to build up a new, independently managed, low-price clothing chain in what they saw as a growth area in the price-conscious 1990s, learning from experience as they converted shops and tested merchandise in a venture that was somewhat different from their existing chain – a strategy of product development. *(Note that the product is not merely the goods sold but the nature of the shopping experience itself.)*

These are examples of a *planned* strategy, and although that of Phileas Fogg is formally described as market development and that of BhS as product development, both rely on a match between the environment and organisational resources – as must all strategies, even if the resources have to be acquired specifically for the purpose. A firm may adopt different strategies in the same or different markets at the same time.

When Toshiba re-entered the satellite receiver market this was a strategy of market development, *but at the same time they exploited their competitive advantage in advanced audio TVs, a strategy of* product development.

Planned strategies are based on a number of assumptions, particularly concerning the future. If the assumptions are incorrect then the plans will almost certainly be inappropriate to a greater or lesser degree, and it is possible that to adhere to such a plan could result in disaster. In circumstances where the future is so uncertain that it would be unwise to make detailed plans, a more flexible approach is needed.

Logical incrementalism

If an organisation knows where it wants to go and, in broad terms, how it wants to get there, it may be able to feel its way tentatively towards its goal, setting short-term targets, proactively probing and adapting to the environment, learning from experience as it goes and continuing in the desired direction as it meets success, otherwise changing direction or branching off on a different track. This approach is not uncommon in the public sector, and is often the strategy of political parties at local level. It is a strategy of *logical incrementalism,* but is different from implementing a preplanned strategy such as that of BhS described above. The difference is, perhaps, one of degree and illustrates the point that, while it is convenient to label and pigeon-hole activities, there is often a continuous spectrum and one strategic approach blends into the next. Thus, logical incrementalism, in turn, blends into *emergent strategy.*

Emergent strategy

Strategies may, of course, be virtually unplanned and develop almost unintentionally – an emergent strategy – this is probably the most common way in which many strategies do develop.

A large firm in the fiercely competitive defence industry was asked by an important Middle Eastern customer to provide computer-based training in the use of the equipment they were supplying. They naturally complied – although they had no previous experience in this field and were obliged to hire experts to prepare the material. Realising the potential, however, they set up an autonomous division offering to develop computer-based training courses in the open market.

A number of computer manufacturers in a highly competitive and price-conscious market found that they were making more profit from servicing equipment than from manufacturing it, and so switched completely to maintenance contracts for other manufacturers.

Muddling through (incrementalism)

Sometimes, the circumstances within both the organisation and its environment are so complex that to weight up all the relevant factors and draw clear-cut conclusions on which to base a planned strategy is just not possible. For example, there may be more or less equally powerful groups within the organisation with different interpretations of the environment, conflicting interests and opposing views on what should be done, while the organisational objectives may not be entirely clear-cut. This frequently occurs in the public sector or a local authority with a hung council.

Decisions concerning the future must nevertheless be made but, in these circumstances, the planning processes described above are not only inappropriate, but probably impossible. Merely avoiding a stalemate by obtaining agreement to proceed may be an achievement – in fact Lindblom, who studied this problem, suggested that in these circumstances, 'A good policy is an agreed policy.'[7] As the agreed policy will almost certainly be a compromise, such a strategy is likely to be very close to what had been done in the past, and Lindblom termed this *incrementalism*, or less formally, 'the science of muddling through'.

Unrealised strategy

An organisation may have planned a particular course of action – its intended strategy – but for some reason it was not pursued; an *unrealised* strategy. This may happen when the environment becomes less favourable, or when it becomes clear that forecasts or predictions were incorrect.

As in virtually all areas of strategic management, there is no one right way to develop a strategy; all that can be said is that a particular approach may be more appropriate for an organisation of a particular type with a particular culture at a particular stage of its development in a particular environment. A small firm, newly started by a couple of entrepreneurs, will probably adopt an approach that is opportunistic – an emergent strategy. Ten years later, if it has grown and settled down in a stable environment and is employing professional managers, its approach will probably be closer to deliberate strategy formulation: more reactive, responding to opportunities rather than seeking them.

Changes to objectives or strategy, both deliberate and emergent, usually occur because the world outside has changed, or is expected to change, thus making the current approach inappropriate. Perhaps it never really had been appropriate and the organisation is now adapting to that fact, or perhaps an opportunity has presented itself which suggests a change in strategy, objectives or both.

The approaches discussed here all rely on attempting a match between the organisation and its environment in order to achieve objectives. Some will be oriented towards the environment by emphasising market development, others will focus on the products or services being offered – strategies of product development.

SUMMARY

- **Deliberate**, planned strategy results from intentions which were carried out.
- **Emergent** strategy arises in the absence of, or despite, previous intentions.
- **Logical incrementalism** describes a process between deliberate and emergent in which the strategy evolves.
- **Incrementalism** is not necessarily 'logical', but at least 'muddling through' results in agreed progress towards a goal.
- **Unrealised strategy** doesn't happen.
- **Realised strategy** does.

When the environment is so turbulent and unpredictable that none of these approaches is suitable, a different model is needed. This problem is considered in Chapter 12. For the time being, however, this book assumes a reasonably predictable environment in order to describe current approaches to strategic management.

EXERCISES

1 Do you agree with the following statements?

(a) The focus of strategic management is on long-range planning.

(b) It is important to distinguish between objectives and strategy.

(c) The most important corporate objective is to maximise profit.

(d) Maximising profit in the short-term will result in maximising profit in the long-term.

(e) Once objectives have been decided they should not be altered.

(f) The best way of achieving objectives is to make a plan and stick to it.

(g) Logical incrementalism is the process of developing a detailed plan in a logical manner.

(h) An effective strategy can result only from detailed planning.

(i) 'Positioning' is how a firm fights competition.

2 Using your own knowledge, or based on case studies, identify two organisations that you would describe as highly successful or as unsuccessful. Which approach to strategy formulation did they adopt and what conclusions do you draw from this?

FURTHER READING

Ansoff, I. *Implanting Strategic Management*, Prentice Hall, 1990, provides a contrary perspective to Mintzberg, H., *The Rise and Fall of Strategic Planning* (*see* below).

Johnson, G. and Scholes, K., *Exploring Corporate Strategy*, Prentice Hall, 1993. Chapters 1–2 offer a model which has been adopted by a number of other authors.

For readers who enjoy challenges to received wisdom, Mintzberg, H., *The Rise and Fall of Strategic Planning*, Prentice Hall, 1994, evoked strong reactions from authorities whose ideas were contested.

Mintzberg, H. and Quinn, J. B., *The Strategy Process*, Prentice Hall, 1991. Chapters 1–5 give a more detailed discussion of strategy.

Stacey, R. D., *Strategic Management and Organisational Dynamics*, Pitman Publishing, 1993. Chapters 1–3 offer a challenging review of strategic management.

REFERENCES

1 *Marketing Week*, 8 October 1993.
2 *Marketing Week*, 9 July 1993.
3 *Financial Times*, 12 October 1993.
4 *Marketing Week*, 20 January 1995.
5 *Marketing Week*, 16 December 1994.
6 *Marketing Week*, 15 October 1993.
7 Lindblom, C. E.,The Science of Muddling Through, *Public Admin Review*, Spring 1959.

CHAPTER 2

Influences on strategic management

The forces influencing strategic management decisions can be divided into two groups: *environmental* – those outside the organisation – and *internal*. This chapter provides an overview of both, and an introduction to the strategies that may result.

ENVIRONMENTAL INFLUENCES

An organisation does not exist in a vacuum; it interacts with its environment. A business offers its goods or services in the market-place – usually against competition – while the environment provides sources of labour, energy, raw materials, finance, information, etc., over which it has little control.

If the environment were relatively unchanging, an organisation might, after a period of adaptation, settle down to a fairly stable relationship with its customers, suppliers, competitors, channels of distribution and investors. There would then be little motivation to make major changes to the objectives or strategy if all parties more or less accepted the status quo. However, this stable state is rare; customers' needs change, a new competitor arises or a superior product is offered, sales decline, shareholders become dissatisfied with the return on their investment, a source of supply dries up or important retail outlets are denied to a manufacturer, a new market opens up – these, or innumerable other changes in the environment, might require a rethink about objectives, strategy, or both. In other words, changes in strategy or objectives are frequently – although not always – made in response to, or in anticipation of, an environmental change; either reacting to a threat, or taking advantage of an opportunity. They may be major changes, they could be minor tweaks in order to make the strategy work better, and sometimes they will have been preplanned, ready for anticipated contingencies if and when they occur. These changes may, in turn, provoke a response in the environment which must then be dealt with; for example, reducing prices in order to gain market share may spark off a price war, or launching a new product might trigger competitors to take their new product off the shelf, where it had been awaiting just such an eventuality. Conversely, if an organisation responds too late to environmental changes, it runs the risk of failure.

A leading retail chain that grew rapidly in the 1960s was Montague Burton. They then manufactured and sold modestly priced made-to-measure men's suits. To achieve low costs they had developed extremely efficient sales and production systems but, although they had a major high street presence, their 'centre of gravity' still lay in their factories; their focus was inwards, on operational efficiency rather than outwards, on what customers wanted; in marketing terms, they were product-oriented *rather than* market-oriented.

Despite offering a very wide range of suits, they failed to respond to the trend towards less formal wear and nearly collapsed as a result of 'sticking to their knitting' until it was nearly too late. In the event, they disposed of their factories and refocused on retailing. Since then the group has undergone several more crises, changes of chairman and reorganisations, largely due to failure to respond to changing conditions – as did many other high-street giants.

Hence:

Adapting an organisation to its environment is an essential aspect of strategic management

If the environment were, as described above, relatively unchanging, the process of strategic management would be appear to be fairly simple, largely a matter of keeping an eye on the environment just to make sure that nothing much has changed – or is likely to do so – and concentrating mainly on good housekeeping: keeping costs under control, maintaining quality and productivity levels by monitoring actual performance against established standards, taking any necessary corrective action to keep on course. In other words, the emphasis would be on *maintenance* of the existing strategy – keeping the trains clean and running on time – rather than *adapting* or changing it, although the strategy may still need to be tweaked because of slight changes in the environment or in order to make it more effective.

In a more turbulent environment, the process of strategic management becomes more complex and demanding. Information systems must be sufficiently sensitive to detect change as early as possible in order to analyse the existing, and probable future, situation and to adapt to it in good time. Matching the organisation to its environment may require, among other characteristics, a more suitable structure, different systems and, in particular, an appropriate organisational culture, all of which are aspects of strategic management.

INTERNAL INFLUENCES

Culture

Although strategy is ultimately constrained by the resources available to an organisation, it is nevertheless largely determined by the firm's *culture*: its basic beliefs, assumptions and values. These may play as important a role in the success of a firm as the products themselves.

The Morgan Motor Company produces hand-made classic sports cars. Although the waiting list stretches into years and labour accounts for about a third of production costs, management firmly resist changing traditional methods of manufacture.

The Body Shop is positioned as a socially responsible, ecologically concerned organisation. This positioning plays an important role in its strategy, attracting a significant segment of the market with similar views. When its sincerity was challenged by a magazine article, the price of shares in the company immediately fell – not because the quality of the products was questioned, but because investors feared that the firm's customer base would be alienated.

Stakeholders

Other important influences on strategy are individuals and interest groups within an organisation (*internal stakeholders*) who will naturally exert pressure in order to select a strategy which is to their advantage and according to their views. Their relative power, and the formation or dissolution of coalitions and alliances to achieve their ends – internal politics – often play an important part in deciding strategy, as was suggested in describing incrementalism (*see* Chapter 1).

Another factor might be a change in the ideas of one or more influential *senior managers*, or the influence of a new manager joining the organisation, although these might themselves be triggered by environmental factors.

When, after a troubled period, a new Chief Executive was appointed to run IBM, he did not wait until a comprehensive audit of the situation had been undertaken, he acted to change the organisational structure very rapidly. He was replaced shortly afterwards, and his successor quickly changed the approach yet again. IBM was in a near-crisis at the time and urgent action was essential. In other circumstances, the time-scale might have been very different.

When ASDA, the supermarket chain, appointed a new marketing director in early 1992, he reviewed the concept on which the Dales discount stores was based. 'The original approach was not a strategy but a set of tactics. So I started to look at what the next generation of discounters would be like'.[1] *However, ASDA did not rush into discounting; in 1994 he announced that they would concentrate in the South East before a national roll-out 'by the end of the decade'.*

Time-scale

This long-term perspective is a vital aspect of strategic management; for example, Dowty's strategy is to look ten years ahead and ask what enabling technologies (R&D) the company will have to undertake to meet business objectives, and how it will acquire and fund these technologies. Hence:

The time-horizon for strategic planning must be at least as long as the lead time necessary to meet change

For example, if the profitable life of a product is anticipated to be five years, and it takes two years from planning to marketing, then preparing for its replacement – a strategy of *product development* – must actively commence not more than three years after its launch, when it may well be at its peak of success and this does not allow for contingencies. This can create considerable problems when predicting the future is difficult.

Construction of the Sellafield Thorp nuclear reprocessing plant started in 1977. By the time it was ready in 1993 there were grave doubts whether it was commercially viable and whether it was needed, while the public's attitude towards the risks of reprocessing had hardened considerably. The government had the problem of seriously considering whether or not to commission the plant which had cost £2.8 billion to build.

Lead time is, however, equally relevant in the short-term. Because of the highly competitive nature of many markets together with their shorter life-cycles, there is considerable pressure on firms to reduce lead times. This has in turn led to organisational structures and systems that facilitate this, often based on Japanese practice – another example of the way in which a firm must adapt to match its environment.

Resources

Another possible internal influence is the opportunity offered by the acquisition or development of additional *resources* such as a new production technology that might enable new or superior products to be manufactured, or an improved distribution system. Thus, many organisations, having invested very heavily in advanced information technology (IT) and communication facilities, try to market them to other non-competitive organisations.

Barclays Bank set up a company to produce direct-mail marketing material for other companies, using the equipment it employs to send information to its own customers.

An example of this particular resource actually saving a firm from extinction due to changes in the environment was Club 24.

Club 24 was the financial services subsidiary of a consortium which ran the credit customer accounts for a number of chains such as Woolworth, Next, Comet, and B&Q. It was very successful during the credit boom of the late 1980s but, as the recession hit, bad debts put the firm in the red and recovery seemed distant. The business was on the point of being closed down in 1991 when senior management realised that their systems, skills and experience in managing millions of small transactions was a marketable resource.

There was a management buy-out, and they became a bureau, managing high-volume, telephone-based operations for other companies, but not carrying any debt themselves. Despite – or because of – the recession, business grew; the service was particularly attractive to their clients who could avoid investment in a time of recession, and because the economies of scale which Club 24 achieved were reflected in their pricing.

Organisations such as Club 24's clients are increasingly using third parties – a strategy of *outsourcing* – to provide goods and services which they previously produced themselves. There are many benefits, among which is that it enables them to concentrate on their core activities, reduce investment in peripheral activities and use their resources to the greatest advantage.

Similarly, in the public sector, organisations market-test to see if it is cheaper to contract-out various services, concentrating their resources on their primary or core activities. It would be possible to brief a research organisation to identify a market opportunity, then commission consultants to research and find a suitable name, hire design consultants to design suitable products and their packaging, contract manufacturers to produce them, employ distributors to sell them and an advertising agency to promote them – a 'virtual organisation' with a minimum of resources – other than money. Resources are the ultimate constraint on strategic management.

Strategic decisions are basically about the use to be made of the organisation's resources – existing or potential – in order to achieve organisational objectives

These resources could, for example, include such strengths as management skills, an expert work-force, a factory, a production line, a sales force, spare cash, the ability to raise money, a research laboratory, a firm's reputation, a patent, technology, an information or delivery system or friends in high places. Conventional wisdom advises that it usually makes sense to base an organisation's strategy on its existing strengths, although there is no inherent need to do so.

IBM has had a stringent environmental policy for the last 20 years and is very experienced in the field. Based on this expertise, which is unrelated to its core activities, IBM has diversified into environmental consultancy such as help with formulating policy and green auditing, as well as air-quality measurement and other environmental data processing. This could be classified as a strategy of unrelated diversification *since green consultancy was not related to its then activities.*

The decision could concern the acquisition of resources.

In order to exploit the opportunities presented by the Single Market – a strategy of market development *– Tibbett & Britten, a distributor and warehouser to the garment industry, acquired Silcock Express, a firm in the business of car distribution which already had a network in Europe. There was further advantage since Silcock benefited from the expertise in sophisticated distribution and warehousing practices which Tibbett possessed in the retailing sector.*

Finally, the uses to be made of resources might also include their disposal, a strategy of *divestiture*; for example: a corporation might sell a profitable subsidiary in order to concentrate on its core activities. Alternatively, it may re-invest the money in an even more profitable business or one with greater potential. This could be a business that it already owns, or one it proposes to set up or intends to acquire.

An example of the interaction of environmental forces and internal resource issues was the sale in 1994 by Van den Bergh of a subsidiary, Mattessons Wall's chilled meat business. One of the reasons for the sale was increased competition, particularly from own-label brands, which created the need for further investment which could not be justified. A spokesman for Van den Burgh said: 'We have limited resources, and have decided that they are better redirected to our core areas of margarines and low-fat spreads.'[2]

A single issue of the *Financial Times*[3] reported three examples of the reallocation of resources in response to environmental forces. First, the effect of a new broom with new ideas is illustrated by Fig 2.1. Since Levercrest is staying in broadly the same industry but manufacturing new products, this strategy is classified as *product development*.

The same issue reported that Bristol-Myers Squibb, the world's third-biggest pharmaceuticals company, was selling its Drackett household product business *which contributed over 50 per cent to their sales* '. . . in a move to

Levercrest launches £1.3m rights issue to fund fresh strategy.

Levercrest, the playground equipment, street furniture and rubber safety surfacing maker, is raising £1.3m through a rights issue and will execute a new strategy to pursue acquisitions in the engineering sector. This will be achieved under a new chairman, Mr Ian Orrock.

Mr Orrock, assisting the board for the last three months as a consultant, is now a director and will become chairman on 19 November.

Fig 2.1 New broom at Levercrest
Source: *Financial Times*, 28 October 1992.

sharpen its competitive edge in the drugs industry'. In other words, it was disposing of one successful business in order to improve its performance in another, a further example of a strategy of *divestiture* combined with that of *consolidation* in an existing market, as was that of Van den Burgh.

The third example reported that Greenalls, the brewers, had reconsidered their strategy in the light of environmental changes.

Following the 1989 Monopolies and Mergers Commission report on the brewing industry, together with a shift in taste from beer to lager, Greenalls had realised that there was more profit to be made selling beer than in brewing it, so they closed their breweries (a strategy of divestiture*) and concentrated on their pubs, hotels, inns, off-licences and leisure services, a strategy of* consolidation.

Shortly after this, the economic recession ruined many hotel businesses, thus creating opportunities to acquire the properties at low prices. Greenalls raised £86 million to have ready for 'piece-meal, add-on acquisitions' as and when they become available – such as a newly built hotel and golf complex bought for £10.3 million from the receiver at half its development cost – an emergent *strategy that could be described as either* product *or* market development.

To outsiders and to brewery employees who were unaware of the reasons, the changes might seem incomprehensible – try to imagine the puzzlement of many employees of Drackett's, a successful business that was sold off under their feet by Bristol-Myers Squibb. This is, however, not at all unusual.

In 1995, Dalgety put up for sale the very popular Golden Wonder and Homepride brands. Golden Wonder alone had sales of £220 million a year, is the second leading brand of bagged snacks, and has been improving its market position. It was, however, in need of further investment and, rather than make this investment, Dalgety proposed to concentrate on Quaker petfood in Europe.[4]

These examples illustrate the difference between *corporate* strategy and *business* strategy. *Corporate-level strategy* is broad in scope and concerned with the long-term financial performance of the organisation as a whole, rather than that of individual divisions or businesses within it. One subsidiary may be disposed of to create, support or acquire another if that makes financial sense. It is, for example, at this level that decisions, such as taking revenue from one subsidiary to invest in another, disposing of assets, entering joint ventures with third parties or raising funds from outside the organisation, will be made.

Business-level strategy focuses on how to compete in a particular business area or market segment. The business-level strategy will be influenced or even determined by the corporate strategy or policy, but the ultimate driving force will almost invariably be to gain *competitive advantage* at the business level.

The business may be a firm in its entirety, or it may be only a part of a firm. If its strategy can be planned independently and its profit performance can be measured, then it may be called a strategic business unit (SBU). An SBU is any unit that has management able to control factors that significantly affect performance and whose performance can be measured. It operates in a distinct segment of a competitive market, and the independence enables it to respond more closely to the particular circumstances in that segment.

The sale by Van den Bergh of certain businesses is an example of strategy at the corporate level; how the resources made available by the sale were used to support other existing brands, is strategy at the business level. For many organisations, particularly small businesses, there will be no distinction between corporate and business strategy, but the term *competitive advantage* has a particular meaning in the context of strategic management. Although advantage over a competitor may be gained by, for example, a lower price or a quality image which result in higher market share, it must be stressed that in the context of strategic management, the term competitive advantage means:

Long-term profitability which is above the average for the industry

A firm which has higher profitability than its competitors can better afford to invest in new product development, staff training, promotional activity, capital equipment or other forms of expenditure that will help to perpetuate its competitive advantage while still maintaining a satisfactory return on investment – which is the prime purpose of the firm.

SUMMARY

The distinction between corporate and business strategies raises the issue of how the organisation is structured. (Changes in strategy may well require changes in structure, and this is explored in Chapter 6.) We can summarise this chapter with four features of strategic management. Strategic management is concerned with:

1 The organisation *as a whole* and *at all levels* – making sure that what should happen does happen.

2 *Long-term* and *short-term* issues.

3 *What* it does or should do, *how* it does it and *when*.

4 *Why* it does what it does – achieving the organisation's objectives.

Items 1 and 2 stress that strategic management is not merely concerned with the 'big issues'. Item 3 is essentially the process of strategic planning, but must be conducted within this overall framework, and with recognition that the *how* of implementation is as important as the strategy itself. Item 4 suggests that objectives lie at the root of strategic decisions, and these are considered in Chapter 3.

A number of strategies (considered in more detail in Chapter 8) are:

- **Consolidation:** e.g. Van den Bergh strengthening their existing position in margarine.
- **Divestiture:** e.g. Bristol-Myers Squibb selling off a subsidiary.
- **Market development:** e.g. Club 24 extending their activities in new markets.
- **Product development:** e.g. Levercrest introducing new products in an existing market.
- **Related diversification:** e.g. ASDA diversifying into discount stores within the grocery retail industry.
- **Unrelated diversification:** New activities in a different industry – e.g. IBM offering 'green' consultancy.

EXERCISES

1 Match the appropriate strategy A–D to activities a–l:

A Consolidation
B Product development
C Market development
D Related diversification
E Unrelated diversification

(a) A computer manufacturer acquiring a competitor to be run independently.

(b) A computer manufacturer acquiring a chain of computer stores.

(c) A hi-fi manufacturer making computers.

(d) A computer manufacturer producing computer software.

(e) A chain of computer stores acquiring a chain of tobacconists.

(f) A tobacco company acquiring a chain of computer stores.

(g) A computer manufacturer acquiring a competitor whose products they will sell as their own.

(h) A computer manufacturer starting to export through an overseas agent.

(i) A computer manufacturer acquiring an overseas agency in order to export.

(j) A computer manufacturer licensing an overseas manufacturer to produce their computers.

(k) A computer manufacturer adapting its product to sell as a games machine.

(l) A computer manufacturer disposing of its software subsidiary.

2 'Strategic decisions are basically about the use to be made of organisational resources in order to achieve organisational objectives.' What are the major resources required for success in question 1 cases **a** to **g** above? Suggest possible reasons for adopting these strategies.

REFERENCES

1 *Marketing Week*, 30 October 1992.
2 *Marketing Week*, 8 July 1994.
3 *Financial Times*, 28 October 1992.
4 *Marketing Week*, 10 February 1995.

CHAPTER 3

What business are we in?

THE MISSION

While strategic decisions are made in order to achieve objectives, both objectives and strategy are themselves constrained by the organisation's *mission*. Traditionally, defining the mission answers the question, 'What business are we in?', but therein lies a trap; obvious answers such as 'engineering' or 'retailing' miss the point.

All organisations, in both the private and public sectors, are set up in order to satisfy external needs or wants; an organisation that fails to do so or does so unprofitably will not survive, however efficiently it conducts its operations. Thus, retailing and engineering are merely activities that serve the end of meeting customers' needs.

Missions must therefore be tied *in the first place* to the needs met, rather than to markets or industries. This *customer orientation* is the essence of what is described as the marketing concept. Thus, the Chartered Institute of Marketing defines marketing as 'The management process which identifies, anticipates and supplies customer requirements efficiently and profitably.' The mission, then, should clearly identify:

- The customers/clients to be served
- The needs to be satisfied
- The means – products and/or technologies – by which these will be achieved

This approach should not be confined to the marketing department but adopted by every person, function and department in the organisation. This point is developed when discussing the value chain in Chapter 5.

The mission statement

In some organisations these points are explicitly documented in a mission statement which often includes references to the organisation's philosophy, culture, commitment to the community and employees, growth, profitability etc., but these should not blur vision of the organisation's basic mission. Mission statements are frequently so broad and general as to be virtually useless for giving strategic direction, while many organisations have no mission – stated or unstated – at all. In these circumstances it is hardly surprising if the organisation has no sense of direction, flounders or even fails.

IBM's mission statement until the shake-up in 1990 read that they would be: '... Guided by three basic beliefs: respect for the individual, the pursuit of excellence and service to the customer. These form the foundations for our five corporate goals for the future: to enhance our customer partnerships; to be the leader in products and services; to grow with the industry; to be the most efficient in everything we do; and to sustain profitability, which funds growth.'

Worthy sentiments, but hardly a guide to strategic thrust.

The Automobile Association's mission is 'To be the UK's leading and most successful motoring and personal services organisation.'

What do 'leading' and 'successful' mean? How do you measure them? Does this include commercial motorists? The statement seems to imply that the purpose is to beat the RAC in some way, a curious mission for a service organisation.

In the 1960s and 1970s, high street retailing was dominated by Marks & Spencer, F W Woolworth and British Home Stores (later to become BhS). Although Woolworth had provided the model for the other two chains, they themselves completely failed to adapt to changes in the shopping environment and, by the 1970s, Woolworth trading results were so poor that the share price had halved.

Meanwhile and throughout the 1970s, Marks & Spencer and British Home Stores were virtually neck and neck both in the high street and in the hearts of investors. Both firms had benefited from the booming 1960s and 1970s but, while Marks & Spencer had a clear, specific mission: providing high quality clothing and textiles at prices that working class and lower-middle class families could afford; British Home Stores had no such mission, and lacked an overall sense of direction.

By the 1980s, Marks & Spencer, with a clear strategy, had shot ahead and was making as much profit as BhS made in sales. By 1990, when BhS's profits had slumped from £71 million three years earlier down to £27 million, senior management realised that drastic action was needed in order to correct the mismatch that had been allowed to develop between the firm and its environment.

To spearhead this, the following mission statement was produced: 'The BhS mission is to be the first-choice store for dressing the modern woman and family. We are committed to service, quality, harmony, innovation and excitement in all that we do. We will succeed by being a focused organisation in dynamic partnership with our customers, suppliers and each one of us.'

Shortly afterwards a new Chief Executive was appointed. He sacked 10 of the 15 managers who had drawn up the mission statement and transformed the organisation.[1] *After successfully turning BhS around, he left – taking a total of £3.3 million in pay and bonuses in his last year.*

BhS had asked itself the classic essential questions:

1. *Who are our target market?*
2. *What are their needs and wants?*
3. *How do we satisfy them better than our competitors – and make a satisfactory profit?*

They had identified the working mother as their core customer, introduced baby-changing facilities and wider aisles that could accommodate prams and revised their product range accordingly. As a result, in 1994 they announced profits of £56.2 million, more than double those of 1990.

Marks & Spencer, however, announced profits of £851.5 million. They had developed their mission much earlier and had acted upon it accordingly and very thoroughly throughout the organisation. By defining their target market they were able to decide the type of store needed, pricing policy, product range and all of the components of a marketing strategy together with marketing objectives. As social and economic circumstances changed, so they adapted by going up-market. Marketing, however, was only one of many aspects of management that were influenced by the mission. In order to maintain quality they not only built quality control laboratories, but also developed new fabrics and processes and even helped new manufacturers start up to ensure supplies – production objectives.

Marks & Spencer stores are some of the most efficient in the world as a result of achieving productivity objectives – sales per square foot were three times those of BhS. Social objectives *stressed social responsibility towards employees and suppliers, as well as towards customers.*

Finally, Marks & Spencer are extremely responsive to environmental changes, and adapt incrementally, rather than deferring the decision to adjust until the mismatch becomes too great – as many organisations do. They constantly test new products and ideas, and learn from experience.

Although highly profitable, Marks & Spencer did not have profit objectives. As in the case of GEC, profit was seen as the result of doing things right rather than the purpose of doing them.

While a well-formulated mission statement provides the framework for defining organisational objectives, nevertheless as the nature and the needs and wants of target markets change, so the objectives and strategy must reflect these. Internal and external factors may, in fact, require that the mission itself be reformulated to meet a changing situation, particularly if the technology or industry itself is clearly in decline.

In 1982, Peters and Waterman published *In Search of Excellence*[2], a book which created a considerable stir. They identified 43 companies as being 'excellent', and listed the eight features that resulted in this performance, among which was 'sticking to their knitting', i.e. maintaining a focus. Almost immediately after publication some of the firms had lost their place in the list and, eight years later, 37 of the original 43 no longer met the criteria, many having disappeared completely. It has been argued that it was their very success that sowed the seeds of their subsequent failure – as so often happens. A firm, having found 'the formula for success' and defined its mission, continues to build on it, but then, when the world about them changes, cannot accept that the formula is no longer valid.

Robert Heller, an authority on management topics, said of IBM: '. . . the company had been so phenomenally successful. As a result, it was impossible for people who had grown up in the system to understand that it didn't work any more. In entirely new circumstances that were changing very rapidly they attempted to follow the old policies that were no longer effective.'[3]

Perhaps the most famous example of this is Henry Ford's 'Give them any colour so long as it's black.' His outstanding success through mass production of a standard product led to near-failure as the market demanded variety and he stubbornly stuck to his recipe for success.

The above examples illustrate the need for:

- A clearly expressed mission which is understood – and acted upon – by everyone in the organisation
- Objectives that are in accord with the mission
- The flexibility to adapt not only strategies but even the mission of the organisation if changing circumstances demand it

OBJECTIVES

The mission provides a framework for the organisation's objectives, and the objectives should be consistent with, and promote, the mission. However, while the word 'mission' implies a singularity of purpose, organisations will have multiple objectives because of the many aspects of the organisation's performance and behaviour that contribute to the mission, and which should therefore be explicitly identified. For example, in discussing Marks & Spencer a number of objectives were mentioned, including those related to marketing, production, productivity, social responsibility and profit. It was the thoroughness with which these objectives – and those which in turn derived from them – were pursued, that ensured their outstanding success.

Organisations will have multiple objectives

In order to satisfy investors, one objective may be to improve short-term profitability and this could be achieved by reducing investment, although doing so might adversely affect long-term profitability objectives.

Organisations will have long-term and short-term objectives

However, many of these objectives will conflict with each other. For example, if a retail group opens larger stores in pursuit of growth objectives, total annual profit should rise, but average profit per square foot will possibly fall. In the short-term, costs may, in fact, erode profit.

In Autumn 1994, the chairman of Kingfisher said that the electrical chain Comet was making a loss because its retail space had risen by 50 per cent in five years but demand had not grown correspondingly.

Objectives may conflict

It is important to note that major conflict between objectives can rarely be resolved satisfactorily by compromise; they are usually incompatible and it may be necessary to alternate their relative importance, emphasising one and then the other over a period of time as a deliberate aspect of corporate strategy.

In contrast to Comet, and within the same week, the chairman of Next announced half-year profits up by 60 per cent and said that everything that Next did would be in existing stores, profit objectives being more appropriate than growth objectives at that time.

Because of these conflicts, the relative importance of objectives is a key factor in strategic management since this will influence the strategy adopted. For example, if the mission implies that a firm should be a market leader – as is the case with some firms – then this suggests that maximising profit is less important than obtaining and maximising market share.

Objectives must be prioritised

The hierarchy of objectives

There is a hierarchy of objectives, and their nature and relative importance will vary from firm to firm and according to the particular circumstances at the time. For example, one firm whose strategy is based on high volume sales may set a particular high share of the market as an important *corporate* and *business* objective but, for another firm whose positioning and strategy are based on exclusivity and high price, market share may be deliberately limited – as is the case with certain luxury watches and cars. In this case, although maintaining a certain level of market share may be an objective of the *marketing strategy*, it may not be of sufficient importance to be considered as a *corporate* objective, that is to say, influencing the strategic thrust of the organisation as a whole. Thus, corporate or business objectives will generate lower-level departmental and functional objectives, and it is important that *all* objectives derive from and are consistent with corporate objectives and with each other. For example, if the sales department exceed their sales target, this might require overtime working in the factory which, by increasing costs prevents profit targets from being achieved. Three organisational functions are involved: sales, operations and finance, and their roles and targets must therefore be co-ordinated. Since the results of exceeding the sales target are measurable, they could, in theory, be anticipated and controlled – hence an important reason for setting objectives is to provide a standard against which to monitor and control performance.

In the public sector, hospitals and the public have had to learn the need to match operations – sometimes literally – against resources; operating theatres are sometimes closed down towards the end of the financial year because budgets have been spent.

The hierarchy of objectives can be divided into four levels which broadly correspond with the levels in which management is frequently divided.

Corporate objectives

This is the level that is implied by corporate strategy. In the case of an organisation such as Unilever, with subsidiaries which are themselves of major importance in their markets, the parent company will be concerned with long-term *overall* optimisation. Thus, profit earned by one subsidiary – a cash cow – might, to that subsidiary's considerable annoyance, be allocated to a different subsidiary that is in an expanding market and would benefit more from the investment, rather than being ploughed back into its originator.

Divisional or business unit objectives

Each subsidiary or SBU should have its own corporate objectives and strategies, long-term and short-term, which will be influenced – or imposed – by its parent in accordance with the parent's corporate objectives. Thus, the Burton Group consists of a number of autonomous chains such as Dorothy Perkins, Debenhams, Burton, Top Shop, etc.; a chemical manufacturer may have a Fine Chemical Division and a Heavy Chemical Division; and a food manufacturer may be split into a retail and a catering company, each serving a different market quite independently of the other, having its own objectives and strategy and possibly competing for corporate resources.

Functional and administrative objectives

Having decided on objectives for the organisation as a whole – corporate or subsidiary – objectives must be set for the various functions such as production, marketing, R&D, finance, human resource management, etc., to ensure that they are all contributing appropriately. In most firms these functions and divisions devise their own strategic plans in order to achieve their objectives – for example, the marketing strategy which will determine the marketing mix, the production strategy which will deal with decisions such as whether to manufacture or whether to buy-in certain components, although these decisions may well be subject to control and approval by senior levels of management.

Operational objectives

The functions and divisions will, in turn, set objectives for their various subsections, and sub-subsections, such as productivity targets for each production line within a factory within a division, within a subsidiary of a firm that is part of a multinational conglomerate. Objectives at the top levels tend to be long-term and less specific than those at lower levels, which may be very short-term, and usually quantified and closely controlled.

Some objectives can be measured fairly simply; growth rate, market share, sales, orders, or profit. Others, particularly non-economic or behavioural objectives, do not lend themselves so easily to this approach but are not necessarily less important. For example, it is crucially important that an investment trust creates a favourable image in order to attract funds, while in the public sector, where profit and sales objectives are not necessarily appropriate, effort is made to measure, such as customer satisfaction.

Some, but not all objectives can be quantified

It is important that when an objective is quantified and a target set, the appropriate unit of measurement is applied. Take profit, for example; this is the ultimate measurement of success, but should it be profit before tax? Profit as a percentage of sales? Profit per square foot of selling space? Annual profit? Long-term profit? Return on capital? Return on shareholders' investment? There is no 'correct' list of objectives, they must relate back to the mission; objectives are important motivators since they are the means whereby performance is judged individually, departmentally, or organisationally.

The yardstick(s) by which an objective is measured must be carefully chosen and defined

It is important that performance is not measured by means of a single yardstick which would oversimplify a complex problem. This is particularly important when the performance is difficult to evaluate directly, making indirect measures necessary instead. For example, in many cases it is difficult to obtain a direct measure of customer satisfaction, and a number of indicators are needed. Nevertheless, in the for-profit sector, the ultimate objective is almost invariably profit related. This raises the fundamental issue of who determines organisational objectives and decides on the appropriate yardstick and target value.

HOW ARE THE MISSION AND OBJECTIVES DETERMINED?

In some organisations, an individual is in such a position of power that he or she is able to impose the agenda; for example, the founder of the firm. It may also occur when an organisation is close to collapse and an outsider is brought in to rescue the firm, as appeared to be the case with Levercrest. It is not unusual in these circumstances for the 'new broom' to sweep away a large number of senior managers and bring in people with similar views to his or her own, which radically differ from those of the old guard, as was the case with BhS. These are, however, exceptional circumstances. Generally, the views of a number of people, or groups, will influence or even determine decisions. Most of these will be within the organisation; for example, members of the board of directors. Others, such as important investors, trade union officials or even customers, may be outside the organisation but in a strong position to exert pressure. This is particularly true in the public sector, where local and national government exert very strong influence on, for example, local educational, health and social services. Their influence may support or oppose a particular objective, and they may do so, not only to further the ends of the organisation, but for their personal or other interests. For example, important outside investors seeking income by buying shares in a firm because it offered a high dividend yield rather than long-term capital growth might be unhappy about a programme of heavy capital expenditure that will not become profitable for a relatively long time, even if the yield would eventually be very high; trade union officials – who may be within or outside the firm – might consider their first priority is to further the interests of the union. A production director would possibly oppose any proposal to transfer production to an overseas location despite lower costs if this diminished his personal position; a sales director might argue that the sales force should be enlarged instead of employing outside distributors, because his own position would thereby be enhanced. *Personal*, as well as *organisational* objectives may therefore be influential in determining corporate objectives and strategy. So, whose priorities *do* determine objectives?

STAKEHOLDER ANALYSIS

The simple answer is, that directly or indirectly, any individuals and organisations with the power to do so, i.e. the *stakeholders*. Stakeholders may be within or outside the organisation and are defined as:

Those individuals or organisations who influence, or are influenced by, the decisions of the organisation

Although this seems obvious, stakeholder analysis – determining who the individuals or bodies are, and what their aims and interests are – does much to provide the rationale behind the behaviour and strategic decisions of both private and public sector organisations. For example, in the public sector, the objectives of educational, health and social services are largely determined by the particular priorities of local and national government, i.e. by politicians, by the needs of those they serve (who are obviously an important group of stakeholders) as well as by the professionals who actually provide the services.

Until the 1980s, these services were constrained by budgets and, in general, objectives reflected political attitudes; financial objectives as such had a lower priority and were rarely quantified. Because political priorities have changed, financial objectives have, in some cases, become supreme. Furthermore, with sanctions such as capping available, the power of national government to influence objectives may now be greater than that of other stakeholders such as local councillors, officials, pressure groups or the local community. These stakeholders' objectives may still be considered, but only within the constraints set by financial objectives.

Turning to the private sector, at one time investors and company directors were the most powerful stakeholders; today the expectations of others – pressure groups, customers, suppliers and employees – may influence decisions to a much greater degree.

Levi Strauss were influenced by considerations of public opinion when they cancelled contracts with Chinese clothing manufacturers because of 'pervasive violations of basic human rights'. They also withdrew from Burma, and a number of other countries where the workers were being exploited, not only for ethical reasons, but because 'We needed to ensure that our products were made in a manner . . . that would not be damaging to our brand image.'

In the past, therefore, the private sector was mainly motivated by profit objectives, while public sector organisations were largely driven by politics – national, local and internal. Today, however, this simple view no longer applies, and a full *stakeholder analysis* is necessary both to understand and to determine organisational objectives and strategy.

Formal or informal trade-offs, bargaining or compromises between the various stakeholders may occur in negotiating an organisation's objectives, or it may be that the decision-makers will take others' interests into account in order to avoid, or settle, conflict. For example, there is always a conflict between the interests of customers and of shareholders: if extra value is added to the product in order to make it more attractive and ensure high market share, the cost could be at the expense of returns to investors. One must therefore consider not only the influence of stakeholders on the organisation, but also interactions between them. Ultimately, objectives and strategy will be influenced by the following considerations:

1 Who are the stakeholders concerned?
2 What is their relative power?
3 How great is the importance to them of a particular issue – which they will therefore support or oppose?
4 Where and how will they exert their influence and power?

Even a powerful stakeholder would probably be prepared to accept a decision to which he or she is almost indifferent, while a weaker stakeholder might fight hard for or against a proposal that arouses strong feelings. In some cases, stakeholder groups with little else in common may form a temporary coalition for a particular end, or one group may support another on one issue in return for a similar favour on another issue. In the event of conflict, either some equilibrium point – a compromise – must be found that balances opposing forces, or opposing stakeholders must be convinced, give way, or be overruled. However, the surrender may be only temporary; the opposition may regroup and make another attack, or there may be an understanding that their turn will come later. Internal politics of this sort frequently play an important part in determining strategy, and should be anticipated by decision-makers.

One particularly significant potential conflict mentioned earlier is between the interests of customers, investors and management, which frequently pull in different directions. For example, in order to make the product more attractive to consumers, management could lower the price or add features in order to increase perceived value, but the cost of either of these strategies would possibly reduce profit margins at the financial expense of investors. Management must therefore balance benefits to the consumer against benefits to the investor, and when there is enough in the kitty to satisfy both, everybody will be content: some will go to investors in the form of dividends and the value of their shares may rise; some will be ploughed back, perhaps as new plant; some will go into the bottom drawer to be used either for business purposes when required or to be drawn on to pay investors when results are poor; and management may themselves receive a bonus or a pay rise.

However, particularly in a highly competitive market or in times of recession, profits may be slim and, if investors were dissatisfied with the financial performance, management's position could be under threat – the better their past performance, the greater the dissatisfaction of investors when it declines. In these circumstances it would be natural for management to concentrate on increasing profitability by the direct means of cutting costs or reducing investment, rather than indirectly by attempting to increase sales as the result of improved customer satisfaction. There is always a degree of tension between adding value to a product and the cost of doing so, which influences strategy, and this may be exacerbated by environmental forces such as governmental actions.

Following the 1994 Autumn budget, the CEO of Northern Foods commented that high interest rates resulted in low investment, and advocated increasing the tax on dividends instead. This would encourage management to reinvest profit rather than pay it out in the form of dividends: 'I've got greedy investors who insist on high dividends', he said.

These environmental factors are explored in Chapter 4.

SUMMARY

The mission

This should clearly identify:

- the customers/clients to be served
- the needs to be satisfied
- the means – products and/or technologies by which these will be achieved.

Objectives

- Organisations will have multiple objectives
- Organisations will have long-term and short-term objectives
- Objectives may conflict
- Objectives must be prioritised
- The yardstick(s) by which an objective is measured must be carefully chosen and defined.

Stakeholder analysis

- Stakeholders are those individuals or organisations who influence, or are influenced by the decisions of the organisation
- These questions need to be asked:
  1. Who are the stakeholders concerned?
  2. What is their relative power?
  3. How great is the importance to them of a particular issue – which they will therefore support or oppose?
  4. Where and how will they exert their influence and power?

EXERCISES

1 Write a mission statement for an organisation of your choice.

2 Helena Rubinstein, the beauty specialist, said 'I don't sell cosmetics, I sell hope', and an insurance company advertises that it sells 'Peace of Mind'. How might the following organisations answer the question, 'What business are we in?':

(a) A luxury ice-cream manufacturer.

(b) A travel agent.

(c) The Automobile Association.

(d) A hypermarket.

(e) A house-builder.

3 What *quantifiable* measurements might these stakeholders consider to be the most important way to judge the performance of a firm?

4 Who are the stakeholders of the following organisations?

(a) A hypermarket.

(b) A medical centre.

(c) A village cricket team or theatre group.

FURTHER READING

Ansoff, I., *Corporate Strategy*, Rev Edn, Penguin Books 1988. This classic text offers a comprehensive treatment of objectives, including some ideas that have been neglected by some later writers.

Johnson, G. and Scholes, K., *Exploring Corporate Strategy*, Prentice Hall, 1993. Their discussions on stakeholders, and other behavioural topics such as culture, are authoratative.

Pearce, J. and Robinson Jr, R. B., *Strategic Management: Formulation, Implementations and Control*, Irwin, 1994. Chapter 2 contains a detailed treatment of organisational missions.

Rowe, A. J., Mason, R. O., Dickel, K. E., Mann, R. B. and Mockler, R. J., *Strategic Management: A Methodological Approach*, Addison-Wesley, 1994. Chapter 4 contains one of the fuller approaches to stakeholder analysis in considerable depth.

REFERENCES

1 *Financial Times*, 28 October 1992, 4 November 1992.
2 Peters, T. J. and Waterman, R. H., *In Search of Excellence*, Harper & Row, 1982.
3 Heller, R., *Management Decision*, Vol 32, No 8, 1994.

CHAPTER 4

The environment

Previous chapters have stressed the importance of an organisation responding to or anticipating changes in its environment – taking advantage of opportunities and countering threats. The action could range from making a small price change to deciding to quit the industry. On the other hand, the organisation may decide not to act, or it may adopt a wait-and-see approach. These are strategic decisions which should follow environmental analysis and evaluation of the consequences. In this chapter we consider some of the forces at work in the environment and how firms may respond to them. The view is that of someone conducting a formal analysis in order to review corporate strategy.

MONITORING THE ENVIRONMENT

In order to maintain contact with environmental trends, the departments or functions of an organisation should continuously monitor developments in their own particular areas. For example, the Marketing department will keep an eye on competitors' new products, the Buying department will monitor the price of raw materials, etc. This is not only in order to perform their own function more effectively, but also, as the specialists, they are best placed to identify the strategic significance of developments in their particular fields, and their interpretation of events and their forecasts should be fed into day-to-day management decisions and long-term planning.

Before the National Lottery commenced, Nestlé Rowntree spent six months researching the probable impact on retailers. They anticipated that participating stores would gain customers, but feared that consumers' disposable income could be diverted from confectionery to lottery tickets. They may have also had in mind the fact that a major competitor, Cadbury, was a member of the lottery operator.[1]

Each department will, however, see the environment from its own particular perspective, and their views will not necessarily give a complete or an objective picture. For example, what might seem at the time to be merely a competitor's short-term tactic and, therefore ignored, may in fact be a strategic move – or become so when they realise how effective it is, i.e. an emergent strategy.

Although the newspaper market is one of the most heavily researched, the extent to which it is price sensitive had not been appreciated. When the price of The Times *was reduced, other papers thought it merely a flash in the pan; however, the effect on the industry was traumatic, and* The Times *obtained a lead that other papers found very difficult to counter.*

In obtaining a corporate overview, there are three major standpoints from which the environment should be viewed, the first being that of the industry within which the firm operates.

INDUSTRY ANALYSIS

The perspective is from within the firm, an *industry analysis* – looking at, for example, trends concerning the industry as a whole, competition within the industry, technologies employed, what it takes to succeed – the key success factors (KSF) – and comparing the firm, its products, its systems, its technology and so on with others in the industry, particularly the most successful.

This process, termed *benchmarking*, is increasingly being adopted by organisations in many industries, and a survey by the Confederation of British Industries (CBI) found that 82 per cent of the firms that practised benchmarking believed it was successful. It should not, however, be limited to organisations of a similar type; much can be learned and applied by studying how things are done in other industries.

A chocolate manufacturer who wanted to make its product more shiny, benchmarked with a cosmetics company which was doing the same with its lipstick.[2]

LIFE-CYCLES

Just as products frequently go through the life-cycle stages of introduction, growth, maturity and decline, so too do industries and the technologies they employ. These must therefore be carefully considered when analysing trends. Although industries and products may come and go, the basic needs they satisfy remain; there is no likelihood of a decline in the demand for the means of cooking food, for clothing, shelter, for less basic needs such as means of communicating over distance, travel, home entertainment, artificial light, although demand will fluctuate and be dependent upon environmental factors such as demographics and economic considerations. There are, however, many ways of satisfying these needs; for example, one can communicate by letter, telephone, radio, fax or electronic mail, and these means give rise to technologies and industries that do have life-cycles.

An industry may adopt successively superior production or superior product technologies – or both – to meet the ongoing need. For example, the first incandescent electric lights had carbon filaments made by burning cotton thread within the bulb. These were superseded first by metal filaments and then by gas-filled lamps, while the technology of production also improved under competitive pressure and to meet growing demand. As the use of electricity grew, the same manufacturers also produced neon lights, fluorescent lamps, sodium lamps, etc., based on different *product* technologies but using broadly similar *production* technologies. However, these products did not replace incandescent lamps but supplemented them, since their applications and uses met different needs or provided different benefits. Electric light did, however, end the career of the street gas-lamp lighter; candles are now rarely found outside churches or on birthday cakes, while the site previously occupied by The Gaslight and Coke Company has long been an office block.

In these cases, new technology meant the death of those firms in an industry that did not or could not adapt to the changed circumstances. However, a firm could, perhaps, survive if it did adopt the new technology. IBM was a manufacturer of punched-card equipment but switched to making computers just in time; others failed to do so or left it too late. Similarly, most manufacturers of steam-powered road vehicles failed to adopt the internal combustion engine and are now forgotten. This phenomenon occurs frequently because, when a new technology arises, the existing technological leaders attempt to protect and maintain the current technology, particularly when committed to a large customer base. This may leave an opportunity for a challenger to enter the market with the superior technology and others will then follow. The existing customer base may help to prolong the life of what is clearly an obsolete product and provide a breathing space which will enable existing firms to adopt the new technology, but there is the danger that they will be unable to catch up if they leave it too late.

Solex manufactured carburettors in the UK and had a very high market share. Although fuel injection systems were increasingly being adopted, Solex failed to develop a product and lost sales of original equipment to car manufacturers, although replacement and spare-part sales continued satisfactorily. When they finally decided to respond, the market was dominated by Bosch and other highly regarded manufacturers who had well-established products that would be virtually impossible to displace. The parent French company decided that the cost of developing a system and trying to compete was not worth while, and Solex went under.

In some cases, the rise of an alternative competitive technology can be met by product improvement; this is the basic strategy of cross-channel ferry companies in meeting the threat of the Channel tunnel – they have little choice since they cannot drill another tunnel – although other considerations such as pricing and identification of target markets are crucial to their strategy. In other circumstances, however, when an industry is in the maturity stage of its life-cycle, there may not be much scope for further product improvement, and this could result in a different strategy. This is currently the case with a number of electronic consumer products.

In the early stages of the product life-cycle of CD players, when the product technology was improving rapidly, manufacturers constantly leap-frogged their competitors with superior equipment in order to gain competitive advantage, and invested heavily in new product development. However, the rate of technological advance has now levelled out and slowed down, and so too has the rate of new product introduction.

In these circumstances, the product life-cycle is longer, resulting in less pressure for expenditure on product development. Nevertheless, profits will be low because of the intense competition which invariably occurs in the maturity stage. The emphasis will therefore probably switch from product development to production methods in order to cut costs and thus improve profitability.

Conversely, however, in some industries, particularly when the production technology lends itself to product variety, the opposite effect occurs: product proliferation is then often a characteristic of the maturity stage. Although a market may have stopped growing overall, it frequently develops into different segments with different needs as consumers become more sophisticated. Consider the variety of personal stereos or microwave ovens: although the basic technology has remained unchanged for years, new products continue to be launched. Manufacturers desperately seeking improved profit performance attempt to develop new products for particular segments that could provide a breakthrough in higher profits and at the same time increase their overall market share.

The technology of baking is easily adaptable to producing a range of products. As a result, the variety of biscuits now available on supermarket shelves is bewildering. Similarly, many bakeries are now producing speciality loaves at much higher profit margins than sliced white bread can provide for both the baker and the supermarket.

Although the car industry's origins lay in the mass production of a single, standard product, the technologies of production and distribution, together with the pressure of competition, have resulted in Ford offering 24 variants of the Escort alone.

However, in a well-developed market which has reached the maturity stage, production technology will probably be capital intensive with a high level of expensive automation, resulting in correspondingly high fixed costs that can only be paid for by high production levels. As a result, a mature, highly automated industry will almost invariably have a production capacity that is greater than demand, so that factories will often be working below optimum capacity. Market pressures will therefore force prices down as firms fight for market share to pay for the high overheads. Despite the low profitability and intense competition, major firms will be reluctant to leave the industry because of the heavy investments they have already made, so that they may make even further investment in an effort to squeeze out even more efficiency and reduce costs. This will be difficult, however, because the most significant improvements will have already been obtained. The effect will be to increase fixed costs while reducing variable costs. This means that the less efficient and smaller-scale manufacturers who cannot compete on cost will be forced out of the market unless they can find a niche where competition is less fierce, or can offer some differential advantage to justify higher prices. This happened in the sliced white bread market where there is considerable over-capacity of production. The product was used by supermarkets as a loss-leader to attract shoppers, typically charging 21 pence for a loaf that cost some bakers 27 pence to produce. Only the largest and most efficient bakeries could meet these conditions.

It is not only smaller manufacturers who are affected by intense competition in mature markets. Research by the marketing consultancy Added Value showed that the typical marketing cost of being one of the top 70 grocery brands is nearly £8 million.[3] In 1994, Heinz had an advertising budget of £15 million – to divide among more than 20 product categories. The implications of this were far-reaching.

It will be seen that the forces at work within an industry can be extremely complex, requiring a wide-ranging depth of analysis, but this is only one aspect of the environment.

MARKET-PLACE ANALYSIS

Another view is from a vantage point a step further away: that of the marketplace, in particular taking the perspective of existing and prospective customers. The marketplace overlaps, but does not necessarily coincide with 'the industry'. It is where prospective customers seek solutions to their problems, and it may be that other, different, competing industries could provide those solutions either at present, or in the future.

Coal is only one of several alternatives in the energy market, and the coal industry must be viewed in that context; the manufacturer of baked beans is in the convenience food market – parents seeking something easily prepared for the children's supper could also solve the problem with fish fingers, tinned spaghetti, a microwave meal, or might telephone for a pizza to be delivered; glass-fibre is only one of half-a-dozen different materials for insulating a loft, and is produced by a different industry from say, rock wool or expanded polystyrene. This raises the question of how 'the market' is defined. Consider the photographic camera market: the sales of single-lens reflex cameras were very badly hit by the development of compact cameras – in many cases made by the same manufacturers. The camera market, as a whole, has been affected by the sale of video-cameras – in some cases made by the same manufacturers; video-cameras virtually killed off cine-cameras – some of which were made by . . . etc. A firm may operate in several markets; one may be growing while another is declining; one may be very attractive because of its size, but might also be fiercely competitive when compared to another, smaller arena. Each market or market segment – *and their trends* – must be considered separately.

The Investors Chronicle, *commenting on the performance of different chains within the Burton Group, said: 'For the fashionable 15–25 year old, Top Shop is doing well, but Top Man is doing badly. Dorothy Perkins, aimed at an older woman, is doing well; Burton, which targets older men is struggling, while Principals is doing worst of all.'*

Some firms may confine themselves to a very narrow niche of a large market, and although quite small, could nevertheless dominate it.

Morgan Cars produce fewer than ten cars a week, but are the market leader in the classic sports car market. Ford, Vauxhall and other mass-market manufacturers do not compete in this market, and are unlikely to do so because it is too small a market to interest them.

There may, nevertheless, be interactions between market segments. Another relatively small car manufacturer, Mazda, with a market share of only about 1 per cent, offers a wide range of cars, albeit at above-average prices. In order to compete with the giants, they must differentiate their cars in some way.

The Marketing Director of Mazda said: 'We are not chasing the same market as the Ford Fiesta or the Vauxhall Astra, and would never pretend to do so.' Mazda's range of models includes three different luxury sports cars (MX3, MX5 and MX6). 'It is our sports models that are helping us to build a brand identity . . . that is different from the herd.'

Firms operating in one clearly defined segment should nevertheless also monitor developments beyond the boundaries of their activities; those which take too narrow a view run the danger of being overtaken by unforeseen events.

A major frozen food company had, for some time, been correctly claiming about 70 per cent of the frozen food market – as they defined it. They did not include products they did not sell, nor did they include grocers' own-label and certain other goods such as frozen chickens in their definition because they did not supply those products, and therefore did not perceive them as competition. However, a survey of typical shopping centres – the market-place – showed that their market share of total frozen food sales was closer to 35 per cent and declining. This led to a rapid reappraisal of their strategy.

The focus of this analysis should be on the market, not on the firm, and it is crucially important to take care in defining the market – think of the market for Morgan cars. Consumers choose between competing offerings, not between competing firms – although the firms' relative strengths, strategies, images, etc. will largely determine success. For this reason, it is advisable to conduct a *competitor analysis*, considering not merely the nature and extent of competition but also identifying major competitors, their strengths and weaknesses and those of their products, their objectives, their strategies and their technologies. In addition to identifying individual competitors, the *market structure* as a whole must be examined. Does it consist of a lot of little fish – suppliers or customers? Is it dominated by relatively few large firms, or is the structure somewhere between these extremes? And so on.

It is also important to recognise that the marketplace includes not only customers and competitors, but that other parties are also involved. Consider the power of retailers in the grocery industry; five supermarket chains account for about 80 per cent of all sales. Located at the head office of each of these are the buyers who negotiate with suppliers. If they don't like your product, or your terms of trade – or possibly you or your firm – then 80 per cent of the market could be denied to you – by five people.

A Tesco market controller was reported as saying that me-too products (products that are basically copies of leading brands) nevertheless have a place in retailers' minds as a 'profit opportunity' because their manufacturers are forced to offer very fat margins just to keep their products on the shelves.[4]

THE POWER OF CUSTOMERS

In an important sense, retailers are also buyers, and the major groups have considerable power which they naturally exercise. In a highly competitive market they are in a very strong position and can negotiate favourable terms of trade from manufacturers. Furthermore, the growing popularity of retailers' own-label goods can make them direct competitors of branded goods manufacturers, thus adding further to their power. It was reported that Unilever withdrew its advertising from a publisher's magazines – resulting in a loss of about £1 million of advertising revenue – because the publisher stood out and refused to accept the terms offered by Unilever's agents.[5]

THE POWER OF SUPPLIERS

In other situations – sellers' markets – power may lie with suppliers, such as manufacturers of vital components in short supply who can thereby charge high prices and choose their customers, or whose product is in high demand so that they can pick and choose distributors.

In 1995, Levi-Strauss delisted more than 450 retailers who failed to meet their standards for product range and display, service, and location and design of stores. At the same time they were severely restricting supplies to one of the UK's largest discount clothes retailers which claimed that Levi's did so because of the chain's status as a membership club.[6]

They referred the case to the Office of Fair Trading, who declined to investigate because they had less than 25 per cent of the market but, in another case, the Office of Fair Trading said that Trebor Bassett, a major confectionary manufacturer with 25 per cent value share of the market, exerted pressure on a number of retailers to stop them stocking the products of a smaller sweet manufacturer, Sweetmate.

PORTER'S FIVE-FORCE MODEL

The *power of customers* and the *power of suppliers* are two of the five forces that are identified in *Porter's five-force model*[7] as factors that influence the profitability of a particular market and hence of the firm, and which should be taken into account in strategic decisions concerning the market.

Competitive rivalry is Porter's third force. Intense competition will force down prices and profits, but conversely, if competition is weak, there will be less need for price trimming or heavy expenditure on anti-competitive activity, thus improving profitability.

Ease of entry into the market is another important factor. Unless this is difficult – due, for example, to the high capital investment or special expertise needed, or problems in obtaining distribution, components or raw materials, then an attractive market is likely to attract new entrants who by increasing competition will reduce its profitability.

Porter's fifth force concerns the threat of *substitutes and alternatives* which could make the market less attractive. As previously mentioned, the roof-insulation market offers a number of alternatives such as glass-fibre, rock-wool, expanded polystyrene, etc. A customer's choice will depend upon how they perceive the benefits and value of the alternatives, and a cheap substitute will depress prices and profits.

These five forces are major influences on the profitability of a market, but other factors such as trends in demand, production, distribution, marketing and other costs must also be considered in deciding the appropriate strategy.

It is not only customers, suppliers, competitors and distributors that may be important, and it is for this reason that, in a formal study, a *stakeholder analysis* should be conducted in order to identify all parties whose interests must be taken into account, for example, consider the pharmaceutical market. The influence of the medical profession on the sales of pharmaceutical products both to National Health Service hospitals and to individual patients is enormous, yet their own direct purchases are a small proportion of total sales. Another important force in this market is the government; their politics, policy, legislation, and regulations concerning, for example, prescription charges, choice of drugs, funding and so on, have a profound effect on particular firms and the market as a whole. The government's efforts to reduce NHS prescriptions, together with higher prescription charges, increased the public's demand for over-the-counter (OTC) preparations that do not require a prescription – particularly if they cost less than the prescription charge. This in turn led to a strong response from the industry to take advantage of the new market opportunity, perhaps offering the same drug in both markets. However, the characteristics of the OTC market require a very different strategy; the entire marketing mix – product, place, promotion and price – had to be matched to a consumer market, rather than that of the medical profession.

Another important feature is legislation such as patent law which may be a barrier to entry – for a while. Prescription-only drugs can earn huge profits – until the patent runs out. The UK patent for Tagamet ran out in 1988 and in 1994 in the USA, where it failed to obtain OTC approval. The manufacturers had to reduce the price by 80 per cent and, because the patent had expired, competitors were able to enter the market. Sales fell by 76 per cent.[8]

Governmental action affected the economy: the public's attitude to medication; the industry; the pattern of demand for existing and new OTC and prescription-only products; pharmacies and other channels of distribution such as chemists and other suppliers. In other words, governmental politico-legal activity affects not only the market and industry, but may be a major force at work in the wider environment within which they are located, the *macro-environment*. The macro-environment provides the setting for, and affects all organisations and individuals: customers, suppliers and channels of distribution as well as the market-place and the industry.

THE MACRO-ENVIRONMENT

A global perspective is essential. For example, world-wide, the pharmaceutical industry underwent major shake-ups as a result of changes in the healthcare market, not only in the UK, but also in Japan, Europe and, in particular, in the world's biggest market, the USA. There the changes were traumatic: the average profit growth rate fell from about 19 per cent in the late 1980s to about 8 per cent in 1993, while overall market growth fell from 8 per cent in 1992 to 1.4 per cent in 1993. These inevitably affected the UK, as firms – particularly American firms – adjusted to the new circumstances. When some markets become less attractive, manufacturers will seek opportunities elsewhere and transfer their efforts to other markets. American drug-houses were therefore attracted to the UK market, intensifying competition with domestic manufacturers.

Similarly, because the British economy was the first to show signs of recovery from the recession in early 1994 – it was the only western European country in which the demand for new cars increased – the UK immediately became the target for car manufacturers from all over the world. However, this higher demand resulted in fierce competition with the result that promotional expenditure hit the roof and eroded profits.

Pharmaceuticals and cars are both examples of highly competitive markets which are highly volatile, with buy-outs, take-overs and changes of ownership occurring on a global scale, resulting in concentration in the industry – the market becoming dominated by fewer giants. In 1994 alone, SmithKline Beecham acquired Sterling Health, American Home Products bought Cyanamid, Merck bought Medco, Eli Lilly bought PCS, Roche bought Syntex, and Sanboz bought Gerber; 1995 started with Glaxo acquiring Wellcome to form Britain's largest firm in any industry and more than £30 billion changed hands.

For many organisations their environment will extend to the other side of the world; their competitors' home bases may be there, their future markets may well be developing there, their raw materials, components or even their products may be sourced there. Not merely firms, but whole industries may well be affected by *politico-legal, ecological, socio-cultural, economic, technological* or other developments and trends half-way round the globe.

PEST ANALYSIS

The first stage of a formal environmental analysis – as distinct from this discussion – is to examine this global macro-environment which embraces the industry and the marketplace, considering each of the aspects mentioned in the paragraph above in order to understand the past and present, and to develop a strategy to match the future environment. This is sometimes referred to as the *PEST analysis* (Politico-legal, Economic, Social, Technological).

It is important, however, not to treat these aspects as a mere check-list. The environment is a complex system the components of which interact, so that the analysis should not only consider each heading in turn, but also look for interrelationships which could reinforce their effect. Although we speak of the 'economic environment', it is important to bear in mind that in many cases the economic aspects are only part of the total situation, and to understand the complete picture it is necessary to examine interactions between different features of the total environment.

The British coal industry has been the focus of interactions between all six factors. Just a few of these are: the social impact on whole communities of coal mines closing; social pressures on the government to review their decisions; the political decisions by the government; legislation restricting the industrial action that trade unions might take; reactions of trade unions; advances in the technology of coal mining which made smaller mines uneconomic; the economic environment both at the time of the closure decision and subsequently; the complex economics of investment in, and prices of, different sources of energy; the ecological implications of the use of fossil fuels and their alternatives such as nuclear power; and societal attitudes concerning these ecological considerations.

Within this overall environment, the industry is under attack by, for example, cheap opencast coal from the antipodes and cheap deep-mined coal from eastern Europe.

Finally, one should not think of the environment as consisting of a series of nesting Russian dolls; the macro-environment, market-place and industry provide different points of view giving particular perspectives to the position of the organisation, and they interpenetrate at their interfaces (*see* Fig 4.1). Furthermore, developments in one industry may impact another even when they are not substitutes or alternatives.

An obvious example of this is the way component suppliers are affected by the sales of the manufacturers they supply – and vice versa.

When a fire occurred at a factory which made the resin used by computer microchip manufacturers to encapsulate the microchips, the computer manufacturers that they in turn supplied immediately raised their prices in anticipation of a shortage of chips.

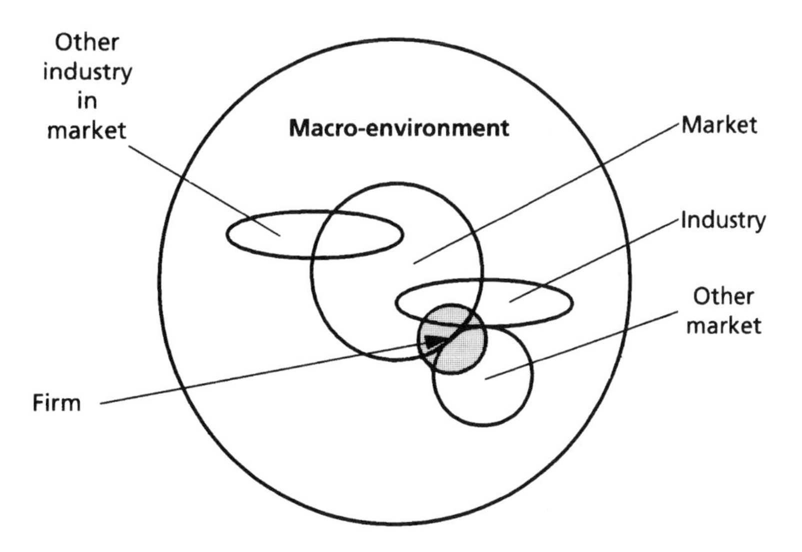

Fig 4.1 Markets in the macro-environment

Another example is the degree to which carpet and furniture sales depend upon the state of the housing market – a very high proportion are bought on moving home.

The technique of *impact analysis* – estimating the probability and effect of such events may identify potentially dangerous environmental threats that could erupt unexpectedly – raises issues that can be summarised under the heading of environmental *turbulence*. The term will be explored in more detail in Chapter 12, but to illustrate the significance of the point, consider a firm operating in a very stable environment: demand has been growing at a steady rate and all the signs suggest this will continue; the nature and extent of competition are stable; the technologies of the product, of production and the channels of distribution are well established and there is no reason to suppose that they will change. In these circumstances, the past is an excellent guide to the future which can therefore be forecast with confidence. The firm can make plans with a high degree of certainty; it can be managed on the basis of rules, procedures or policies for virtually every eventuality because rarely does anything new ever happen. Hence, individual initiative, entrepreneurship or creativity are unnecessary and might even be discouraged; a bureaucratic organisation is the most appropriate and efficient, everyone having a clearly defined job specification.

At the other extreme, for a firm in a highly turbulent environment – where the past never repeats itself; when the unexpected must be expected; when plans cannot be based on forecasts because it is impossible to predict the future – a completely different culture, structure and management style would be essential. For them, the best way to predict the future is to invent it, to make it happen, rather as adept canoeists in turbulent white water can use the force of the flow to avoid the rocks and speed them on their way. This, however, is within the power of very few organisations; the others must find alternative ways to deal with the problem, and this is considered in Chapter 12.

While few organisations lie at these extremes, the point illustrates the important fact that matching an organisation to its environment implies much more than developing an appropriate strategy.

Formal analysis of an organisation's circumstances for the purpose of reviewing its strategy should start with the macro-environment since this provides a context for considering the market-place, the industry in which the firm operates, and then, with an understanding of its environment, the firm itself. This sequence, rather than starting with the firm and then considering its environment, militates against the danger of interpreting the environment from the existing perspective of the firm. This may not only have become outdated, but could itself prevent that fact from being recognised.

Before proceeding to the next stage of a formal analysis, that of considering the organisation itself, it is essential to draw conclusions from the environmental audit, and to identify and record the particular features that are, or will be, or could become, of strategic importance: the environmental *key issues*.

There are, of course, innumerable forces at work in the environment but, in developing a strategy, they must for three reasons be narrowed down to a handful. First, if strategists attempt to take too many factors into account, there is a danger of not being able to see the wood for the trees, resulting in a confused picture and a confused analysis – Lindblom's 'muddling through'.[9] Second, organisational strategy must have a distinctly defined thrust that is clear to both those inside and outside the organisation. Finally, there usually are only very few *really* important factors; on the other hand the analyst must not resort to 'reductionism', which is to ignore what are, in fact, important considerations in order to simplify the situation.

EXERCISES

1 Conduct PEST analyses for the macro-environment of an industry of your choice *and* one of the following. Identify and compare the key issues.

The defence industry.
The motor car industry.
The fresh vegetable industry.
The public house industry.

2 Use Porter's five-force model to evaluate the markets of the industries in Question 1.

FURTHER READING

Lehmann, D. R. and Winer, R. S., *Analysis for Marketing Planning*, Irwin, 1991. As the title indicates, this book takes a marketing perspective and is a practical guide rather than an academic treatise and is recommended to anyone needing to conduct PEST analyses.

Palmer, A. and Worthington, I., *The Business and Marketing Environment*, McGraw-Hill, 1992. This is one of the few books entirely devoted to PEST analysis. This is a readable volume that treats each aspect at some length and reasonable depth, and like the previous title, takes a marketing perspective.

Porter, M. E., *Competitive Strategy*, Free Press, 1980. This is by far the best and clearest source of Porter's own ideas.

Rowe, A. J., Mason, R. O., Dickel, K. E., Mann, R. B. and Mockler, R. J., *Strategic Management: A Methodological Approach*, Addison-Wesley, 1994. This title offers a very comprehensive framework for conducting PEST analysis.

REFERENCES

1 *Marketing Week*, 2 September 1994.
2 *Marketing Week*, p. 55, 4 November 1994.
3 *Marketing Week*, 7 October 1994.
4 *Marketing Week*, 7 October 1994.
5 *Marketing Week*, 11 December 1992.
6 *Marketing Week*, 10 February 1995.
7 Porter, M. E., *Competitive Strategy*, Free Press, 1980.
8 *Marketing Week*, 4 November 1994.
9 Lindblom, C. E., The Science of Muddling Through. *Public Admin Review*, Spring 1959.

CHAPTER 5

Analysing the organisation

Just as everyday strategic management requires the environment to be continuously monitored, so too must many aspects of the organisation itself. Much of this activity will be the normal process of monitoring and control – ensuring that the organisation is on track. This is discussed further in Chapter 11. However, on occasion, a more intensive study may be undertaken, either when the overall strategy is under review, or when the monitoring suggests that all is not well.

The purpose is to identify those internal weaknesses that, either at present or in the future, could adversely affect performance. Some can be ignored as relatively trivial or not requiring action unless they worsen; some can be corrected immediately or programmed for later action; some may be identified as being of considerable consequence but not requiring a change in strategy; but others – and there will be relatively few – may clearly be of major strategic importance, and should be identified as such. Conversely, the analysis should evaluate those internal strengths which are the bases of the organisation's current strategy in order not only to ensure that they continue to be both effective and relevant to the present and future environment, but also to seek additional strengths that could contribute to success.

An important aspect of the evaluation is comparison. Unless the data are compared to those of competitors, the industry and the broader environment, they cannot be properly evaluated. For example, management may consider that achieving an annual sales increase of 10 per cent is satisfactory. This may be so when compared to an increase in GNP of 2 per cent, but not if its particular market is growing by 12 per cent, and that of the market-leader by 18 per cent.

There are two features to the evaluation: first, how *efficiently* the organisation is carrying out its tasks and second, how *effectively* it is operating.

Efficiency is concerned with how well inputs such as budgets, labour or management time, and resources such as shop premises, production capacity, technologies or skills are converted into outputs. For example, a firm might have a very high level of both machine and labour productivity, a very low reject rate, low costs, and various other characteristics that would label production as highly *efficient*. Efficiency usually refers to internal aspects of the organisation. If, however, it is producing an obsolete product for which there is little demand, or one which is not generating a satisfactory profit because intense competition keeps prices low, then resources are not being used *effectively*. Effectiveness may refer both to the internal application of resources and to the organisation in relation to its environment.

A Swedish firm, Sonessons, was very efficient in producing low-value stainless steel stovepipes and kitchen sinks. When, however, it diversified by applying its skills and technology to produce medical equipment, its profits rose phenomenally – it was using its resources more effectively by making different products.

In the case of an obsolete product, the firm is not well matched to its environment; in the case of low margins, it is not achieving its profit objectives.

There are four aspects to the analysis:

1 The organisation as a whole, and what is going on within it.
2 The organisation in relation to its objectives.
3 The organisation in relation to the environment.
4 The products or services in relation to the environment.

ANALYSING THE ORGANISATION AS A WHOLE

The internal audit

As is the case with the environmental analysis, trends and forecasts are as important as the current situation, and every effort should be made to look to the future. The customary framework for internal analysis is to consider the following four aspects of the organisation: financial performance; function or department; organisational structure; intangibles.

First, the *financial performance* of the organisation as a whole. This should cover several past years if the data are available, in order to analyse trends which can then be compared with those of the industry as a whole and with those of competitors, and to identify scope for improvement or danger signals. There is a standard list of parameters for financial analysis largely consisting of a number of financial ratios, and these are easily calculated or, in the case of the larger public companies, possibly obtained from a database.

Second, each *function or department* should be considered in turn – production, finance, human resource management, R&D, marketing, etc., examining its efficiency and effectiveness, strengths and weaknesses. The importance of the findings will depend on the particular circumstances. For example, the analysis may reveal that credit control is poor and the average length of credit is longer than desirable. In some firms, remedying this may merely be a question of better housekeeping with no strategic significance, but for other organisations it could result in an expensive overdraft that inhibits expansion or, as was the case with Club 24, result in near ruin.

Third, in addition to analysis of each function, the *organisational structure* – the skeleton that holds them in their relative positions – should be considered.

In an organisation that has grown in size or range of activities, this is frequently no longer appropriate. Sometimes environmental changes create or expose a mismatch between the structure and the environment. Structure is considered in Chapter 6.

At one time United Biscuits' two subsidiaries, KP selling snacks and McVities selling biscuits, had separate sales forces. This simplified management and control, but they were merged in 1994 in the interests of efficiency.

Birds Eye was structured with one sales force calling on caterers and another on retailers. A catering salesperson could therefore be calling on a restaurant while a retail colleague was calling on the supermarket next door. This may appear to be inefficient, but is much more effective *since each understands the particular product/market requirements which differ considerably.*

Finally, within this framework are two sets of features that although labelled as *intangibles,* are at least as important as the other attributes. These include characteristics such as attitude to risk, the organisational 'formula for success', management ethos, style, etc. These are features that determine how things are done and what is acceptable to the decision makers – broadly, the culture of the organisation which is considered in Chapter 7. In other words, they shape strategy and must be taken into account in any recommendations – which perhaps include a change in these attitudes and beliefs themselves. The others are features such as brand images, quality of relationships with customers, suppliers, stockists and sources of finance. These may be important assets – or liabilities.

An incalculably valuable asset of Coca-Cola was their worldwide image which enabled them to charge a premium price for their cola – which did not fare particularly well in blind tests, when drinkers did not know the brand they were tasting. Suddenly, in late 1994, not only retailers such as Sainsbury and Safeway but new entrants such as Virgin deflated this balloon with their own brands.

Will consumers continue to pay the 'brand tax', 'the extra costs of hiring rock stars and the like to promote and sustain a brand's image', as the CEO of the firm that makes most of these rival colas described it?

One of the shortcomings of analysing an organisation department by department is its inevitable emphasis on what is being done and how it is done at present, although this may expose shortcomings that can and should be remedied. Another, more fundamental approach is to stand back and identify as the starting point what *needs* to be done. This will reduce the dangers of concentrating on efficiency rather than effectiveness, of not seeing the wood for the trees and of adopting existing, perhaps outdated, perspectives.

There is an increasing trend in organisations towards breaking down departmental barriers, looking at what needs to be done regardless of who is currently doing it, and then designing an appropriate organisation – and perhaps product too. This approach, sometimes called 'business re-engineering' – where the emphasis is on *processes* rather than functions, divisions or products – has achieved remarkable results in a number of organisations. For example, credit control has been mentioned above; in many organisations an important part of a salesperson's job may be the collection of outstanding debt; although members of the sales department, they are also part of the financial system.

The major competitive advantage of a frozen food manufacturer lay in providing delivery within 24 hours of a salesperson taking the order, when the industry norm was often more than three days. This was much valued by retailers who, as a result, favoured that brand, and it resulted in high market share. As demand grew, however, so did the number of important customers complaining of late delivery – to the annoyance of the Sales Director who naturally blamed distribution.

On investigation, however, it was found that the fault lay not with distribution, but with his own sales team who were not transmitting the orders back to the office in time for them to be processed and packed for next-day delivery: the sales force was a crucial part of the order-processing system.

For a firm whose major competitive differential advantage was next-day delivery, this was *of strategic importance; for another firm in different circumstances, providing next-day delivery might be a completely unnecessary cost and, in fact, when this service was no longer of value to retailers because they had installed more storage capacity, it was stopped.*

Making it easy for a customer to place an order, speedy order taking, order processing, and delivery all play an important role in providing customer satisfaction which is now recognised as one of the major driving forces of every organisation, and therefore a focus for business re-engineering, the thrust often being provided by information technology.

Citibank's credit analysis system was overhauled and staff, instead of processing paper, were able to spend a higher proportion of their time – 43 per cent instead of 9 per cent – on getting new business. Profits increased by more than 750 per cent over a period of two years.[1]

The Seven S framework

A different and very powerful framework for internal analysis which also adopts a systems approach in that it considers interactions between sub-systems, but which focuses on the organisation as a whole rather than on individual components is 'The Seven S framework'.[2] This is additional, not alternative, to the internal audit approach, although they do overlap.

The underlying principle is that an organisation consists of seven subsystems which are all of importance in achieving success. They interact with each other: change one, and any or all of the others may need to be changed for optimum organisational efficiency and effectiveness. Many organisations recognise the relationship between strategy and structure, but neglect other, equally important relationships. Even the most appropriate strategy may fail if the other factors do not fit – all of the needles must point in the same direction.

The 'every day low price' strategy of Woolworths, mentioned in Chapter 1, is that of its parent company, Kingfisher. A Financial Times *analyst commented 'Marks & Spencer's surging profits are living proof that Kingfisher's every day low-pricing strategy works. Sadly, there is little evidence that it works at Kingfisher.'*[3] *The reason for this failure was given by another analyst: 'Every day low-pricing is not all about low-pricing, it is about delivering a better deal and a fair deal every time. It is probable that the other ingredients of the strategy have been on the back-burner because Kingfisher does not have the systems to deliver.' Three months after that comment, major structural changes were announced, '. . . designed to improve performance and enable the stores to react quickly. . . .'*[4]

The Seven Ss are:

Structure. The emphasis should be not on how to divide up tasks but on how to co-ordinate them.

Strategy. Actions planned in response to environmental changes in order to achieve organisational objectives.

Systems. How the organisation gets things done: in particular, information systems, but also, for example, training, budgeting, and accounting.

Style. The way managers manage; the way they do things.

Staff. 'People' issues: both 'hard', such as recruitment, promotion and payment, and 'soft', such as appraisal, morale and, in particular, staff development.

Skills. What the organisation and personnel do best or need to do well in order to be successful.

Superordinate goals/shared values. The organisational guiding principles, ethos, values, aspirations, mission.

The framework was specifically designed to relate to interactions between the factors when one or more are changed – particularly the implications of changes in strategy – rather than as a basis for auditing an organisation, and for this reason should be considered when change is contemplated. It is particularly valuable when used together with a business re-engineering approach since this almost invariably challenges every aspect of the existing organisation.

THE ORGANISATION IN RELATION TO ITS OBJECTIVES

An organisation exists to achieve its primary objectives and these must always be present in the mind of management, who should resist being tempted to pursue improvements for their own sake, perhaps concentrating on efficiency and thereby losing sight of the ends they should serve.

In examining various aspects of the organisation, their contribution to achieving departmental and organisational objectives should be continuously questioned. Are there better, more effective ways of achieving the same ends? Are they a resource – a strength – with untapped potential? Conversely, are they unduly costly for what they accomplish – in other words, poor value for the resources they employ – over-engineered?

THE ORGANISATION IN RELATION TO THE ENVIRONMENT

Since strategic management is largely concerned with matching an organisation to its environment in order to achieve organisational objectives, this aspect of the internal analysis formally relates the two sections above to the findings of Chapter 4.

Portfolio analysis

It is the organisation's products or services that are at the interface between itself and its environment, and therefore it is these that are the main focus of this part of the analysis. Just as each function or department should be considered, so too should each individual subsidiary, division, product or service which is above a minimum size. As a general rule of thumb, each one of these that contributes more than 5 per cent to sales, profit, revenue, costs or any other important parameter should, if possible, be analysed individually (the remainder can be lumped together).

The analysis should consider how well each product or service meets the needs of its target market, and in particular, how it compares with competitors' products, how its market and demand are expected to develop and other implications of the environmental audit.

The future contributions of each product or service should be forecast. If these are totalled and plotted on a chart it may be seen whether, in the future, the total will match the quantifiable objectives. If not, the chart will show the *planning gap* between targets for the next few years and what will probably happen if no new decisions are made. It is this planning gap that must be filled by a revision of the corporate strategy (*see* Fig 5.1).

The review may strongly suggest that certain changes should be made. However, decisions should not be finalised at this stage; a coherent picture of the future organisation must be created, rather than a set of recommendations that may not be mutually compatible. Furthermore, there is the danger

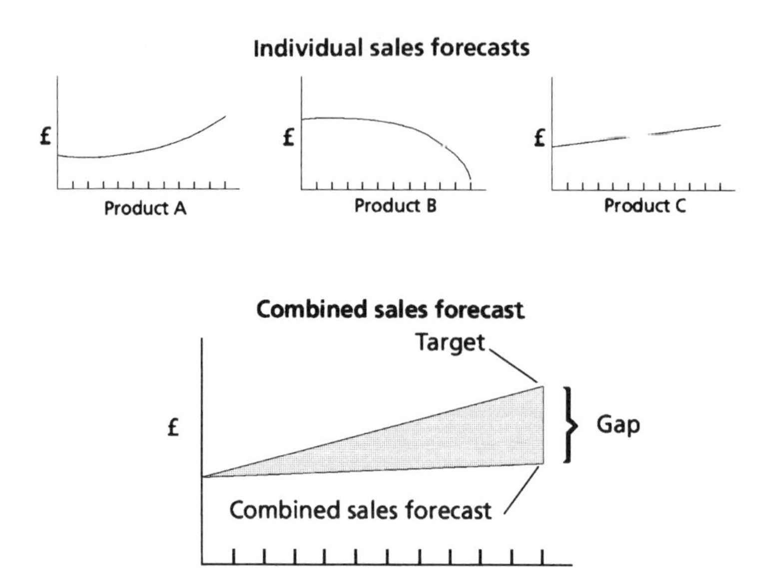

Fig 5.1 Portfolio analysis, showing the planning gap

that the analyst, having drawn certain conclusions, may be inclined to seek evidence that supports them and overlook or neglect uncomfortable facts that do not. This means that an overall strategy, based on full internal and environmental audits, should first be developed, and demands on resources and implications for the other components of the Seven S framework then considered. This may necessitate a rethink of the proposed strategy. An appraisal may show that there will not be enough money available for all of the proposals, that the time-scale is over-ambitious, that managerial resources may be over-stretched, too much is put at risk, a radical change in culture is needed, etc. A firm having a number of divisions or products should consider not only each individual product or service, but the portfolio as a whole. For example, if the firm operates in an environment where products have a relatively short life-cycle, then it is important that new products – *fledglings* – are under development to replace the *dogs* reaching the end of their useful life. There should also be sufficient *cash cows* to generate the funds necessary to pay for the development and launch of the fledglings, and to sustain the *stars* that are still growing but not yet generating high profit.

The portfolio must be balanced; too many *fledglings* – or *problem children* as they are sometimes called – can be a strain on financial and management resources. Conversely, *dogs*, having reached the end of their useful life, are generally best put to sleep unless they are still performing a useful function – even if this is merely making a contribution to overheads, not using any resources that could be put to achieve better ends.

The components of a portfolio could range from what are virtually independent companies with their own research, production and marketing resources (in the case of a conglomerate) to a variety of products, such as shampoos, jams or CD players. If they are aimed at different market segments and it is possible to adopt different strategies for them, they may be described as Strategic Business Units (SBUs), even if they share certain resources, such as production or distribution, in common.

A number of approaches have been devised for analysing a portfolio, each offering advantages and disadvantages. Most plot the positions of the products in the firm's portfolio of products on a chart. The horizontal axis usually denotes some internal characteristic such as relative market share or relative competitive strength, while the vertical axis relates to an environmental factor such as stages of the industry life-cycle or growth rate of the industry. Each axis is divided into ranges or has a scale. The best known of these is the original *Boston Consulting Group (BCG) product portfolio matrix* (also called the growth/share matrix) which uses the descriptions fledglings, question marks, stars, cash cows and dogs (*see* Fig 5.2). In this case, the vertical axis represents the rate of industry growth, an important environmental factor; if the industry is growing then, everything else being equal, the prospects are favourable and vice versa. The horizontal axis shows the market share relative to that of the biggest competitor. *Relative* market share is a better indicator of strength in the marketplace than the percentage itself. In some markets the leading brand may have 60 per cent market share, but in more fragmented markets, the leader may have only 10 per cent, but that could be more than twice that of their biggest rival; for example, Mazola is the brand-leader in the cooking-oil market – with about a 3 per cent share.

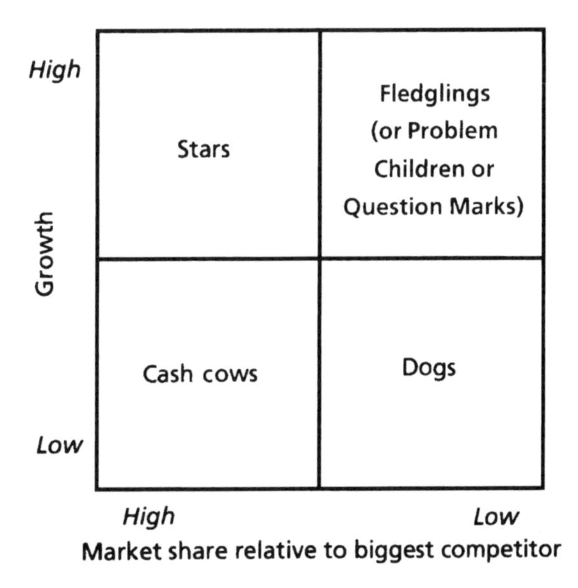

Fig 5.2 The Boston Consulting Group product portfolio matrix

Crucial to portfolio analysis, as to all market analyses, is the way in which the market is defined: if a product competes only in a particular well-defined sector of a larger generic market, then its market is that sector, not the market as a whole; each product, division or SBU should be plotted on the matrix in relation to its own market. The *Investors Chronicle* comment on the performance of different chains within the Burton Group, quoted in Chapter 4, illustrates this point.

The BCG matrix is a very simple tool, and frequently criticised for its shortcomings. It takes into account only three factors: the firm's market share, that of its biggest competitor and the rate of growth of the industry. The scales on the axes are frequently omitted and the names in the cells used as descriptions only, in order to assign strategic roles to products or services, for example, labelling those products – stars – which might warrant further investment, stressing the problematic nature of fledglings, or the important role of cash cows in providing revenue or the questionable future of dogs. The matrix can make a useful contribution to determining strategy at both the corporate and the business level, but it would obviously be foolhardy to base a strategy upon this picture alone. Nevertheless, the original model sometimes has bells and whistles attached in order to increase its sophistication. For example, it provides a fuller picture of the portfolio, not merely to plot the positions of products by points on the chart, but using circles, the sizes of which are proportional to their contribution to revenue. Some add further complications such as arrows showing the direction in which the product is moving, in order to overcome the lack of the dimension of time, but there are many other tools with which to supplement the BCG matrix which are specifically designed for a particular purpose.

It will be seen that there *may* be a correspondence between stages of the product life-cycle and the BCG matrix but this is not necessarily the case as they are based on different parameters:

Product life-cycle	**BCG matrix**
Introduction	Fledgling
Growth	Star
Maturity	Cash cow
Decline	Dog

A more sophisticated approach is that of the General Electric business screen, also known as the directional policy matrix (*see* Fig. 5.3). This shows a firm's strength in the market place on the horizontal axis, but allows the analyst to take into account all of the factors that contribute to a strong competitive position. These might include the relative market share, as with the BCG matrix, as well as production capacity, R&D strength, image, etc. The vertical axis is also more complex and attempts to assess the attractiveness of the industry under a number of headings in addition to market

Competitive strength

Industry attractiveness	*Strong*	*Medium*	*Weak*
High	A		C
Medium		D	
Low	E		B

Fig 5.3 The General Electric business screen

growth, such as Porter's five forces, profitability, seasonality and any others considered relevant by the analyst. The matrix that results may be used to suggest a strategic approach for each of the products mapped. Thus a product which has a strong competitive position in an attractive market (Position A in Fig 5.3) would obviously be cherished, while at the other extreme, those having a weak competitive position in an unattractive market (position B) are candidates for divestment or retrenchment. Decisions concerning those in other cells will depend on the circumstances. For example, it may be possible to remedy the factors that resulted in product C being given a poor anti-competitive rating. However, this may not be the best use of the resources required, which could be better employed in, for example, supporting product D. Although product E is in an unattractive market, its strong position may be yielding a satisfactory return on investment.

A factor to be considered when analysing a portfolio of products is interaction between them. For example, they might share production or distribution facilities, or share advertising expenses; a change in volume production or sales of one might affect the profitability of another; the sale of single-lens reflex cameras provides the market for additional lenses, as do razors for razor blades.

Although the importance of systematic and thorough analysis is stressed here, the analysis of data will not by itself produce new ideas, and it may be that a completely novel approach is what the organisation needs in order to meet its objectives – or even to survive. This was the situation that many firms in the defence industry found themselves in when the cold war ended and the most detailed analysis did not solve their problems, it merely identified and confirmed them.

The value chain

The focus of contemporary business strategy is consumer satisfaction. Until relatively recently, this meant identifying and satisfying customer needs and wants, providing the benefits sought and doing so better than competitors while making a satisfactory profit – in other words, gaining a differential advantage by giving better value from the perspective of the customer, value being the relationship between the benefits provided, as perceived by the customer, and the price paid.

Today, however, competition is often so fierce that merely satisfying needs and wants may not be an adequate goal; a firm should perhaps aim to exceed customers' expectations if it is to retain their loyalty. Repeat sales from a loyal existing customer generates far more profit than trying to switch a customer from a competitor. Furthermore, the description 'customer' must be interpreted broadly: in a real sense, wholesalers and retailers and any others in the chain from manufacturer to end-user are being served, and are therefore customers and should be treated as such – a chain is only as strong as its weakest link. For that reason, it is also important for manufacturers to look upstream at the firm's inputs and forge links with their suppliers – and possibly their suppliers' suppliers, to their mutual advantage (*see* Fig 5.4).

The first conclusion from this approach is that a firm should identify what features each member of the chain values, and provide them more effectively and efficiently than competitors. Thus some retailers, The Body Shop for example, place a high value on reliable and prompt scheduled delivery, even paying a bonus for it; in the industrial market just-in-time (JIT) delivery and guaranteed zero defects from a component supplier are becoming common practice. These are different benefits from those that end-users of the product seek, and the need to *consider all of the links* in the chain is one of three implications of the term 'value chain'.

Providing the additional benefits identified by the analysis will frequently impose unfamiliar demands on the firm, particularly if it is an innovative move. For example, providing JIT delivery requires a very different organisation from say, delivery three weeks after receipt of order. The sales function,

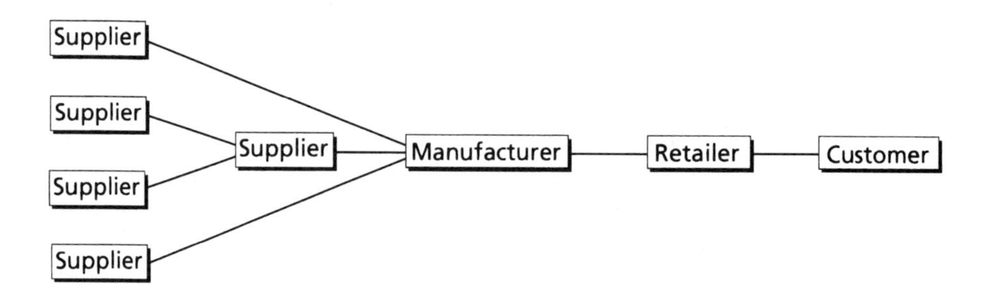

Fig 5.4 The value chain

finance, production, production control, stock-holding, delivery, quality control, internal communications, order receipt and processing and management attitude are only the most obvious areas affected, and a careful study of the implications must be made. The changes necessary in one department may well impose strains on another – as was the case with the frozen food company providing 24-hour delivery – so that these interactions too must be considered.

The second implication of the value chain then, is the need to *identify the internal links* and interrelationships between departments and functions required to provide specific competitive advantages. There is, however, the other side of the coin: perhaps resources are being expended on providing features that do not add as much to perceived value as the costs they incur. (Note that although a form of value analysis, the focus is on value as perceived by the customer rather than as a mere cost-cutting exercise.)

The third aspect of the value chain is to *evaluate the contribution* to perceived value made by every stage, or link in the chain, from the process of deciding how, when and where to place orders for the raw materials and components, through the stages of manufacture, marketing and delivery of the finished product to the end-user – including any after-sales service.

The purpose of the analysis is to identify, from the perspective of all parties in the chain of distribution, any operations or features that add less to perceived value than they cost or, as sometimes occurs, that are not valued by the purchaser at all and which should be considered for elimination.

Conversely, the analysis might identify features – go-fast stripes – that would add more to the value as perceived by those in the chain than the costs they would incur. The decision whether or not the price charged should be increased and if so, by how much, must also be evaluated.

As the result of market research among their clients, Avis Rent-a-Car spent £2 million on the launch of a new premium car rental service aimed at increasing the speed of car rental at airports in order to gain a competitive edge with an important market segment prepared to pay for the convenience.

Conversely, most major computer software manufacturers stopped offering a free telephone help-line or after-sales support despite the highly competitive nature of a market where this might have been a differential advantage. It now costs £150 a year to obtain advice that had been provided free.

There is a negative aspect to the value chain that is sometimes overlooked: while the benefit of fostering a mutually advantageous relationship between links in the chain from manufacturer, supplier and distributor was described above, they are nevertheless, in a sense, also competitors. They vie for the profit generated by the process of adding value to raw materials which go through several stages and intermediaries before ending up as glistening products on shop shelves. There is, however, a limit to how much customers will pay for go-fast stripes, image, convenience, etc., so that if one member of the chain adds desirable value, it may be at the expense of the potential profit of another. Retailers will attempt to squeeze suppliers for discounts; suppliers may not be able to raise their profit margins to pay for discounts, but might counter by trying to make their brand highly attractive to consumers by adding perceived value thus creating demand which the retailer is forced to satisfy. Similarly, component manufacturers may direct advertising not only to manufacturers using their products, but also to the end consumers. Thus Nutrasweet is promoted by the manufacturer as *the* sweetener for soft drinks, Intel as *the* chip inside computers and Kodak as *the* paper for your photographs to be printed on. These tensions play an important part in the relationship between members of the chain.

EXERCISES

1 What are the attributes of the products or services provided by the following organisations which should be reflected in their value chain?

   (a) A furniture store.
   (b) A fast-food outlet.
   (c) The outpatients' department of a hospital.
   (d) A travel agent.

2 Compare the relative importance of *efficiency* and *effectiveness* in the following enterprises:

   (a) A portrait painter/a house painter.
   (b) A press photographer/a fashion photographer.
   (c) A hospital operating theatre/a municipal theatre.

FURTHER READING

Glautier, W. E. and Underdown, B., *Accounting Theory and Practice*, Pitman Publishing, 1991. This is the most comprehensive text devoted to financial analysis.

Rowe, A. J., Mason, R. O., Dickel, K. E., Mann, R. B. and Mockler, R. J., *Strategic Management: A Methodological Approach*, Addison-Wesley, 1994. This text covers financial analysis with some breadth and depth, including a number of frameworks for internal and environmental analysis such as Ethical audit, Vulnerability analysis and Strategic position and action evaluation.

Thompson, J. L., *Strategic Management, Awareness and Change*, Chapman and Hall. Chapter 6 provides one of the fuller treatments for the non-financial, based on British practice and examples.

REFERENCES

1 Heller, R. *Management Decision*, Vol. 32, No. 8, 1994.
2 Waterman, R. H., Peters, T. J. and Phillips, J. R. 'Structure is Not Organization', *Business Horizons*, June 1980.
3 *Marketing Week*, 15 April 1994.
4 *Marketing Week*, 16 September 1994.

CHAPTER 6

Structure

An organisation is basically a group of people who act together in a purposeful way. How they are organised, who does what and reports to whom is largely – but certainly not entirely – determined by the organisational structure. Structure specifies responsibility, authority, tasks and relationships, and the image that usually comes to mind is that of the organisation tree which shows, in a hierarchy of descending importance, the various departments of the organisation and their titles summarising their areas of responsibility.

Structure was the focus of the article describing the Seven-S framework, *Structure is Not Organization*[1] where 'The central problem in structuring is ... how to make the whole thing work', implying that for a given set of circumstances there will be an optimum structure. Making it work may include the need to adapt to new circumstances: as the environment changes, or as the organisation grows older and larger or as its strategy, culture, systems, technologies, ownership or other characteristics change, so the existing structure may no longer be entirely appropriate. Despite such changes, the structure may nevertheless remain unaltered. There are several possible reasons for this, the most common being resistance to change. Many environmental or internal changes are gradual, so that while the organisation could be growing out of one structural form, the mismatch is no worse than would be the case with an alternative form for which it is not yet quite ready. This implies that there is a limited number of forms, and for the classifying of structures that is so: the traditional forms include simple, functional, divisional, matrix, etc. Organisations rarely make quantum leaps from one form to another; they usually evolve through hybrid or transitional forms. To illustrate these, this chapter traces – with minor adaptations – the development of a two-partner business into a multinational corporation.

THE SIMPLE STRUCTURE

Richard Branson started Virgin with little money and less commercial experience – hence its title. He had a minority partner, and between them they ran a mail-order business selling cut-price records, using the cash received with the orders to buy the stock required. The organisation could hardly be simpler; there was no need for a formal marketing function or any other department and, although additional staff were needed as the business grew,

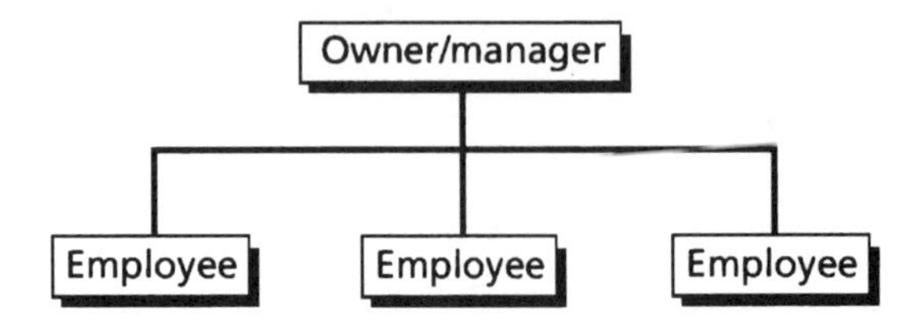

Fig 6.1 The simple structure

the scale and scope of operations were such that the partners knew exactly what was going on and could control it between them without a formal division of responsibility.

Successful growth was, to an extent, the result of their closeness to the market and their ability to respond quickly and flexibly to changing tastes. This is described as the *simple*, or sometimes the *entrepreneurial* structure (*see* Fig 6.1).

THE FUNCTIONAL STRUCTURE

There came a time, however, when growth was inhibited by two factors. First, the difficulty and burden the partners had in controlling what had now become a large operation; and second, the need for the professional expertise they themselves lacked in matters of finance, marketing, etc. The obvious solution was, of course, to employ specialist functional managers to whom responsibility could be delegated, leaving the partners to concentrate on strategic issues. The basic form is called the *functional* structure and, typically, appears as illustrated in Fig 6.2.

THE DIVISIONAL STRUCTURE

With this injection of professionalism, the firm continued to grow and develop, while the partners, relieved of day-to-day responsibility, continued to seek new opportunities and provide a sense of direction.

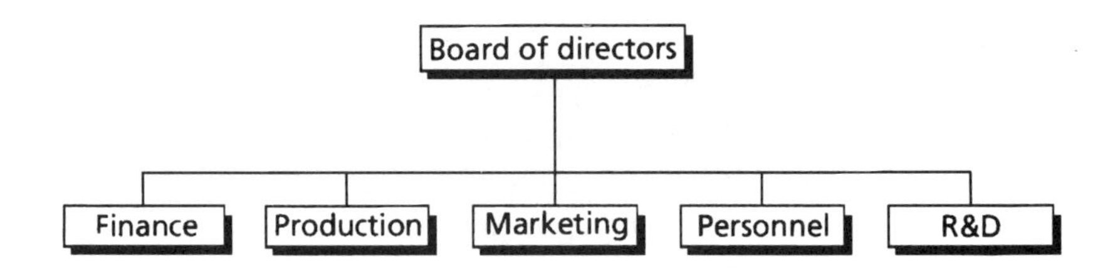

Fig 6.2 The functional structure

Having gained considerable experience and skills in the mail-order business, they might have been tempted into a strategy of *product development* by selling other products by mail order. However, a postal strike nearly ruined the business and so, in order to reduce this vulnerability, they opened a retail store to sell records, a strategy of *market development* – selling the same product through different channels.

Additional stores were opened, and another development resulted from Mike Oldfield turning up and offering some tapes he had recorded. Branson was impressed and became his manager; others such as the Sex Pistols followed, and the Virgin record label was formed. Virgin had now adopted a strategy of *related diversification*, related in that they were all in the music industry. Nevertheless, the activities were sufficiently different to warrant individual management as semi-autonomous strategic business units, i.e. a *divisional* structure (*see* Fig 6.3).

This form offers a number of other benefits: while the functional structure is suitable for a single-product, single-market and a relatively small firm, as the firm grows and the product/market mixture becomes more complex and the interests of the different functions will start to conflict. For example, the marketing department may press for greater product variety to suit different customer requirements, but this may be opposed by the finance department because of costs, and by the production department who prefer long, simple production runs.

In a divisional structure, however, many of the functions will be provided within a division, thus reducing conflict. Others, or certain aspects of them,

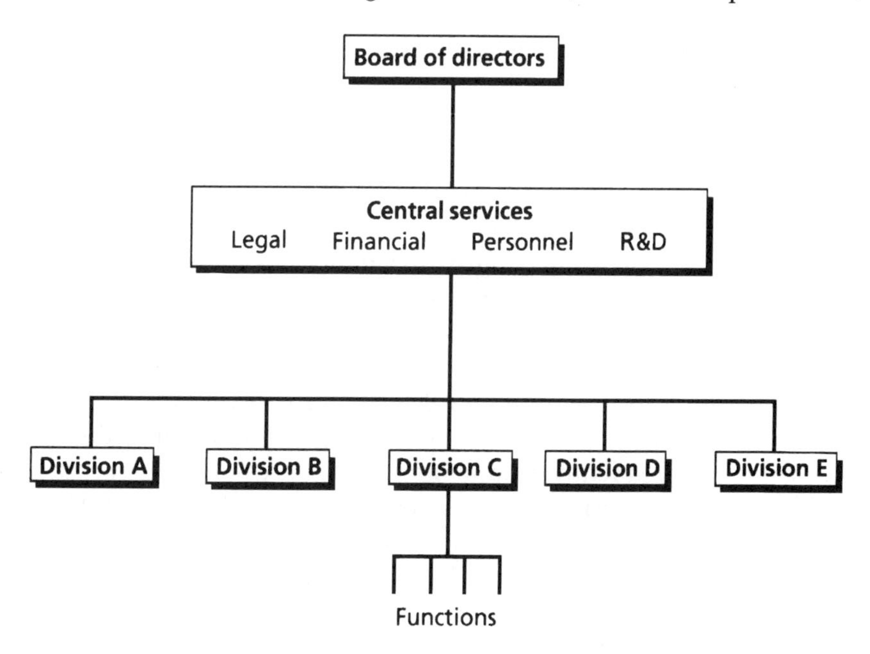

Fig 6.3 The divisional structure

may be located as central services covering all divisions. This is illustrated in Fig 6.3. The degree of centralisation will depend not only on the number, variety and size of divisions, but also on the organisational culture. In some organisations, divisions will merely be profit centres, concentrating on relatively short-term profit while the longer-term strategy is determined at a higher level. In others, they may be highly autonomous SBUs, concerned with long-term strategic issues.

Boots the Chemist has four business centres: health and food; beauty and personal care; baby; and gift and photo. Each have their own business general managers, marketing departments, etc., and develop their own business plans, but are accountable to the director of merchandising and marketing.

Branson had a relaxed management style and encouraged initiative amongst his enthusiastic team of managers who were allowed a high degree of autonomy. The business continued to grow in size as a result of encouraging entrepreneurship, while senior management continued to concentrate on corporate strategy.

In other organisations, although the divisions may have grown in size and complexity, the centre often continues to maintain tight control, but may be less knowledgeable than divisional managers who may therefore feel frustrated and seek greater responsibility – or leave. Setting the right balance requires fine judgement.

THE MULTIDIVISIONAL STRUCTURE

Despite the structural changes and growth in size, the organisation was not financially successful. This was partly due to the state of the music industry and so, in an attempt to reduce its dependence on this market, Virgin adopted a strategy of *unrelated diversification*. For example, they founded an entertainments-listing magazine to rival *Time Out*, and acquired a 75 per cent holding in an ailing airline that was renamed Virgin Atlantic. These too, were semi-autonomous, each concentrating on its own particular area of business.

The poor financial performance was, however, also attributable to lack of strong central control of what had by now become a large conglomerate. This is not uncommon at this stage of an organisation's development; there is frequently a trade-off between greater autonomy and strong central direction. An outsider was therefore hired as Group Managing Director to take overall control, and the group grew successfully under his management.

The record label acquired about 15 overseas subsidiaries, and there were about 120 overseas companies in 23 different countries. Overseas turnover grew to equal UK revenue. Management of the group remained centralised, but divided into three major divisions: Music, Retail and Property, and

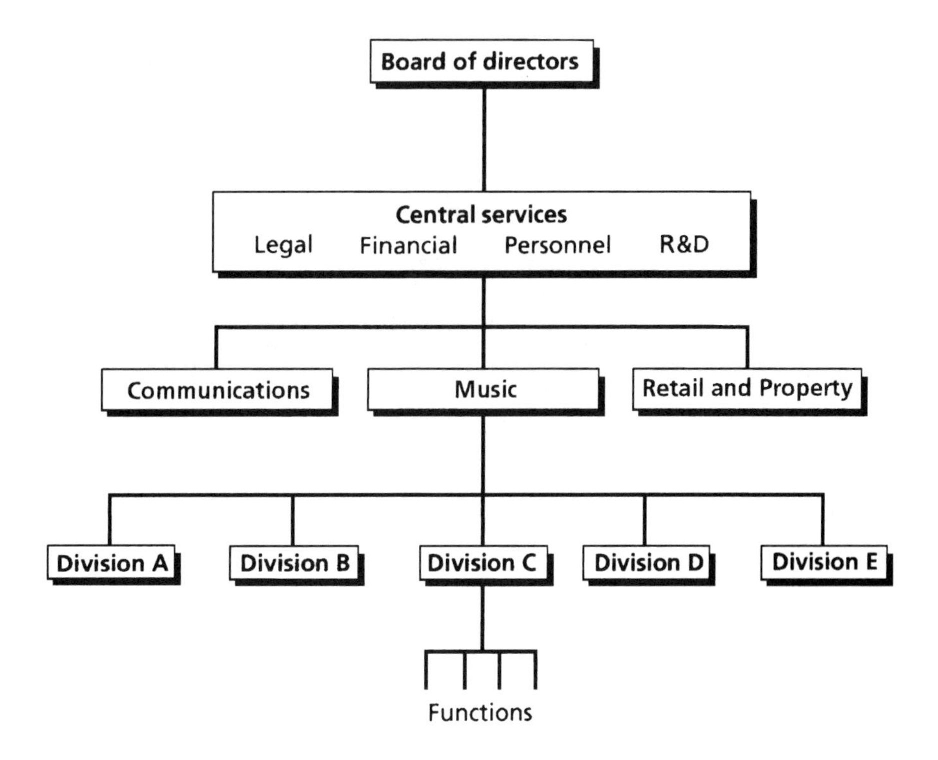

Fig 6.4 The multidivisional structure

Communications. The organisation chart is similar to that of Fig 6.3, but with an additional layer (*see* Fig 6.4).

THE MATRIX STRUCTURE

Because of the range of activities on a global basis, the organisational structure had now become quite complex. For example, within the music division there was not only the usual central roles of Chairman, Managing Director, Finance Director, etc. – i.e. *functional* management – but, under a Director-International, there was a Managing Director for France, another for Germany, and two joint Managing Directors for the USA, i.e. a *geographical* management structure. However, there was also a Managing Director for each of the business areas, i.e. a *product/market* management structure. Hence both the French and the Merchandising management would be involved in decisions concerning a store in France. This is an example of a matrix structure where each unit in the organisation reports to two different management roles – a dual authority structure (*see* Fig 6.5). The two arms are frequently geography related and product/service related, as in this case, but could also be geography and function related.

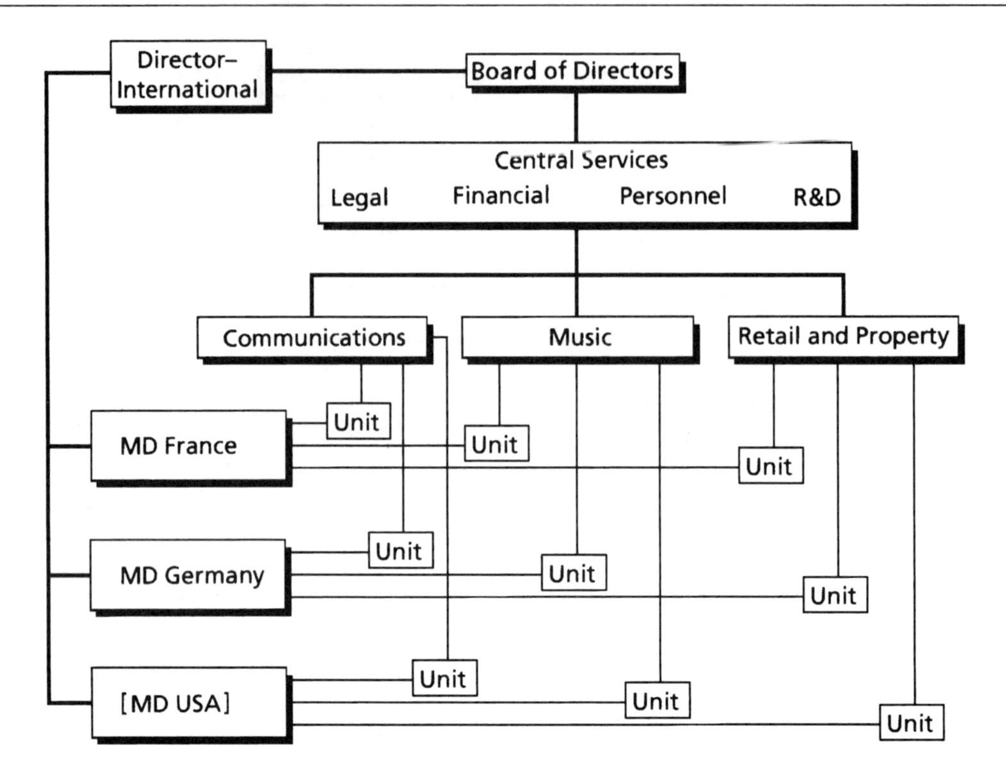

Fig 6.5 The matrix structure

The matrix structure is particularly appropriate in an organisation which frequently sets up a project team with a limited life, such as in the construction industry, and where there is less likelihood of a clash of interests or confusion of priorities between the two arms – as may occur when a servant has two masters.

THE HOLDING COMPANY

Whatever the future of the Virgin Group – which continues to diversify into unrelated activities and now has over 200 companies – it is unlikely to grant such a degree of autonomy to its constituent businesses that they will run virtually independently. That is, however, the nature of a holding company which owns, or has a major interest in, a number of businesses but does not get involved in their management. This is usually found only in very large and widely diversified organisations – conglomerates – when the task of monitoring and controlling the performance of the subsidiaries at headquarters would be formidable.

The degree of head office involvement is usually lowest in organisations such as investment companies, whose major concern and activity is in the investment industry rather than in managing the actual strategies of their investments. Nevertheless, even the large and diversified Hanson Group keeps a close eye on the activities of its investments, and recent events suggest that head office involvement is increasing.

The problems of managing mega-organisations are considerable, and two trends are discernible. First, concentration in certain specific areas of activity; for example, although Lord Hanson has stated that Hanson Trust does not want to be involved in businesses where decision making has to be centralised, they are now concentrating on five specific industries and have disposed of a number of companies outside these. Similarly, BTR – another conglomerate – is concentrating on manufacturing businesses and has disposed of several successful wholesale distributors and merchants.

By restricting investment to certain specific industries, it is possible to have a limited number of business groups which are fairly homogeneous, so that management at group level can have the expertise and knowledge to monitor, contribute to, or even determine and control strategy at corporate and company level without requiring numerous staff.

Second, is to split them into smaller, completely independent groups which are themselves more homogeneous, and therefore simpler to control – although many members of the boards of directors may be common to both. IBM moved in this direction under one newly appointed chief executive – but then moved away under his successor.

THE AD-HOCRACY OR INNOVATIVE ORGANISATION

This structure is found in organisations whose business is solving clients' problems by drawing on a range of skills and disciplines, such as a firm of solicitors or an advertising agency. This frequently calls for a flexible, innovative and participative organisation with a loose structure that may approach a state of no-structure in some cases.

The design group Imagination handles a wide variety of projects such as airport design, car design and water privatisation. While project teams are set up from within functional departments, these are seen as 'somewhere to sit'. Structures are configured around each assignment as circumstances demand, and the teams evolve as projects develop.[3]

THE POSITION OF POWER

Running through this account of changes in structure are shifts in the location of power and authority. At some stages of its development an organisation may be decentralised with divisions able to act with a high degree of independence, and at other times it is more tightly controlled by head office.

Tension frequently results from a pull for greater autonomy at middle levels of management, countered by a pull for greater control at the top. Both approaches have advantages and disadvantages. When authority to make decisions and appropriate financial and other resources have been distributed downwards, then lower-level management can respond more closely and quickly to the local circumstances in which they find themselves than if head office must first approve the proposed action. This also relieves the centre of relatively routine information processing and involvement in lower-level decision making, and may thereby permit a smaller and less bureaucratic head office which can concentrate on strategic issues.

In 1994, the supermarket chain Safeway decided on a change of strategic direction in order to differentiate itself from Tesco and Sainsbury. Their new positioning stressed customer service and innovation. They scrapped the conventional line management structure and adopted a flatter structure with fewer levels of management based on business units, each being allocated a sector such as fresh fruit, with senior managers and directors taking responsibility for more managers at lower levels.[4]

There is the danger that unless managers are given training and support, a 'leaner, fitter organisation' may result in overloading lower levels of management who will therefore concentrate on fire fighting urgent issues at the expense of strategic management. Although involvement in decision-making is an important motivating factor for lower-level management, their decisions may not be entirely consistent with corporate policy, strategy or interests, and if the number of divisions or SBUs is large the problems of overall co-ordination could be considerable. Furthermore, the use of resources such as R&D laboratories may not be as efficiently or effectively employed in the corporate interest as they would have been if centralised. This is particularly important for corporations with subsidiaries employing related technologies or those with the potential for synergy.

Unilever has a number of subsidiaries that were the result of related diversification. They began in the soap industry, then integrated backwards into producing their own fatty acids from oil-seed to make the soap. The oil-seed residues were sold as animal feedstuffs and, having entered the industry, additional firms were acquired. The fatty acids were also used to make ice-cream, margarine and cosmetics which led to diversification into related industries such as toiletries and perfumes.

While these are now well-established major businesses in their own right, Unilever recently set up the Exploratory Research Council, 'operating for the overall health of the company, rather than that of their own labs', which concentrates on certain identified core sciences which span the activities of the subsidiaries.[5]

Clearly, a balance between a centralised and a decentralised structure must be found which is appropriate to the size and complexity of the organisation, the turbulence of the environments in which it operates and, of course, the other Seven-Ss, in particular the organisational culture which is considered in Chapter 7.

Finally, one factor which will have a profound influence on organisational structure and design, and distribution in particular, is information technology (IT). It is not merely that department-based information systems are no longer adequate, nor that the later generation of integrated systems providing information concerning suppliers, production, marketing, R&D and distribution tasks are causing a rethink about departments themselves, resulting in major organisational process redesign. IT has the potential to enable one person simultaneously to do a number of jobs that were previously carried out sequentially in different departments. It presents new opportunities and could eliminate whole layers of middle management in virtually every industry. Expert systems and neural networks enable relatively inexperienced staff to make decisions that previously required judgement based on considerable experience. When that experience is, in any case, no longer relevant to a changed world, the future for management is uncertain.

The explosive growth of Direct Line motor insurance which gained 20 per cent market share in a very short time exemplifies this.

Customers of the Co-operative Bank can book holidays from unmanned kiosks via a telephone video link instead of going to a travel agent.

Communication and stock-control systems enable the correct quantity of lettuce, ordered from a supplier at 6 a.m., to be delivered to a centralised Marks & Spencer depot that afternoon and to be on the shelves of a store when it opens the following morning.

IT enables many tasks to be performed either at home or hundreds – or thousands – of miles away from the office, and international conferences may be held via a telephone video link – perhaps without leaving home. These forces, together with the growth of outsourcing and the pressure of environmental changes, will inevitably lead to new approaches to organisational design which will not be constrained by the need to represent an organisation by a neat pyramid of boxes and job titles on an organisation chart. Competitors of firms adopting these approaches will be forced to adopt them too if they are not to be left behind.

IT will affect not only the production side, but also the demand side; for example, here is a system currently under development in the USA:

'You're watching LA Law *and you like the suit one of the cast is wearing? Click on the garment and you'll find out who makes it, where to buy it, and how much it is.'*[6]

Interactive TV and virtual reality will transform consumer-buying behaviour.

EXERCISES

1 Draw an outline organisation chart for an international bank which has the following divisions at head office:

- Investment banking.
- Consumer retail banking.
- Domestic corporate banking.
- Multinational corporate banking.
- International banking.

2 Each of these divisions is in turn subdivided in appropriate ways. For example, International Banking is divided into the following continental regions:

- Europe.
- Asia.
- North America.
- South America.
- Australasia.

While Multinational corporate banking is separated into a number of specialist divisions to provide expertise in particular industries such as:

- Consumer products
- Electronics
- Petroleum and chemicals
- Electric and mechanical engineering

(a) How might the bank allocate responsibility for the development of multinational corporate banking in the petroleum industry in Saudi Arabia?

(b) Describe the inherent problems of this structure.

FURTHER READING

Mintzberg, H. and Quinn, J. B., *The Strategy Process*, Prentice Hall, 1991. Henry Mintzberg has written extensively on structure – as well as many other aspects of strategic management. If you are interested in this topic, he *must* be on your reading lists. Alternatively, this text is an accessible treatment on structure; it is out of the mainstream of books on strategic management but contains a wealth of interesting readings. An earlier edition included an analysis of Robin Hood's strategy (the current edition starts with the description of a battle that took place in 338 B.C.) to make some points concerning strategy that are crucial today.

REFERENCES

1 Waterman, R. H., Peters, T. J. and Phillips, J. R. 'Structure is Not Organization', *Business Horizons*, June 1980.
2. *Financial Times*, 21 March 1990.
3. *Marketing Week*, 30 September 1994.
4. *Unilever Magazine*, p. 10, January 1994.
5. Douglas, T. *Marketing Week*, 30 September 1994.

CHAPTER 7

Culture and management style

CULTURE

Goering is reported to have said 'When I hear the word "culture" I reach for my gun.'

Culture refers to the basic values, assumptions and beliefs of a group that provide a template for their members' values, norms, attitudes, perceptions, ways of thinking and behaviour. In an organisation with a strong culture the new member of a group will absorb, for example, 'That's *how* we do things around here' and, conversely, '*That*'s just not done.' Established members will have internalised these features and will conform instinctively; deviants will suppress their differences if they want to make progress.

The individuals in an organisation will each be influenced by the culture of a number of groups to which they belong or aspire. First, there are those groups which are not occupationally related such as social class, political affiliation, etc. More relevant, second, may be professional training before actually joining an organisation and the culture of the particular department, function, level of management or informal group with which they identify.

Within an organisation there will therefore be a number of subcultures, some of which may be at variance with the organisational culture – they may even take a pride in this difference; this form of internal politics can be disruptive and divisive. On the other hand, a strong culture can foster loyalty to, and identification with, the group, hence encouraging co-operation between subgroups, while the nature of the culture can itself promote the organisation's mission.

A firm's culture could, for example, be *industry-oriented*; this is particularly so in traditional industries such as mining or shipbuilding. Others may be locked into their *technology* and find it difficult to adapt to change; for example, quartz watches were invented in Switzerland, but the Swiss watch industry rejected them until it was nearly too late because it was proud of its tradition of craftsmanship.

Market-oriented cultures, being outward looking, are usually more flexible in meeting a changing environment, but a firm's culture may have a narrower focus or nature than the industry, technology or market. It could, for example, be quality driven, sales-oriented, customer-oriented, cost conscious, entrepreneurial, conservative, prepared to take risks or risk-averse. Deliberately developing a strong and relevant culture may be a powerful aid to giving a sense of direction or fostering a particular distinctive competence that provides a competitive advantage. Furthermore, it is manageable and it can be deliberately developed.

This fact has been exploited by nation states, religious and political movements throughout the ages, and some present-day organisations do so to a greater or lesser extent: encouraging myths and legends concerning heroes and heroic deeds or the fate of wrong-doers and non-conformists; exhorting members at conferences and meetings; publishing notices, newsletters and house-magazines; imposing conformity through uniforms and approved attire; granting status symbols, recognition and rewards such as the key to the executive toilet, the company car, nomination as salesperson of the month or year, rolls of honour and long-service awards; using special jargon terms and acronyms that only insiders understand; encouraging routines, rituals and forms of behaviour such as always arriving early, always leaving the office late regardless of the work-load and use of particular forms of address; but above all in the selection and self-selection of compatible recruits, their training, socialisation, promotion and reward systems; and the visible progress of conformists who act as role models to the rest.

In providing this template, culture may therefore act as a filter to perceptions, and could – either deliberately or quite unconsciously – colour, distort, or block inputs to a decision-making process if they are contrary to the basic assumptions, beliefs, previous experience or received wisdom of the organisation – particularly if they actually threaten them. This means that warning signals from the environment may go undetected, their significance underestimated or their implications misunderstood. Subordinates may also deliberately underplay or suppress them if they fear the consequences of being the bearers of bad news. Thus, it may be very difficult to accept that a firm's historic strengths are no longer relevant, or that a major product on which the business was founded has reached the end of its life-cycle; the sales force may be blamed or a temporary drop in demand assumed. It is even more difficult to accept that a whole technology or industry is in decline; that is why a new technology is often adopted by those outside an industry: it was not carriage-makers that developed the horseless carriage – later called automobiles – nor main-frame computer manufacturers that first developed personal computers.

The middle-to-low end of the Swiss watch industry continued making mechanical watches when they obviously could not compete with quartz watches from the Far East, and nearly collapsed as a result. A quartz watch is basically a printed circuit in a case with knobs – ideal for mass-production by the Japanese electronic industry. The Swiss watch industry was fragmented and small scale, with a culture that took pride in craftsmanship and mechanical skills. One Swiss manufacturer advertises: 'Since 1735 there has never been a quartz Blancpain watch and there never will be.'

It will be seen that culture has the potential to be one of the most powerful influences on strategic management. Although an organisation's culture will initially derive from its mission and strategy and will therefore be fully consistent with them, as circumstances change it could become less so; an inward-looking, production-oriented, cost-conscious culture could become completely inappropriate as the market evolves and becomes more competitive and dynamic, but the culture itself may prevent this from being perceived or acted upon. The given examples of the car, computer and watch industries, underwent quantum changes in a relatively short time. In other circumstances an organisation may adapt progressively to minor changes in the environment almost unconsciously. However, the stronger the culture, the more likely is it to resist change.

Organisational development (OD) is deliberately planned culture-change in order to improve organisational effectiveness. It aims at more open management based on participation and co-operation in decision making, and on a reduction in conflict. This attempt to improve harmony is, however, internally directed and does not usually try to develop a culture specifically related to the organisation's environment. Nevertheless, in 1994, Mercury Communications introduced 'Imagine 1997', at a cost of several million pounds, in order to 'change the culture for the late 1990s'.[1]

CLASSIFICATIONS OF CULTURE

Several different cultures have been mentioned: liberal, conservative, customer-oriented, entrepreneurial, etc. There have been a number of attempts at classifying organisational cultures and as they adopt dissimilar perspectives they are not merely different labels for the same thing, although there is a degree of overlap. Their underlying approach – like that of all methods of classification – is that an organisation can be given a label because features such as its structure, location of power, people/task orientation, internal/external emphasis, age and size and so on, match those of one of the types. The label then enables behaviour or attitude in a given situation to be better understood or predicted, or problems anticipated. This is helpful when considering strategic change or when anticipating a competitor's response to a strategic move.

One of the two best-known classification systems is that of Miles and Snow[2] who divide organisations into:

- **Defenders** who are basically conservative, inward-looking and risk-averse. They do little planning, but employ tight control systems.
- **Prospectors** who are proactive, innovative, decentralised and prepared to take risks.
- **Analysers** who adopt a rational, analytical stance; planning is important.

- **Reactors** who only respond to a near-crisis situation, and then with hasty action and minimal planning.

The other major classification is that of Handy[3] who has a different approach, classifying cultures into:

- **Power** – where the organisation is dominated from the centre and power radiates outwards.
- **Role** – which is the 'typical' organisation: somewhat bureaucratic, with clearly defined job specifications or roles.
- **Task** – where the emphasis is on solving problems and producing results.
- **Person** – which is people-oriented.

MANAGEMENT STYLE

Closely related to organisational culture is management style. The organisational culture will frequently reflect the management style of a dominant chief executive: Tiny Rowland, Lord Hanson, Alan Sugar and Richard Branson are well-known public figures who – for better or for worse – have imprinted their personalities on the organisations they ran, and the effect of a strong personality can reverberate long after they have gone – John Spedan Lewis is still referred to as 'The Founder' within the John Lewis Partnership, Henry Ford left his mark, etc.

Just as with culture, there are many taxonomies of management style, for example:[4]

- **Leader** – having an ability to communicate and motivate.
- **Administrator** – possessing skills in identifying and solving problems, and in controlling a situation.
- **Planner** – methodical, possessing analytical skills.
- **Entrepreneur** – constantly seeking new ventures and challenges.

Another authority[5] divides them into:

- **Directive** – autocratic, acts rapidly, uses rules.
- **Analytic** – enjoys problem solving, analyses much data.
- **Conceptual** – achievement-oriented, future-oriented, creative.
- **Behavioural** – supportive, empathetic, communicative.

Yet another[6] describes ten management roles, saying: 'They form an integrated whole. No role can be pulled out of the framework and the job left intact.' Their relative importance will vary according to circumstances.

Qualities of leadership may be crucial to organisational success – possibly more important than good and efficient management, particularly in a challenging environment. In less turbulent circumstances, administrative ability is perhaps a more important quality than a strong personality. In a complex situation, analytical skills may be essential qualities in a senior manager whereas, in a simple environment, decisiveness may be more important. There is no one 'best' management style, although a particular style may well be the most appropriate in a particular set of circumstances. Thus, a strong leader may be needed to take a firm out of the wilderness – to be replaced by an administrator when the 'promised land' is reached.

Not only did Compaq, the computer manufacturer, achieve sales of $2 billion within six years of start-up under its co-founder and chief executive officer (CEO) Rod Canion, it was the first manufacturer ever to achieve this level of sales within such a short time-scale.

Three years later Canion was fired by the company's chairman and head of the venture capital group that had funded the firm, who said 'We often have to change the CEOs of our start-up companies. Many of the 70 companies we have invested in are started by . . . very charismatic people who are not good at running a business.'

Under the replacement CEO, profits rose by about 120 per cent and 90 per cent in the two successive years, and in 1994 the firm became the world's largest seller of personal computers.[7]

ORGANISATIONAL LIFE-CYCLE

Another factor that will affect both organisational culture and management style is the stage the organisation has reached in its life-cycle. Chapter 6 described stages in the development of Virgin, and there is some evidence that a particular style may be the more appropriate at a particular stage. For example, during the *functional* stage, when the organisation is going for growth, an *analytical* and *conceptual* style might be appropriate. Later, however, as it reaches the *divisional* stage, when the organisation must be held together, a more autocratic touch may be warranted.

If one considers the multidivisional stage of the organisational life-cycle, then the divisions will themselves be at different stages of their life-cycles, or, to use a different framework, some will be question marks/fledglings/problem children, others stars, cash cows or dogs, each warranting different qualities and styles of management.

BUSINESS ETHICS

Milton Friedman, the Nobel prize-winning economist, wrote an article entitled *The Social Responsibility of Business is to Make a Profit*. He argued that a firm's prime responsibility is to its owners and, therefore, for example, has no brief to make donations to charitable or other causes unless it is in the interest of shareholders who can otherwise themselves choose whether or not to make donations. He says that a firm should avail itself of all legal means to make profit, and if society or the community disapprove of certain means, then it is for them to apply sanctions or legislate accordingly. Business ethics, however, concern an organisation's responsibilities not only to society and the community, but to all stakeholders: employees, customers, suppliers, etc., and apply to the organisation as a whole, and from the level of the chief executive down to shop-floor workers. In some organisations business ethics may extend into private life as well.

There are no present-day tablets of stone which lay down business ethics, and it is for organisations and individuals to set their own standards. However, it has been argued that an organisation should assume some share of social costs over and above those of its legal responsibilities, and that its social responsibility is related to its power and influence, and to that of its industry; the greater their power and influence, the greater their burden of responsibility.

EXERCISES

1 List the characteristics of the 'ideal' organizational culture or suggest which of Miles and Snow's list you would endeavour to foster if you were appointed as a senior manager in three of the following organisations:

   (a) a wheel-clamping contractor

   (b) a research laboratory

   (c) a battleship

   (d) a private hospital

   (e) Pepsico

   (f) a second-hand car business

   (g) a high-fashion clothing store

   (h) a fast-food chain

   (i) an advertising agency.

2 How would you go about fostering that culture if the prevailing culture were different?

3 Rank the management styles listed on page 72 in descending order of relevance to the chief executive of these organisations.

Discussion topic

Some insurance companies train their staff in ways of minimising the amount paid to claimants. There are many ways in which this *could* be achieved:

   (a) list them;

   (b) where and why do you draw the line?

FURTHER READING

Brown, A., *Organisational Culture*, Pitman Publishing, 1995. This is an approachable and highly recommended book.

Johnson, G., *Long Range Planning*, Vol. 25, No. 1. This text contains a description of the concept of the cultural web which takes a comprehensive view of a number of aspects of culture (*see also* Johnson, G. and Scholes, K., *Exploring Corporate Strategy*, Prentice Hall, 1993 in which it is dealt with in reasonable detail).

Schein, E., *Organisation, Culture and Leadership*, Jossey Bass, 1985. This text provides a very comprehensive background.

REFERENCES

1 *Daily Telegraph*, 26 March 1994.
2 Miles, R. E. and Snow, C. C., *Organization Strategy, Structure and Process*, 1978.
3 Handy, C. B., *Understanding Organizations*, Penguin Books, 1976.
4 Ansoff, I. and McDonnell, E., *Implanting Strategic Management*, Prentice Hall, 1990.
5 Rowe, A. J. and Mason, R. O., *Managing with Style*, Jossey Bass, 1987.
6 Mintzberg, H. (1975) 'The Manager's Job: Folklore and Fact', *Harvard Business Review*, July–August, 1975.
7 *Sunday Times*, 13 November 1994.

CHAPTER 8

Strategic options

Management, having conducted a formal analysis of the features described in earlier chapters, will now have a picture of the environment in which the organisation operates, and an understanding of the organisation itself. They should recognise existing or potential problems, and identify the causes or the need for further analysis. They may possibly have some ideas on how problems, existing or potential, might be tackled – although an open mind should be kept at this stage; there are often several ways in which a particular problem can be resolved, and they should *all* be considered.

When formally reviewing corporate strategy, the next stage should be to generate strategic options that at first sight are possible solutions to any strategic problems, and choose the 'best' – whatever that may mean. This chapter considers the first stage, that of generating a list of relevant strategic options. To a large extent this will depend upon what was found: perhaps, at one extreme, a basically healthy organisation which is meeting its objectives in a benign environment – or at any rate – whatever threats exist can be met by the present strategic approach, and with no reasons to suppose that this fortunate state of affairs will change in the foreseeable future. In these circumstances, it might be thought that all that needs to be done is to ensure that the situation – internal and external – is monitored to ensure that changes are detected and acted upon in good time, perhaps improve housekeeping to a greater or lesser degree by cutting costs, improving quality, etc. This, however, is dangerous complacency. Even if not an explicitly stated objective, it is generally agreed that, for a number of reasons, most organisations should *always* strive to do better, to grow or to consider changes of direction; in the absence of strategic problems, strategy should be periodically and critically reviewed.

Although Microsoft, the computer software firm, was probably the most successful in the industry in 1993, in 1994 they decided to reorganise: 'What better time to change than when you are on top' explained an executive.

It is ironic that at almost the same time the Chairman of IBM, in announcing that they were changing the primary focus of their strategy from mainframes to client-server products, said: 'We should have done it a decade ago . . .' – when, of course, IBM were on top – '. . . Failure [to do so] was the single most important mistake IBM has made in the last decade.' he said.[1]

In many sectors, the old formula for success of continuously improving performance is no longer adequate; it may be necessary to become not merely better but radically different: almost 40 per cent of the Fortune 500 of ten years ago – the cream of American industry – no longer exist for this reason – most of Peter's and Waterman's 'excellent' firms dropped out of their list because of their complacency and sticking to their knitting.

There is a growing realisation that the progressive management practices such as just-in-time, value-chain analysis, zero-defects, quality circles, customer orientation, etc., that may originally have provided a successful firm with its competitive advantage are not secret formulas unknown to their competitors. These practices must, *of necessity*, be adopted by them too if they are to compete and will, therefore, before long become standard practice within an industry. Other firms may become leaders through alternative means, the previous competitive advantage being superseded or eroded by new approaches.

URGENCY AND IMPORTANCE

There will probably be a wide choice of possible means to improve results: opening new branches, developing new products, exporting, diversifying into new areas, buying out competitors, investing in modern plant or new technology or perhaps just trying that little bit harder. However, for a firm in a healthy condition, unless a particular window of opportunity closes, such a decision, although important, may not be urgent – although indecision should be avoided.

At the other extreme, an organisation may be on the brink of disaster due to internal weaknesses, environmental threats, or both and will topple over the edge beyond hope of rescue unless drastic and urgent action is taken.

Between these extremes lies a spectrum of issues of varying urgency and importance. A matter may be urgent but not important: imagine that you are on the Underground when you hear a train approaching. It is an *urgent* decision whether or not you run for it; it may not be *important*, because another will be along in a few minutes – but if you are already late for an appointment . . .

Conversely, for example, a fifth-former must decide what subjects to take at A-level; an important but not urgent decision, and one that might well be deferred for as long as possible in order to keep the options open. (Note, however, that in deciding the urgency of an issue, the lead time necessary to resolve it must also be taken into account.)

Clearly, those problems which are both urgent *and* important strategic issues should be given priority and allocated the necessary resources, and this may determine how the other matters are dealt with. Matters which are important but not urgent can be deferred, whilst issues which are urgent only will not be of strategic importance and could probably be delegated to lower levels of management. If, however, the particular environment of an organisation is so turbulent that issues which are both urgent and important are being thrown up with a frequency that interferes with the normal processes of strategic management, then a different approach to that developed here would be more appropriate. This is described in Chapter 12.

The first step in making sense of the comprehensive internal and external analyses is therefore to concentrate on the *strategic* problems, and the findings that may be of strategic importance. Because an analyst should keep an open mind about what the final shape of strategy will be, we cannot be sure which findings may be relevant, but we can, and should, for the moment ignore those which are relatively unimportant, i.e. clearly not of strategic importance, in order to focus on those which may be significant; we must be able to see the wood for the trees.

THE SWOT ANALYSIS

Adapting an organisation to its environment means responding to environmental opportunities, but at the same time coping with environmental threats; it is as important to defend a vulnerable position as it is to exploit an opportunity. The environmental analysis should identify most of these opportunities and threats. Furthermore, 'adapting' implies improvement, not only by correcting existing or potential weaknesses, but also by exploiting strengths which offer a strategic or competitive advantage. These strengths and weaknesses will have been identified by the internal audit. That is the basis of the SWOT analysis, an inventory of *strategically important* internal Strengths and Weaknesses, and environmental Opportunities and Threats – but a pruned list, possibly as few as only three or four of each, with the remainder put aside for delegated or subsequent consideration, depending upon their urgency and importance.

The list is pruned because relatively few will, in fact, be of strategic importance. However, those that are must be clearly identified. A strength could be a particular *competence* such as product design, a *resource* such as strong channels of distribution, or an *attribute* such as a well-established, favourable brand image. In general, a strength is potentially of strategic importance if it provides one or more of the following benefits, while weaknesses inhibit, prevent, or nullify them:

- an anti-competitor advantage
- perceived value in the value chain
- above industry/market average profit or revenue, efficiency or effectiveness
- increased security or reduced risk in the marketplace

Opportunities and threats may extend from the immediate present to the foreseeable future, with probability ranging from certainty to remote possibility – hence the need to consider urgency and importance in evaluating them. Opportunities may be exploited to obtain these benefits but are not themselves strategies. Thus, if a firm identifies a market opportunity in Italy for one of its products, it could be exploited in several ways: by export, by a joint venture with an Italian firm, by granting a licence, by local manufacture, etc. – or the firm may decide to take none of these options.

Although almost universally referred to as the SWOT analysis, it is less an analysis in its own right than a summary of the findings of all of the analyses previously undertaken and a particular finding may be classified as both a strength and a weakness. They are basically situational, defined by the environment or by the existing or previous strategy.

Rolls Royce's image as the *luxury car was undoubtedly a strength – until the recession when it was perceived as inappropriately ostentatious. They concentrate on a very limited product range which is a strength, but is it wise to have all of your eggs in one basket?*

Having completed the SWOT analysis, the next step is to generate strategic options which support organisational objectives based upon:

1 Exploiting environmental opportunities by utilising existing internal strengths, by developing them or by correcting weaknesses.
2 Evaluating the extent to which internal strengths are adequate to meet environmental threats, or whether weaknesses make the organisation vulnerable to them and should therefore be remedied.

That is the 'so what?' of SWOT – adapting an organisation to its environment, matching strengths and weaknesses to opportunities and threats and may well provide adequate answers to the issues identified. It is the first of a number of ways of generating strategic options from which to choose the most appropriate strategy or strategies.

The matching process may be formally conducted by using a matrix in which – as usual – internal characteristics are plotted on the horizontal axis, while environmental features are plotted on the other (*see* Table 8.1).

Cell A of Table 8.1 shows that Strength 1 plus Strength 2 enable the organisation to take advantage of Opportunity 3. Note however, that four threats are listed. Cell C shows that Threat 2 may be met by Strength 1, and Cell D shows that, provided Weakness 3 is corrected, then Threat 3 can be countered. Nevertheless, that still leaves the organisation vulnerable to Threats 1 and 4; the SWOT analysis has not suggested a suitable strategy to overcome this problem. The urgency and importance of the threats must, of course, be evaluated. Conversely, the analysis may identify a strength for which there is no listed opportunity, but which may have considerable potential.

Table 8.1 SWOT analysis matrix

	Strengths **Strength 1 . . .** **Strength 2 . . .** **Strength 3 . . .**	**Weaknesses** **Weakness 1 . . .** **Weakness 2 . . .** **Weakness 3 . . .** **Weakness 4 . . .**
Opportunities **Opportunity 1 . . .** **Opportunity 2 . . .** **Opportunity 3 . . .** **Opportunity 4 . . .**	Cell A *Strategies based on using strengths to exploit opportunites* e.g. Strength 1 + Strength 2 + Opportunity 3	Cell B *Strategies based on correcting weakness to exploit opportunities* e.g. Weakness 1 + Opportunity 1
Threats **Threat 1 . . .** **Threat 2 . . .** **Threat 3 . . .** **Threat 4 . . .**	Cell C *Strategies based on using strengths to combat threats* e.g. Strength 1 + Threat 2	Cell D *Strategies based on correcting weakness to combat threats* e.g. Weakness 3 + Threat 3

One can be wise after the event; who would have forecast that a cassette 'recorder' that could not actually record but could only replay tapes, that was portable but could only be heard through earphones and cost four or five times as much as some portable cassette recorders without these defects, would be the amazing success that the Sony Walkman became?

There was no obvious environmental opportunity; success was due to internal strengths such as design capability, marketing skills and reputation but, above all, the drive and creative vision of Sony's Chief Executive.

CREATIVITY

Although a useful tool, the SWOT analysis is a mechanistic process and unlikely to generate genuine new ideas or provide the major breakthrough so often needed at critical times. While we may be able to identify the cause of a problem, we may not be able to remedy it, particularly if it is environmental. Other problems may be due to a complexity of causes. We must then go beyond the analysis, and *design* a way out of the problem. Analysis of a situation must be followed by synthesis. With hindsight this may be seen as overcoming a weakness or taking advantage of an opportunity, but that may not be evident at the time.

The elderly, electrically powered fleet of an old-established riverside boat-hire firm required frequent and expensive maintenance. The business was highly dependent on the weather, labour costs were high and the firm was not in a strong financial position. A number of options were generated from a SWOT analysis: renovate the fleet, replace them, rent-out rowing boats, etc., all offering some advantages but with major snags. The solution, not arising directly from the SWOT analysis, was to close the business down and open a marina on the site for which capital would be readily available from investors.

There is a need not only for the logical analysis of data, but also for creativity, imagination and lateral thinking. The more turbulent and unpredictable the environment, the greater the need for these qualities, and this in turn demands an appropriate organisational culture. A recent study showed that of 73 successful innovations studied, only nine were the result of identifying a market opportunity and designing a suitable product; the remainder all sprang from innovative ideas.[2]

The 3M organisation has a target, 30 per cent of its annual revenue, that must come from products which did not exist four years previously. Furthermore, staff are given 15 per cent 'bootlegging time' to work on projects of their own choice.

In general, over half of Hewlett-Packard's revenue is for products launched less than two years previously.

A second approach to generating strategic options may be by brainstorming, synectics or similar aids to creativity, but the organisation must have a culture – such as those of 3M or Hewlett-Packard – that encourages this approach; in some organisations, new ideas are often perceived as threats to existing vested interests, as indeed they frequently are.

ANSOFF'S PRODUCT/MARKET MATRIX

A third, more formal approach which lies between the strategic and the SWOT analysis may generate suitable ideas. This too is based on a matrix which relates environmental factors to internal ones: Ansoff's product/market matrix (*see* Table 8.2).[3] The vertical axis denotes either existing or new markets – the environmental factor – the other axis, refers to products, either existing or new. Virtually every possible strategic option can be located in one or other of the cells, and it therefore provides a framework for reviewing them. First, however, one or two points should be made.

Considering the right-hand column, what is implied by 'new product'? Are, for example, 'New Improved Persil' or a completely remodelled car which still bears the old name new or existing products? In strategic terms, they may best be considered as *brands* – and some brand names, such as Persil,

Table 8.2 Ansoff's product/market matrix

	Existing products	New products
Existing markets	*Strategies based on existing markets and existing products:* CONSOLIDATION PENETRATION	*Strategies based on launching new (or improved) products into existing markets:* PRODUCT DEVELOPMENT
New markets	*Strategies based on finding new markets for existing products:* MARKET DEVELOPMENT	*Strategies based on launching new products into new markets:* DIVERSIFICATION

are extremely valuable company assets and continue to be used, although the product itself has been reformulated many times. In other cases, when the image has faded, it may be better to launch a replacement brand. For example, in 1994 Vauxhall announced that in 1996 it will be killing off the Cavalier name after 14 years of service. Conversely, Coca-Cola and Ovaltine have been going strong for over 100 years, although formulation and packaging have changed with the times. Coke only faltered when the change was too great. In other words, the labels of the cells are a useful means of generating ideas, but are less important than how appropriate the strategies are themselves. For example, consider the strategies in the two left-hand cells. Is the strategy of a retail chain buying up a competitor (horizontal diversification) a case of *market penetration* or *market development*? Is a bank or insurance company which starts a telephone service offering a new product or entering a new market? The answer is, to both questions, both: strategic decisions do not always fall neatly into one or other cell of a matrix, and the label itself is not important.

Let us now consider the matrix cell by cell.

Existing products – existing markets

This is the least risky cell as, by definition, both product and market are familiar and the firm can concentrate on what it knows best.

Divestiture/ sell-out

An existing business may be disposed of for several reasons, for example:

- to concentrate on core activities
- to raise cash in a crisis

- to 'harvest' a business when it has reached a peak
- to make alternative use of financial and/or other resources
- poor performance
- poor fit with organisation

Retrenchment

Less radical than divestiture, the firm disposes of parts of the business, usually:

- to reduce costs when results are poor
- when the firm is over-extended

Market consolidation

This means maintaining the current position, possibly building a firm base in preparation for more dynamic activity when this is appropriate. After a firm has undertaken a major strategic change, for example having acquired a competitor, it may be advisable to allow a settling-down period before embarking on more activity. It may also be appropriate in hard times.

Market penetration

This is a strategy of increasing the market share of existing products in existing markets through greater marketing effort, i.e. by use of the marketing mix, for example, by better selling methods; more advertising or promotion; using additional channels of distribution such as wholesalers or direct selling; lowering the price; improving service and often a combination of several of these.

Another approach to market penetration is to buy up competitors, a strategy of *horizontal integration* in order to gain economies of scale and reduce costs, as well as eliminating a competitor.

New products – existing markets

Product development

Product development and the introduction of new products into an existing market is an essential strategy when product life-cycles are short, e.g. personal computers, microchips, videotapes. It is often based on existing skills or technologies, particularly when *adaptable* spare production capacity exists. Adding new products for existing customers is sometimes called *horizontal diversification.* The strategy may be adopted in order to fill a gap in the market and thereby deny an opportunity to a competitor, to gain sales or to spread the risk.

Existing products – new markets

Market development

Market development is particularly appropriate for capital-intensive firms whose fixed costs and production capacity are high, demanding high productivity, but whose production technology cannot easily be adapted to different products (thus allowing *product development*). New markets may consist of:

1 New market segments, e.g. non-users; creating family areas in male-oriented pubs; targeting Savlon antiseptic cream at younger users as a 'skincare product'.
2 New uses of the product by the same market segments, e.g. lining kitchen shelves and backing radiators with aluminium roasting foil.
3 New geographical areas, exporting.
4 New channels of distribution may open new markets, e.g. selling domestic goods in petrol station forecourts, renting out as well as selling.

Diversification

Related diversification

Related diversification is activity beyond the present product and market, but still in the same industry, e.g. a manufacturer opening retail outlets or a retailer going into production. A manufacturer opening retail outlets is an example of *forward integration*: i.e. becoming involved in activities concerned with the firm's *outputs* – activities which are *downstream* in the flow to the end-user.

Backward integration is involvement in activities which are *inputs* to the business, for example, a retailer starting to manufacture; a manufacturer starting to produce components; a chain of pubs acquiring a brewery – activities which are *upstream* in the flow towards the end-user.

Unrelated diversification

Unrelated diversification is activity which is not in the same product/market area – although possibly capitalising on existing resources such as skills or technology. A firm with a number of such activities is described as a *conglomerate*, and the strategy may also be called *conglomerate diversification*. Since, by definition, the firm is going into the unknown, it could be a risky strategy. To reduce the risk, entry could be by joint development with a firm that has expertise in the field, or by acquiring a firm already active in the business – which is also faster than internal development – or by franchising or licencing another manufacturer which avoids capital investment.

When Amstrad acquired the Dancall mobile phone brand in late 1993, their marketing director said: 'We have effectively leap-frogged ahead by at least two years by not having to spend that time building up the know-how.'

The strategy spreads the risk of having all of one's eggs in one basket.

Walls diversified from pork products into ice-cream because the sale of bacon and pork products dropped dramatically in summer at the time when domestic refrigerators were rare. Ice-cream was the obvious seasonal product to compensate for this.

Using a number of approaches to identify appropriate strategies increases the likelihood of obtaining a satisfactory outcome, while the differing perspectives increase the analyst's understanding of the situation. The result of the process should be a shortlist of strategic options from which one – or possibly more – will be chosen as the 'best'. For example, the decision may be taken to combine a strategy of *market development* by exporting existing products, together with a strategy of *product development*, i.e. developing a new product to exploit a gap in the existing home market.

This chapter has listed about a dozen strategies; how to make a choice between them is considered in Chapter 10. First, since profit is such an important influence on choice, it is considered in some detail in Chapter 9.

EXERCISES

1 This is a SWOT analysis for a manufacturer of a narrow range of audio equipment which is the subsidiary of a tobacco manufacturer that is diversifying into other industries.

Strengths

- Strong financial position of parent company.
- Adaptable and efficient production facilities.
- Good reputation for quality and style in industry and market-place.
- Well located, near Channel ports and motorways.
- Ready availability of skilled labour.

Weaknesses

- Obsolescent product range.
- Poor marketing skills.
- Low profitability.
- Low R&D expenditure and effort.
- Conservative management style.

Opportunities

- Growing home market for domestic electronic equipment.
- Increasing prosperity and availability of Third World markets.
- European Single Market.
- Demographic/economic changes – increased attractiveness of over-55s market.

Threats

- Increasing competition from Europe and Asia.
- Parent company dissatisfied with performance.
- No signs of current recession ending.
- Market share declining.
- Profit margins in industry under strong pressure due to competition.

(a) List possible appropriate strategies.

(b) What data are needed to narrow the choice?

2 (a) Give an example of a product or service that is marketed largely on the basis of each of the following attributes:

– Packaging	– Quality
– High price	– Low price
– Back-up service	– Channel of distribution
– Uniqueness	– Availability
– Rarity	– Technological simplicity
– Technological superiority	– Agelessness
– Novelty	– Versatility
– Product brand name	– Manufacturer's brand name

(b) Are the products/services aimed at particular market segments – a focus strategy, or at the general market – a differentiation strategy?

FURTHER READING

Porter, M. E., *Competitive Strategy*, Free Press, 1980. This text is a very comprehensive treatment of strategic decisions in a range of circumstances such as fragmented, emerging and declining industries, and so on.

Porter, M. E., *Competitive Advantage*, Free Press, 1985. Five years after the publication of *Competitive Strategy*, this text developed some of the previous ideas.

Both titles can be recommended to readers who wish to explore the subject in considerable depth.

REFERENCES

1 *PC User*, 232, pp 14, 22.
2 Berth, Rolf,
3 Ansoff, I. *Corporate Strategy*, McGraw-Hill, 1966.

CHAPTER 9

Money matters

The driving force in a market economy is naturally profit: it is the ultimate reason for the existence of the enterprise, and it is consideration of profit and, in particular, competitive advantage – the pursuit of profit which is above the average for the industry as a whole – that underpins this chapter. The firm that achieves profit levels above those of its competitors has a competitive advantage: it can better afford to invest in whatever will perpetuate its lead over its competitors.

PROFIT

There are two routes to above-industry average profitability:

- achieving lower **costs** than the industry as a whole
- **differentiating** the product from those of competitors in a way that justifies a higher price and higher profit margins.

COSTS

All firms in a highly competitive, low-profit industry will, of course, constantly attempt to cut costs in order to remain competitive and achieve satisfactory profit levels, but only those capable of notable cost-reduction will succeed in achieving cost leadership, that is, costs which are *significantly* below those of their competitors. In a mass market, these are most likely to be the brand leaders with high market share, the corresponding benefits of scale, and greater ability to meet the bargaining power of customers and suppliers. Other factors such as experience, production technology, the design of the product, cheaper sources of raw materials or channels of distribution could also contribute to lower costs. However, a competitor adopting a breakthrough as a result of new, lower-cost production technology or other means of reducing costs could destroy a firm's cost leadership. An example of this is the way that the direct selling by telephone of banking services, insurance and holidays has affected these industries, all of which operate on tight profit margins.

In a highly competitive mass market with strong pressure on *all* manufacturers to reduce costs, it would appear that, although in theory cost leadership is a means of obtaining above-average profitability, only a few firms can or should base their strategic thrust *mainly or entirely* on cost leadership; it is a risky strategy unless the leadership is secure.

So far, we have concentrated on mass markets, but a low-cost strategy could, in some circumstances, be appropriate for a firm which focuses on one segment of a market rather than competing in the mass market, a strategy of *cost focus*. A small local courier service with a limited catchment area could have lower costs than a larger competitor which provides a national service with heavy overheads. Similarly, many family-run shops can compete with multiples because they pay themselves less than they would earn if they worked for their larger competitors.

THE EXPERIENCE CURVE

In view of the importance of costs, particularly in highly competitive markets, the work of the Boston Consulting Group concerning the *experience curve* should be noted. They investigated a range of factors thought to affect costs, and found that one of the most important was the experience gained in producing the product – experience being measured as the cumulative total of units produced, not the rate of production, nor the length of time the manufacturer had been in the business. They found that, in many cases, every time experience doubled, costs declined by between 10 per cent and 30 per cent. This is the result of management learning and applying the lessons of experience, the scale effect, product redesign, improved methods, etc.

The costs per unit when two million units had been made would be, say, 20 per cent lower than at the one million stage; at the four million stage, they would be about 20 per cent lower than these, and so on. Note, however, that there is a law of diminishing returns, so that the rate of decline is greatest in the earlier stages: costs are 20 per cent lower at the two million stage, decline by a further 16 per cent by four million, but are only a further 13 per cent lower at the eight million mark.

COSTS AND MARKET SHARE

Firms with high market share who are therefore producing more than their competitors with a lower market share could gain a cost advantage, particularly if they gain this share in the early stages of the product life-cycle when the greatest savings occur. Furthermore, it is easier and relatively cheaper to gain market share when the market is growing.

The Chief Executive of Bulmer Holdings, the cider manufacturer, welcomed the decision when their main rival, Taunton Cider, went public. He predicted this would further expand the growing market.[1]

When the battle for market share is intense, the only way extra sales can be achieved is at the expense of a competitor who is also fighting for share.

The experience curve has clear implications for the choice of strategy, but has important resource implications too: to benefit from the effect could require heavy investment in both production capacity and in marketing effort. (Sources of finance are considered later in this chapter.) Furthermore, there is some evidence that the magnitude of the effect is currently less than when the research was undertaken in the late 1960s, so that basing a strategy on assumptions concerning the way a business's own or its competitors' costs could decline with experience should be treated with caution.

PIMS

Finally, a further finding concerning the importance of high market share should be mentioned: the Profit Impact of Marketing Strategy (PIMS) research.[2] This demonstrates a relationship between high relative market share and high return on investment (ROI). However, although statistical evidence for the relationship is strong, there is no proof that high ROI is the *result* of high market share; it has been argued that both could result from a third factor – good management – while other research has shown that the correlation is far from universal. Nevertheless, there is considerable food for thought in this and other published research, in particular the correlation between high relative quality and high ROI.

DIFFERENTIATION

If a cost-leadership strategy is not really an appropriate way for most firms to achieve above-average profitability – particularly in a mass market (and how can *most* be above average?) – the alternative is to charge more for the product or service while endeavouring to maintain costs at the industry average. This means differentiating the product by adding perceived value for which customers are prepared to pay extra, an approach considered when discussing the value chain in Chapter 5.

As before, the target market could be either:

(a) the mass-market, a strategy of *differentiation*; or
(b) by focusing on the special needs of a particular market segment, a strategy of *differentiation focus*.

Both strategies adopt the classic textbook approach of adding value in order to obtain higher margins in competitive, relatively undifferentiated markets.

Five-Pints powdered milk succeeded in gaining 50 per cent market share in its first year because it came in a bottle-shaped plastic container. The product was, however, basically the same as its competitors which were sold in cardboard boxes.

Oil companies add detergent to petrol. Bakers add fibre made from pea-shells to sliced white bread. Some mineral-water suppliers add a label to tap-water.

All of them can charge more as a result of adding perceived value.

PORTER'S GENERIC STRATEGIES

We have now derived Michael Porter's three *Generic Strategies*[3] – a widely respected model – for achieving competitive advantage through above industry-average profitability:

- **Cost leadership** – selling at the market price, but with the lowest costs in the industry.
- **Differentiation** – maintaining costs at the industry average while adding perceived value for which customers in the mass market will pay.
- **Focus** – focusing on a particular market segment with either a differentiation or low-cost strategy.

The actual competitive advantage results from providing extra funds to plough back into the business and thus maintain the competitive edge. However, in practice, in order to achieve a competitive edge in a highly competitive marketplace, the *cost*-leadership strategy is frequently translated into a *price*-leadership strategy in order to undercut competitors. This is, in effect, a form of price differentiation, and erodes the cost advantage of that strategy, so that Porter's framework *usually* reduces to a choice of two segmentation strategies:

- **Differentiation** – a *mass-market* strategy of distinguishing the product or service from those of competitors by such features as price, image, quality, packaging, support services, design or channels of distribution.
- **Focus** – a *niche* or *segmentation* strategy which concentrates on satisfying the needs, wants and benefits sought of one or more particular market segments.

This is consistent with conventional market segmentation theory which, however, recognises that there is a *spectrum* of product/market strategies ranging from marketing a product aimed at the mass market at one end to one aimed at a very narrow niche at the other extreme. Furthermore, although Porter claims that it is necessary to make a choice between these strategies and avoid being 'stuck in the middle', the example he gives of this, the failure of Laker Airways, was due to many other causes and, in practice, a combination of strategies may well be appropriate. For example, the car insurance industry was transformed by direct selling by telephone which eliminated agents and expensive offices, reduced staffing costs and became highly profitable as a result of cost leadership in a very short time. In addition, however, it is aimed specifically at – and available only to – the market segment of careful drivers, and at the same time is differentiated by very competitive prices.

INTERACTIONS

The simplistic model outlined here does not take price elasticity of demand into account, that is to say, the effect that price may have on total sales, on profit and, in particular, on market share which is often a key consideration in strategic choice, nor on the implications of the life-cycle or changes in demand. Porter deals at length with these and other important issues, discussing, in particular, appropriate strategies for different circumstances.

The impact of a new CEO on Compaq also illustrates a mixture of strategies. Their early success was based on innovation – a differentiation strategy; they beat IBM to the market with a PC based on the then new '386' chip.

Compaq works on the basis of products having a nine-month life-cycle, so that the expenditure on new product development is vast – 35 new products were launched in 1994. Nevertheless their pricing strategy allows them to make price cuts averaging almost 30 per cent per annum while achieving profit margins ranging from 40 per cent–20 per cent – a mixture of cost leadership and differentiation strategies. Their stated future strategy lies in developing innovative, multimedia consumer products – a return to a strategy of differentiation.

PRICE

For Compaq, pricing is obviously more than one of the components of the marketing mix; it is an important consideration in the corporate strategy. In some markets a change in the price of a brand has considerable effect on sales. This effect is measured by the *price elasticity* of demand – the percentage change in demand for a given percentage change in price.

Some products, notably those that are unique, luxuries or self-indulgences such as beauty preparations or Häagen-Dazs ice-cream are not very price sensitive; they have a low price elasticity of demand. Others, frequently commodities such as petrol – where buyers may not be brand-loyal and the differences between brands are slight and comparable – may show a considerable change in sales. Organisations such as coach or railway companies faced with the need to raise prices can predict the effect of such changes reasonably accurately.

Let us look at what increase in sales is necessary to obtain the same profit as previously when the price is reduced but costs remain constant.

Consider a product which sells for £100 with a profit margin of 20 per cent. A price reduction of 5 per cent – which is not very dramatic – will reduce the profit from £20 to £15. That means that for every 15 units previously sold, they must now sell 20 to make the same amount of profit, a sales increase of 33 per cent. For bigger cuts, the requirement becomes formidable:

Percentage of reduction	*Percentage of sales increase to break even*
5	33
10	100
15	400
17.5	800
20	never

Let us now compare the three ways of increasing profits that we have considered: increasing sales volume, reducing costs or increasing the price.

A firm sets the ambitious target of doubling net profit. They have fixed costs of £30 000. This covers rent, heating, the canteen, management and office staff and other costs incurred just by being in business regardless of the level of production or sales.

They also have variable costs of £60 000. This is the cost of raw materials, labour, selling, energy, etc. which are directly related to the volume of production and sales. If their sales revenue is £100 000, then the net profit is:

Revenue – (Fixed + Variable costs) = Net Profit

100 000 – (30 000 + 60 000) = <u>10 000</u>

They could achieve their profit target if they increased sales by 25 per cent which will also increase variable costs by 25 per cent. That is only so, however, if the sales increase does not affect fixed costs or increase variable costs. (This is unlikely in practice. How *do* you increase sales by this extent without incurring extra production or marketing costs?)

125 000 – (30 000 + 75 000) = <u>20 000</u>

Alternatively, they could trim fixed costs by *a third*:

100 000 – (20 000 + 60 000) = <u>20 000</u>

A pretty savage cut, particularly if the firm is already trim. *But*, if they increase the price by only 10 per cent:

$$110\,000 - (30\,000 + 60\,000) = \underline{20\,000}$$

How might they increase the price without affecting sales? By adding perceived value. In practice, of course, adding value will probably add to costs, but a 10 per cent price increase may well be an easier target than a 25 per cent sales increase if the product is clearly good value.

For firms in a price-sensitive market, the pricing strategy over the life of a product can be crucial, and we return to this topic later.

To demonstrate further how some of the concepts we have covered are interrelated, let us follow the life-cycle of a newly introduced product – a fledgling.

One feasible strategy would be to go for the fastest possible rate of growth that the firm has the resources to sustain. This could be for several reasons: for example, to gain an edge over competition; to recoup sunk costs as quickly as possible; to maximise the return from a product expected to have a limited life; to be seen as the market leader; because it is easier to gain market share in the early stages of the life-cycle than later when customers have become brand-loyal and competition is fiercer; or to benefit from the experience curve.

One means of achieving accelerated growth might be to market the product at a price below that which would yield the normal target profit margin or the 'market price'. As a result of the higher perceived value, it would grow faster than would otherwise be the case, depending upon the price elasticity of demand. Furthermore, the lower price would result in faster growth than that of competitors, and might also deter others from entering the market, so that relative market share would increase. High rate of growth together with high relative market share mean that during the growth stage of the life-cycle,

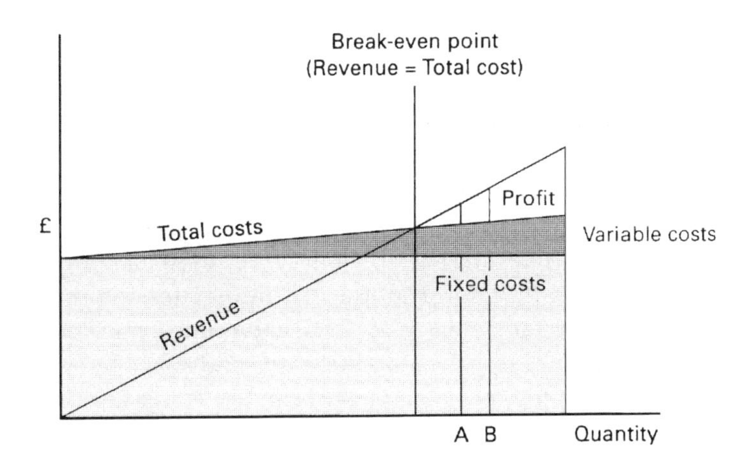

Fig 9.1 Break-even chart

the product is a star (*see* BCG matrix, Chapter 5). Depending upon the cost structure, however, this could have a profound effect upon profits. Figure 9.1 illustrates this effect. With a low price, the manufacturer is operating relatively close to the *break-even point* (where total revenue equals total costs) at point A, with high fixed costs and low variable costs. This is often the case in highly competitive mass markets.

If a firm were able to increase unit sales to point B (possibly by adding value) – which is only a 15 per cent increase in volume – then profits will nearly double. In these circumstances, price/sales volume relationships are a crucial strategic consideration.

Returning to the example, although sales are growing partly as a result of demand, they will also probably respond to marketing effort: advertising, promotion, sales effort and so on. If the rate of growth is to be maximised, this investment should be at the highest possible rate, although the law of diminishing returns will almost certainly apply: beyond a certain level, twice as much spent on, say advertising, will not have twice the effect. Moreover, the greatest cost reductions resulting from the experience curve occur in the earlier stages because of the law of diminishing returns. Hence, the higher the sales rate, the faster will costs decline, and the firm may even consider reducing prices further in order to stimulate demand and to deter competition from entering the market – bearing in mind, however, the implications illustrated in the break-even chart (Fig 9.1). Eventually, however, in the maturity stage of the life-cycle, growth will level off but the product will now dominate the market. Marketing expenditure should then be set at a level that will maintain that dominant position; since growth has ceased, to try to force further growth would not be an effective use of funds.

With high relative market share but low growth, the product is now a cash cow and, in particular, reaping the benefit of the lower costs which result from greater experience. It is generating profit which can be ploughed back in order to maintain its dominant position (which could be expensive as the market becomes more competitive) and which must also fund the development and marketing of products that will become its successors – currently fledglings and stars – when it becomes a dog and is put to rest.

In some circumstances, that fate could be avoided by updating the product, in other words by a strategy of product development. Alternatively, it could perhaps survive by adopting a strategy of consolidation, concentrating on a particular market segment rather than tackling the entire market. This is an oversimplified example, but illustrates the importance of interactions between factors such as costs, experience, market share, stage of the life-cycle, competition, the marketing mix and so on. Because circumstances are always changing, no organisation can hope to adopt the same strategy throughout the life of a product, and in Chapter 10 we turn to some of the criteria that determine strategic choice but, first, we look at where the money to finance all this activity could come from.

SOURCES OF FUNDS

The owners of a small family business who are fortunate enough to have no bank loans or investors to consider may at some time wish to expand, perhaps buying new plant and equipment or perhaps moving to bigger premises. They may be unable or unwilling to finance this themselves and must therefore obtain funds from an outside source. This will cost money. Their expectation is that the investment will earn more than enough to cover this cost and will therefore yield additional profit.

The reverse situation is also true; for several years in the 1980s, when GEC was acknowledged as one of Britain's best-run manufacturers, they had a £1.5 billion cash hoard invested in short-term gilts because they considered that there was no better purpose that they could put it to. They were paying satisfactory dividends to shareholders and they had no need for major investment in their existing activities. The alternative use for the funds was therefore to acquire businesses that would earn more than investing it in gilts – and meet other criteria.

Their criteria for acquisitions, apart from financial appraisal, were that they should have a link with the group's existing skills, should enable it to exploit those skills in the new business and should have market potential;[4] they had not found such businesses, so they made no investments. (A number of subsequent attempts at take-overs were thwarted.)

GEC was in the very fortunate position of being able to fund its activities from retained earnings; even after a very satisfactory record of dividend payment to shareholders it had very healthy reserves. In general, there are three basic sources of funds: retained earnings, borrowing and equity. In addition, assets may be sold, as discussed in Chapter 1. However, they originally grew through both borrowing – *loan capital* and *equity* – share capital. Each has advantages and disadvantages.

Loan capital

Loans are usually for a fixed period after which they must be repaid, and usually at a predetermined rate of interest – which must also be paid according to a given schedule regardless of the firm's financial situation. Loans are almost invariably secured against assets and if the firm is unable to meet the terms of the loan the lender may appoint a receiver to take over the company.

A firm may also borrow in the form of an overdraft. This enables it to borrow money from the bank up to an agreed sum and usually for short-term purposes. The rate of interest will vary according to changes in the market rate, and there is no agreed time period; the bank may demand that the overdraft be repaid if it fears that the business is likely to fail.

Equity capital

Equity capital is often, but not always, raised by offering a rights issue to existing shareholders, for example, they may be given the opportunity to buy one new share for every five they already own, at a price lower than the current market price. Any shares not taken up will then be offered on the open market. One benefit of a rights issue is that it reduces the risk of a take-over by a third party. Furthermore, in difficult times or when there is a need to retain profit, dividend payment can be reduced or even deferred while, unlike a loan, there is no repayment date. Nevertheless, issuing shares does make a business more vulnerable to take-over bids and pressures from influential investors, and the cost of servicing the capital may be higher than some forms of loan.

Alternatives to capital investment

There are two main alternatives to raising capital other than selling assets; first, which is becoming increasingly common, is to lease plant and equipment rather than buy it – to the extent that many firms, in order to raise capital, sell the premises they occupy to a property company and then lease them back.

The second approach, which reduces the capital invested in plant and equipment, is to use third parties to provide goods and services: employ a firm to store and distribute your product rather than invest in a warehouse and a fleet of vehicles yourself; hire the cars for your sales force instead of buying them; many computer firms do not manufacture at all, they merely market products which they obtain from the Far East and 'badge' as their brand. This offers two major advantages. Although the unit cost *may* be higher than if the firm undertook the work itself so that the profit margin per unit of sale may be lower, because the firm has not invested capital, however, the ROI will be higher. The other advantage is the greater flexibility this offers; it may be possible to adjust supplies of the components or services to the demand for the product so that, when demand falls, there is no surplus capacity increasing the fixed costs per unit of sale.

There are many other considerations such as:

- the stability of the industry
- the degree of risk in the enterprise for which capital is required
- the attitude to risk of management and potential sources of capital
- financial custom and practice in the industry
- the cost of capital
- how long it will take for an investment to pay back the outlay
- alternative uses for the investment or for the unused cash
- maintaining an appropriate relationship between fixed interest loan capital and equity, known as *gearing*.

In 1994, Lucas Industries issued shares in order to fund the £56 million purchase of an American car business. A spokesperson said: 'Although we have the resources, we decided to raise the money this way. It prevents our gearing moving up and helps preserve our cash for whatever options we choose.' The CEO claimed that it would enhance earnings per share.[5]

A full treatment of these topics is beyond this brief review.

EXERCISE

The fixed costs of an enterprise making widgets are £100 000 per annum. The variable costs are £10, and a widget is sold for £15.

1. If the annual profit is £100 000, how many are being sold?
2. If the price elasticity of demand is –2, (a 1 per cent drop in price results in a 2 per cent increase in sales), what would the sales volume and annual profit be if the price were reduced to £13.50?
3. If, as a result of the increase in sales volume, the variable production and sales costs were reduced by 10 per cent, what would be the effect on the annual profit?

FURTHER READING

Davies, D., *The Act of Managing Finance – A Guide For Non-financial Managers*, McGraw-Hill, 1985. This is a practical text that covers all of the topics that a non-accountant is likely to need.

REFERENCES

1 *Financial Times*, 17 December 1992.
2 Buzzell, R. D. and Gale, B. T., *The PIMS Principles*, Free Press, 1987.
3 Porter, M. E., *Competitive Advantage: Creating and Sustaining Competitive Advantage*, Free Press, 1985.
4 *Sunday Times*, 8 January 1984.
5 The *Daily Telegraph*, 10 December 1994.

CHAPTER 10

Criteria for strategic choice

To make a choice between a number of alternatives requires criteria against which to evaluate them and choose the 'best'. Some criteria may act as filters; they eliminate options that do not meet their requirements. For example, if, as was the case with United Biscuits, one corporate objective is to obtain a 20 per cent return on investment, that would eliminate an otherwise ideal project returning only 17 per cent. Hence, the first criterion is:

How well does it contribute to meeting corporate objectives?

(Remember, however, that analysis may have revealed that current objectives are not appropriate and should themselves be reviewed.)

Policy decisions may also act as filters, for example, if management had previously decided against any projects requiring capital investment above a certain level because of current financial difficulties, that may eliminate a number of otherwise attractive possibilities; it may be policy to stay very close to the firm's core activity and that could severely restrict diversification or it may be company policy not to be involved in particular activities for ethical or environmental reasons despite their profitability.

The term *policy* should include the firm's culture, ethos and similar intangibles; the firm may be risk-averse and will consider only safe ventures, or it may be a family-controlled firm that is reluctant to seek outside investors. The second criterion is therefore:

Is the project consistent with the organisation's policies/culture?

Again, these policies should perhaps be reviewed in the light of findings of the study; they may have lost their relevance or validity.

Further criteria will result from the SWOT analysis itself, for example, it may have identified a threat, perhaps a gap in the market, that should be filled in order to prevent the entry of a potential competitor – although the gap could also be seen as an opportunity. How well a particular strategy will block this entry is clearly an important criterion. Although strategies may well include the exploitation of opportunities and build on strengths, the negative side must also be considered. It is essential to ask:

Does the strategy overcome strategic weaknesses and counter serious environmental threats?

Even if these are possibilities rather than probabilities, the strategy should include contingency plans to deal with such problems should they arise, rather than be unprepared. For example, if problems were to delay the launch of a proposed new venture or costs were above the estimate – as so often happens – would sufficient funds be available to continue without jeopardising other activities? If so, for how long? What would be the consequences otherwise? In other words:

What would be the consequences of the strategy failing or of only partial success?

There are criteria based on sound management practice that should be applied to every situation. The first of these is the extent to which a strategy provides the firm with a competitive edge. Clearly, unless a product or service offers something which customers value and does so better than its competitors, there is no reason for the customers to prefer it and it must, inevitably, eventually fail.

The competitive edge may lie in a wide range of features of the product or service: price, quality, value, reputation, image, ease of use, reliability, speed of delivery, ready availability, etc. Alternatively, it may result from organisational skills or competences such as innovative ability, flexibility, rapid-response capability and low-cost structure. Whatever their origin, however, these must be features valued in the marketplace – they should take into account previously identified key success factors, and/or meet some newly identified need, not yet satisfied. Furthermore, because we are dealing with strategic issues, the advantage must be one that the firm can maintain, which will continue to be valued for some time and, most importantly, will be difficult for competitors to adopt or leap-frog – thus allowing the advantage to be lost before a satisfactory return has been achieved – by which time its successor must be ready.

Amstrad pioneered compact audio systems, inexpensive personal computers and satellite TV, achieving highly satisfactory results for a while. However, they attracted competitors who undercut them and eroded sales. Alan Sugar, Amstrad's Chairman, said 'We must find ways to make sure that when we create things, we can hold onto it a little longer.' [1] *Almost exactly a year later, having failed to do so, Amstrad attempted an alternative strategy; they reduced prices dramatically by cutting out retailers whom they accused of demanding excessive margins, and set up their own direct sales operation.*

A crucial criterion is therefore:

Is the strategy based on a *sustainable* competitive advantage?

It has to achievable in practice. There is a danger of being carried away by exciting and attractive ideas that will apparently solve difficulties, and consequently not only be over-optimistic about the benefits but minimise the problems. This is not the same as taking a calculated risk, when the dangers are fully evaluated before going ahead, for example, even if a small firm with limited financial and other resources had a new product concept in mind which had a strong competitive edge, should it enter a highly competitive market which is dominated by two or three giants who have a reputation for reacting very aggressively towards new entrants?

The UK firm Wilkinson Sword pioneered the stainless steel razor blade in the 1960s, but when, as a small UK-based firm they decided to enter the US market, they were challenging the giant Gillette on their home ground and were forced to make considerable concessions. They were eventually taken over by an American firm.

Conversely, when the razor market became extremely competitive and, hence, less profitable, Gillette had the resources to diversify into toiletries. Despite this, they were threatened by the growth of the relatively unprofitable disposable razor in the 1980s which eventually accounted for over half the shaving market's turnover, and in particular by competition from France's Bic. As a result of Gillette's poor results a number of predators attempted to acquire them, but they still had the resources to fight them off. They also had the resources to spend around $200 million on research, engineering and tooling to produce the Sensor razor, and they committed the bulk of their advertising budget to launch it. The product was a roaring success, gaining 20 per cent of the US market, and considerably improving profit margins. Razors accounted for 38 per cent of sales but 68 per cent of group profit in 1993. The success led to the launch of its successor, the Sensor Excel.

This poses the question:

Is the strategy feasible?

The feasibility of a strategy is firstly related to the resources required: financial, production, marketing, information systems, skills, etc., and these should be reviewed in the light of the requirements of each strategic option and their possible outcomes.

At least as important, however, is the ability and willingness of staff and management at all levels to understand, accept and adopt the strategy. There will almost certainly be some who will – rightly or wrongly – feel threatened in some way by the proposed changes and who might not only resist, but prevent or actually sabotage them – if only by default.

Willingness to accept the strategy applies not only within the organisation, but also to external stakeholders such as customers, shareholders, the local community and, in particular and most importantly, distributors and competitors. How will they react? What should be done before, during and after the change to ensure success – and will it work? Is it worth the cost and bother? How long will it take? Many projects fail, not because the idea was unsound, but because this aspect of acceptability was not sufficiently thought through. Hence an important criterion is to consider:

What will be stakeholders' reactions?

Finally, while the first criterion matched the options against the organisation's objectives, these are not the only important outcomes. There is a broader question to ask:

What are the potential rewards?

The potential rewards of a strategy should, whenever practical, be evaluated in cost-benefit terms. Thus, if the strategy is intended to increase market share to a target level, the benefits of this must be compared, first, with the costs of achieving it, and second, with alternative uses of the resources. A common objective is, of course, to achieve profit objectives:

In 1994, London International Group, whose core brand is Durex, disposed of well-known products such as Wright's Coal Tar Soap and major cough medicines. These were very successful in their own right – the book value of the cough medicine brands was £500 000 but yielded an annual profit of £700 000. Furthermore, since they were sold through the same channels as their main products, they contributed to sales and distribution costs, a common reason for actually making acquisitions. Nevertheless, the Group Chief Executive said that it was more important to restore the profitability of the group's core business.

Some rewards can be measured financially, and those concerned with profit and profitability are usually key issues: return on capital employed (ROCE), change in costs, sales or profit. Some can be quantified, such as market share, the number of years it will take to recover the net investment (the payback period), or the proportion of tenders converted to orders. Others, such as enhanced quality, improved image, earlier information, greater organisational flexibility or superior customer service may be more difficult to evaluate. It may be possible to quantify their probable effect sufficiently well for the purpose, for example, management could make a 'guesstimate' of the increase in market share that would result from improved quality or better service ('more than three per cent, but less than seven – say five per cent'), and this can then be translated into financial terms.

A further issue is who benefits from the reward. All too often in the past, the main beneficiaries of, for example, growth by acquisition have been company directors rather than shareholders. As the directors of organisations that became larger, not only were they more secure, they also drew higher salaries and received bonuses and other perks. In many cases studied, the return on shareholders' investment did not improve proportionately. This illustrates the difference between ROCE, and return on shareholders' investment. If you invest a sum of money in shares, it is unlikely that you are unduly concerned about ROCE; your criterion is a satisfactory return on your investment by way of dividend payments and capital growth. Whatever the difficulties, if a choice is to made between strategic options, the benefits of alternatives must be made explicit and somehow compared.

This preliminary sift may eliminate a number of options and will almost certainly raise questions concerning others that require further study, again illustrating the point that the process of strategic planning is not linear, passing through a number of stages in sequence; it is often necessary to go backwards and forwards between the steps of the model, a later one feeding back into an earlier step.

The next stage is to choose between the remaining shortlist, and there are usually many factors to take into account. Very rarely will one candidate excel under every criterion, but an overall judgement must nevertheless be made. However, some criteria will, by their nature, be more important than the rest, and some may have a high level of importance mainly because of the current situation, for example, if interest rates are high, then investment might be curtailed or deferred. Nevertheless, short-term considerations should be seen as such, and should not unduly influence long-term decisions.

EVALUATION

The next step is, therefore, to list the criteria and evaluate each of the options against them. A grid such as the one shown in Table 10.1 is helpful not only for this particular purpose, but whenever a number of alternatives must be compared and evaluated. Options are listed in the boxes at the top of the columns, and each criterion considered in turn, the conclusion being inserted in the corresponding cell at the bottom of the column.

The evaluation can be conducted in a number of ways, ranging from simply counting the major advantages and disadvantages of each and comparing the plus and minus points – a crude and misleading approach – to a mathematical method that allocates each criterion a weighting out of a total of 100, according to its relative importance. Each option is given a score from zero to five according to how well it meets each criterion, and the scores are then multiplied by weightings and totalled for each option, the one with the highest total being the 'winner'.

In the example in Table 10.2, Criterion 1 is the most important while Criterion 4 is relatively unimportant and this is reflected in their weightings of 40 and 10 respectively. Option 1, however, does not meet Criterion 1 very well – it only obtains a score of one out of a maximum of five, while Option 2 meets the criterion rather better with a score of four. However, Option 1 does meet criterion five perfectly with a score of five points.

Table 10.1 Evaluation of criteria

	Option 1	Option 2	Option 3	Option 4
Criterion 1				
Criterion 2				
Criterion 3				
Criterion 4				
Criterion 5				
Conclusion:				

Table 10.2 Mathematical method of evaluation

Weighting		Option 1		Option 2	
		Score	Score × Weighting	Score	Score × Weighting
Criterion 1	40	1	40	4	160
Criterion 2	30	2	60	1	30
Criterion 3	20	3	60	2	40
Criterion 4	10	5	50	3	30
Total	100		210		260

Although, with the exception of Criterion 1, Option 2 is worse than Option 1 at meeting the criteria, its total of 260 compared to 210 for Option 1 would appear to make it the better of the two, and this might raise the question of whether the weightings truly reflect the relative importance of the criteria. The pseudo-mathematical nature of this approach should not conceal the fact that it is completely subjective and depends entirely on the opinions of those making judgements. These will depend on their own individual attitudes and backgrounds, and the organisational culture which are therefore key determinants of strategy. Nevertheless it forces them to think in a structured way about relative importance. The benefit of the approach lies in the method not in the answer, and if the decision-makers don't like the answer, they should reconsider their weightings and scores. Intuition is a very important factor in management decision making, and a feeling that, despite the scores, the answer is wrong should not be ignored. This is not intended as criticism of quantitative approaches to evaluating strategy which is unfortunately rarely conducted in sufficient depth. For example, PA Consulting studied the costs of offering ranges of products, and found that among the companies studied, about half their range produced 150 per cent of the final profit, but the other half *consumed* the other 50 per cent to produce the final 100 per cent total.[2]

Finally, although the discussion has referred to *the* strategy, this is an oversimplification; many strategies consist of a number of substrategies, and there is a danger of these conflicting. For example, a small car may be aimed at two different markets; first, the young couple with a baby, but secondly their own parents – elderly couples in retirement. There is a danger that the young couple may be put off buying the car if they perceive it as being a car for the elderly. (Nevertheless, Renault successfully aimed the Clio at two very different markets in their 'Nicole' television advertising campaigns.) Again, in order to gain market share, a firm might aim to use the sales force to open new accounts, while at the same time attempting to improve sales by increasing the range of products bought by existing customers. These are two very different tasks for the sales force, which may not have the resources to do both: the components of a strategy must be mutually compatible and consistent.

Strategies may also have resource implications for other functions, for example, to attempt to increase sales without ensuring that adequate stock is available, together with production capacity to meet the increased demand, could lead to a fiasco. Thus, when first launched, the confectionery bar Whispa had to be withdrawn from the market because production could not meet demand, and the same problem occurred with the test marketing of Galaxy Caramel – it sold three times as many as was planned. It is therefore necessary to ensure that not only finance, but other resources are adequate for the strategy as an entirety, and this may require that the proposed strategy be modified, in other words, returning to an earlier stage of the planning process before finalising the plan for implementation. This is considered in the next chapter.

EXERCISE

A risk-averse firm in a fairly strong financial position and with a good reputation but in a rapidly declining industry has decided it must adopt a strategy of unrelated diversification. It has evaluated a number of industries, identified the one it favours, and is now considering the best method of entering the market.

The alternatives are:

A Develop and manufacture a new product.

B Obtain a licence and manufacture under licence.

C Set up a joint venture with German firm X that has experience in the field.

D Buy out firm Y that is already in the industry.

E Market under their brand name an existing Korean product not currently imported into the UK.

They have established the following criteria, and weighted them as shown:

	Weighting
(a) Low risk	35
(b) Speedy entry into the market	25
(c) Low capital cost	20
(d) Profitability	15
(e) Short payback period	5
	100

1 Discuss the advantages and disadvantages of each method of entry.

2 Using your own judgement, assign scores to each alternative strategy and evaluate them. Try different scores and see how the rankings compare.

FURTHER READING

Ansoff, I. and McDonnell, *Implanting Strategic Management*, Prentice Hall, 1990. This text tackles the subject in a very thorough manner which is different from other writers, and is most likely to apeal to readers who enjoy a quantitative approach.

Johnson, G. and Scholes, K. *Exploring Corporate Strategy*, Prentice Hall, 1993. Chapters 7 and 8 use the criteria of *suitability, feasibility, acceptability*.

Rowe, A. J., Mason, R. O., Dickel, K. E., Mann, R. B. and Mockler, R. J., *Strategic Management: A Methodological Approach*, Addison-Wesley, 1984. This text describes, in some detail, how to use the SPACE matrix to determine the appropriate strategic posture. This is sometimes referred to in other texts.

Thompson, J. L., *Strategic Management, Awareness and Change*, Chapman and Hall. This text uses the criterion of *appropriateness, feasibility, desirability*.

REFERENCES

1 *Financial Times*, 6 October 1993.

2 *Marketing Week*, 7 October 1994.

CHAPTER 11

Planning, implementation and control

THE RELATIONSHIP BETWEEN PLANNING, IMPLEMENTATION AND CONTROL

Although planning and control are often considered as Siamese twins, planning is largely concerned with future change, while, by its very nature, control is concerned with maintaining a present, predetermined situation, although that situation could be dynamic; for example, maintaining a particular position in an expanding market – rather like keeping up with the front-runners in a race. Where they are very closely linked, however, is in planning and controlling the process of implementation. Implementation consists of transforming a plan into action and ensuring that the intended outcomes do result.

The particular way in which the strategic plan was developed will influence the processes of implementation and subsequent control. If this had been highly participative then the proposed strategy may be well understood and accepted within the organisation. If, however, it had been hatched in great secrecy in the board room, then the response could be very different.

The chairman of RTZ believes in agreeing a strategy through a 'bottom-up, top-down process which ensures that everyone is rowing in the same direction. Then, although the operating managements have an unusual degree of discretion, it is within a disciplined framework. Without it they may become robber barons.' [1]

Whether developed top-down, bottom-up, or somehow in-between as at RTZ, in all but the simplest of organisations a corporate plan is implemented and the organisation controlled at a hierarchy of levels. For an international conglomerate such as BTR, the complexity is formidable: more than 1000 operations in 40 countries ranging from airline pilot training in Australia to builders' merchants in the UK, from golf clubs to pillows, and from hearing aids to diesel engines. Clearly, the time-scale for many changes decided at the corporate level must inevitably be long, and would probably not concern the strategy of specific operating units.

THE INFLUENCE OF STRUCTURE

BTR is an example of a multidivisional organisation, and serves to demonstrate how structure affects the planning, implementation and control of strategy.

At the first level in the organisational hierarchy, BTR is divided into five business sectors such as Industrial, Transportation and Construction. Within each sector are Groups: for example, Batteries, Materials handling, Diesel engines, Packaging and so on.

At the next level down, Group management in turn delegates a degree of responsibility to the management of individual companies, many of which are in turn split into some form of strategic business units (SBUs).

An SBU is a group within an organisation that is set up to serve a specific market segment. It has a level of autonomy that enables it to decide its own strategy within given budgetary and other constraints. A division subdivided into a number of SBUs may not only relate and respond more closely to the different market segments it serves, but its performance can be more closely monitored.

Within BTR, Dunlop Slazenger produces and markets golf, tennis and squash equipment, and sports, leisure and industrial footwear, while the Slazenger label is licensed around the world. These highly competitive markets require a considerable degree of flexibility and the centre cannot hope to be sufficiently knowledgeable to decide the strategy for each. Nevertheless, the total effort must somehow be controlled and co-ordinated, and be consistent with corporate strategy and objectives.

The degree of central control will vary from organisation to organisation. Sometimes, head office may set performance targets such as sales volume, return on investment, etc., but leave the units to decide how to achieve them, perhaps controlling only capital expenditure above a certain level. Other organisations will require that all but relatively low-level operational decisions must be referred to head office, a top-down approach. Many retail chains, for example, impose strict merchandising plans on their outlets, deciding which products may be stocked and where they should be displayed, their prices, and which should be promoted and when. They employ senior managers to inspect all aspects of a branch's operations to ensure that it is conforming to the rules. Even painting the canteen may be decided at head office. This is practical when there is little diversity in the activities of the units within an organisation. The centre can then adopt standard monitoring, planning and control systems with a common corporate image and strategy. Because of this standardisation, such organisations lend themselves to the intensive use of information technology to monitor and control operations, sacrificing a degree of flexibility for very close and efficient control. For example, it is possible for the head office of a retail chain to be aware of the sales of products as they are actually occurring at the checkouts (in 'real time'), by using electronic point of sale equipment (EPOS). They may be able to intervene by electronic means in hundreds of branches virtually simultaneously.

When a new season's line goes into Marks & Spencer stores in a variety of colours, information technology enables sales to be monitored during the first few days and production of faster-selling colours and sizes to be stepped up. A supplier can receive an order and dye pre-knitted garments accordingly within 48 hours ready for delivery.[2]

Although a large organisation – 282 stores in the UK – a complex structure is not needed because of the high degree of standardisation that is possible. There are, however, 72 other Marks & Spencer stores in, for example, France, Spain, Holland, Hong Kong and Canada; there are 76 franchises in 18 different countries ranging from Austria to Thailand, 133 Brooks Brothers stores in USA and Japan, 19 Kings Supermarkets in the USA, and 106 D'Allaird's in Canada. Although all are retail outlets, they obviously cannot be controlled within the same system, while financial activities – credit cards, personal loans, unit trusts sales, pensions and life assurance products – is a rapidly growing but completely different market, although available through retail outlets.

It will be seen that even within the Marks & Spencer organisation, a number of different control systems or styles are needed, and the complexity of both the organisation and its environment are influential factors. This is considered further in Chapter 12.

Nevertheless, because of the benefits it brings, Marks & Spencer is investing £100 million a year in its own international information system to connect all its stores to the centre. The Managing Director said that tills and electronic warehousing systems will be the same in Peking as in Bordeaux. 'Once we are all on-line, I will be able to pick up any staff members and put them anywhere in the world and they will be right at home.'[3]

Although a multidivisional organisation, the divisions operate in parallel rather than in series – that is, the output of one division is not the input of another, as would be the case in vertical integration. When divisions are closely coupled, however, much tighter overall planning and control is necessary, particularly if a policy of just-in-time has been adopted.

STYLES OF CONTROL

To a large extent, the degree and type of control exerted over strategic business units will depend on the industry, type of organisation, its environment, its age and its corporate strategy. At one extreme, particularly in the case of a small family firm, head-office control could be absolute. At the other extreme it could be possible for the head office of a holding company to leave management entirely to the subsidiaries, and merely collect the profit they make. Between these extremes there are three major styles:[4]

- Financial control style
- Strategic planning style
- Strategic control style.

BTR adopted the *financial control style*. This consists of setting financial targets and requiring capital expenditure above a certain level to be authorised, but leaving the subsidiaries to decide their own strategies. A BTR executive said: 'We are a fairly low risk organisation. We avoid businesses that require major, risky outlays with long payback periods', while another stated: 'We don't like mass production. We like niche situations that involve customer problem solving.'[5]

This business policy does not rely on tight head office control that would be inappropriate for a highly diversified organisation where local autonomy is essential, and is less necessary where the financial risk is low.

The *strategic planning style*, however, implies that the centre *is* involved in the strategic planning processes of its subsidiaries. In less diverse organisations than BTR, usually involved in fewer than half a dozen and often only two or three industries, the centre can be more knowledgeable about them. As a result, head office can become more involved in strategic planning, controlling the portfolio of enterprises overall – growing not only by organic development of the existing subsidiaries but also by acquiring others, using its knowledge of the industries. Marks & Spencer has adopted this approach in the USA if not the UK.

Between these two approaches is the *strategic control style*. This implies less involvement of the centre, and entails creating groups of similar businesses and delegating much of the strategic responsibility to those groups. Unilever is structured like this.

This approach can – in theory – enable organisations with very different cultures to be accommodated under one umbrella yet go their own way, although, in practice, the centre usually does get involved. It may also be the style adopted by single-industry, horizontally diversified organisations. For example, RTZ sold off all of its industrial activities to concentrate on international mining and adopted this approach. It also stems from the chairman's hands-off management style and the particular organisational culture.

THE INFLUENCE OF CULTURE

As organisations grow and age, they may not only become more complex, they also tend to become more bureaucratic, exerting tighter controls, and this is not necessarily completely inappropriate when the environment is static. However, many large organisations in more dynamic environments face the problem of staying flexible and responsive, despite their size, and innovative despite their age.

One approach that attempts to avoid the problems associated with a successful, mature and large organisation that might inhibit or delay innovation is to set up 'skunkworks'. These are relatively autonomous project teams that are not bound by or influenced by the prevailing organisational culture, beliefs, 'formula for success' and, in particular, the control systems. This may enable a large organisation to have some of the responsiveness of an entrepreneur. An example was the way in which IBM moved into the personal computer market.

The parent company provided capital and premises – a far from prestigious converted warehouse – and put a dynamic entrepreneur in charge. The design teams had a degree of autonomy that was unprecedented for IBM and there was no question of having to conform to corporate policy: they used competitors' microprocessors and software, and marketed their product through different channels of distribution. Within a year they dominated the PC market, leaving the parent company unaffected – until its own crisis a few years later.

In many respects, and particularly during its prime, IBM had an image as the quintessentially conventional organisation; this is often the case with large and mature organisations, although they may have been very different earlier in their history.

In its early days, the supermarket chain ASDA grew very successfully by breaking many of the accepted rules – as do many entrepreneurs.

Unlike most chains, there was no central warehouse to control stock and to obtain better discounts from suppliers as a result of placing larger single orders. Unlike most chains, branch managers had a considerable degree of autonomy and were expected to act entrepreneurially – as though it were their own store – and this was reflected in their bonus payments. Unlike most chains, the premises were not purpose-built supermarkets but low-rent, out-of-town buildings with ample car-parking (for example, a former cattle market, a cotton mill, a large warehouse and similar no-frills buildings), and their prices were correspondingly low.

Because of the high throughput of each outlet, the manager was still able to negotiate quantity discounts, and although this was less than ASDA would have obtained by placing orders centrally, they saved the costs of central storage, distribution and control. Because they did not have to refer to head office, the managers could respond flexibly and quickly to local circumstances.

There came a point, however, when this strategy was considered no longer appropriate; the chain had now grown quite large, and a move up-market was thought desirable. It was therefore decided that further expansion should be only through purpose-built stores, and that central warehousing, standardised procedures, and tighter control over operations were necessary.

Carrying out this strategy greatly affected the organisation; every one of the 7-Ss was modified:

1 New *systems* were needed. The greater emphasis on strong central control

required considerably improved communication, information and control systems, and also meant that financial reward systems needed modification. Logistics were completely transformed with the need for a warehouse stock control and distribution system to be devised, together with complementary systems in the branches, and liaison with suppliers.

2 The management *style* changed from being relatively informal to a *role* culture with a greater emphasis on formally defined functions.
3 *Staff* were recruited and trained in the required *skills* for the new activities. Greater size and central control now demanded more formal approaches to recruitment, training and staff development.
4 The organisational *structure* was considerably changed, with new levels of management, responsibilities and reporting relationships.
5 *Shared values* were changed with the reduction in autonomy and the move up-market.

This example illustrates the degree to which the elements of the 7-S framework are interdependent, and the value of the framework for checking that the implications of strategy implementation are fully taken into account.

It is interesting to note that, in 1993, deliberately attempting to change its culture from a bureaucratic approach to a less authoritarian style while still maintaining central control, ASDA reduced the head-office head count from more than 2000 to about 1300. However, it is also noteworthy that RTZ, which has a culture based on consensus and decentralization, has a head office staff of only about 200, and these control 46 000 people in over 60 major mines in 35 countries.

IMPLEMENTATION

It may be possible or necessary to adapt the organisation and its strategic thrust in stages over a period of time in order to reduce the impact – although some would argue that it is better to make the changes as quickly as possible, for example, the CEO of Barclays Bank said, 'Organization and management changes should be reasonably small and made reasonably often.'[6] However, whenever the proposed changes are of any magnitude, the process of implementation must itself be planned and controlled; it must be programmed, and variations from the programme detected, investigated and appropriate action taken. According to one authority, successful implementation requires:

- Above all, a manager with clear responsibility for the process of implementation.
- A culture that motivates people to participate and co-operate.
- A clear understanding of the proposed strategy at every level of the organisation (*see* Planning processes, later in this chapter).
- An appropriate reporting structure to monitor the progress of change.

- Information and control systems that enable timely decisions to be made and communicated.
- In some circumstances, reward systems that provide the financial and other incentives for people at all levels to implement the strategy, possibly linked to the achievement of 'milestones' along the way.

These must be decided in advance of implementation, and the resources – including budgets – and time-scale implications fully appreciated. The plan may need to be modified if it appears to be too ambitious or impractical.

RESISTANCE TO CHANGE

Once identified, many problems that might arise could – in theory – be solved by spending money: systems can be bought, consultants hired, staff trained, experts recruited, buildings and plant bought and so on. Resistance to change, however, is a major problem in strategy implementation, and if significant stakeholders within – and indeed outside as well – do not understand, accept, believe in, adopt and adapt to the changes, the probability of failure is high, although in some circumstances the brute force approach may succeed.

Commitment is frequently crucial to successful implementation, but it may not be possible to teach an old – or unwilling – dog new tricks; it may be necessary to replace people at any level from the boardroom to the shop floor if they cannot or will not adapt; senior managers upon whom success depends may resist changes that will adversely affect them, and this must be dealt with. How, then, does an organisation obtain commitment?

The answer – as is usually the case with management problems – depends upon the circumstances. At one extreme, in a crisis and if survival is at stake, instant acceptance may be necessary and obtained when the situation and the solution are obvious and those involved trust the leadership, even when implementation is imposed from above: a submarine captain does not consult the crew, nor do they expect him to do so; the organisational culture is such. Hence, in some circumstances, it may be possible to impose the plan because no one has the wish, the power, or the will to oppose it.

At the other extreme, when the reasons for change are controversial or not apparent; when the changes are imposed without consultation let alone participation; when the personal benefits or organisational advantages are questionable; when the organisational culture is particularly conservative and resistant to change; when the new strategy requires a change in organisational culture to succeed, and when management/staff relationships are poor and difficult to improve, then the process of obtaining commitment could be lengthy or even impossible, resulting in a high probability of failure.

In these circumstances the wisdom of adopting a strategy that requires a radical change should be re-examined, and, if possible, either a strategy more in keeping with the characteristics of the organisation adopted, the changes introduced at a slower pace, or the shortcomings remedied over a period. The stronger an organisation's culture, the greater is its influence in resisting change, and the dangers of attempting to force change must be recognised.

PLANNING PROCESSES

What this means is that the most appropriate process for developing and implementing strategy in a particular organisation at a particular time will depend on a number of factors such as urgency, organisational culture, management style, size and complexity of the organisation, degree of autonomy, the need to liaise or consult third parties, etc. In large, complex, or diversified organisations, the co-ordination of change requires particularly careful management. There is no one best way, but a range of possible approaches. These include a working party drawn from different functions that makes recommendations to a committee that actually decides; a standing committee that itself decides; a strategic planning department that develops plans for approval by the board; employing outside consultants who make recommendations to the board, etc.

The approach adopted for developing strategic plans will influence the tactics used to implement the new strategy. Nevertheless, whatever the process, the outcome should be a plan for every level in the hierarchy of the organisation affected by the proposed changes.

In conglomerates such as BTR or Unilever, there will be an overall corporate plan within which plans for each business sector will be prepared. At sector level there will be a general group plan to co-ordinate the plans for each company. Companies will in turn prepare plans for the divisions, and these might be further divided for the SBUs within a division. Beyond plans for the various levels of the business, the various functions at each level will prepare their own plans according to their position and reporting responsibility within the organisation. Thus, based on the sales targets required in the strategic plan, an SBU will probably prepare its marketing plan, deciding the advertising and promotion plan and the sales force plan, and submitting budgets for these.

The production plan will cover such decisions as the production schedule based on the sales plan, what to manufacture and what to buy in, what plant and equipment will be needed, and the budgets for these.

Human resource planning will need to co-ordinate the recruitment needs of other departments and arrange for training programmes, while finance must consolidate all the budgets within the approved organisational budget – probably sending them back to be trimmed – and plan the financial arrangements.

These plans may need to be submitted to the next level of management where they must be approved, then consolidated and co-ordinated with those of the other SBUs, and possibly so on up the hierarchy, though in decreasing detail and possibly with a longer time-scale. The lower-level plans will probably be prepared annually, although possibly updating a rolling five-year plan which is the planning horizon at higher-levels. However it is done, a plan should be a clear statement of:

- Who is in charge
- What will be accomplished
- When it will be accomplished
- Who will do it
- Where it will be done
- How much it will cost
- What it will achieve

These statements then enable the roles of every unit within the organisation to be co-ordinated, and act as a set of benchmarks against which to monitor progress and success, and to trigger corrective action if required – in other words, as a key component of the control process.

CONTROL PROCESSES

The basis of the control of a system is the negative feedback loop, as shown in Fig. 11.1.

The output of a system – for example, product from a production line, sales from a sales force, or profit from a SBU – is monitored and compared with some predetermined standard. Corrective action is then taken to reduce any deviation from the standard if this is outside acceptable limits. Figure 11.1 shows action being taken on the inputs, but it could equally well be applied to the operations. This is *data-management control.*

For a production line, the approach is relatively straightforward, the standards are usually easily defined and quantified. They could be, for example, rate of production, productivity, reject rate or a physical characteristic such as weight or colour. The corrective action could be to the inputs such as a different raw material, or to the production process itself by resetting a tool, or increasing the temperature or pressure.

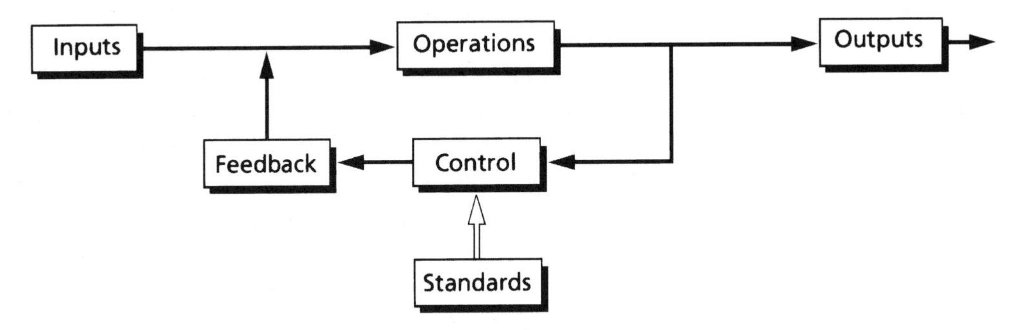

Fig 11.1 Negative feedback loop

Similarly, sales can be monitored as a routine and targets set for each salesperson or sales team on a weekly, monthly or yearly basis. In the latter case, cumulative sales may be monitored against a forecast to see if the trend will enable the year-end target to be achieved. If this appears unlikely, marketing effort could be intensified to remedy the situation. This could be by increased advertising, additional sales effort, trade incentives, consumer incentives, or whatever experience suggests is appropriate. These examples are at the operational level, but are equally appropriate at higher levels when the activities being monitored are routine, when the parameters are clearly identified and measurable, when the standards are appropriate, and when the causes of deviation are identifiable and can be corrected. In these circumstances, particularly when the environment is relatively stable, control by data management can be exercised by people at relatively low levels of the organisation if they have the authority and the appropriate level of expertise and experience needed to identify the cause and solution.

At business or corporate level, the time-scale for taking corrective action will be longer than at the operational level, but the major parameters may still be quantifiable, for example: market share, return on investment (ROI), budgets, growth rate, revenue and so on. In this case data-management control is likely to be the main method of managing the organisation.

Measurements of performance for most industrial organisations include:

- Net profit
- Earnings per share
- Market share
- Sales per employee
- Dividend rate
- Return on capital
- Productivity
- Sales
- Costs
- Staff turnover

For retail outlets, sales as a function of selling space and stock-turn would be important parameters; for a hospital, bed-occupancy and operating theatre utilisation; and for a cinema, 'bums on seats'. It will be seen that most of the parameters measure the efficiency with which resources are used. When the activities are less routine – in other words, in a less certain environment, for example, when bidding for contracts or in certain commodity markets – control may need to be based more on what has been learned by experience or trial and error than on monitoring data. Control must then be exercised further up the hierarchy by more senior managers with greater experience and responsibility.

In a turbulent environment, when causal relationships are obscure and events are not repetitive, control cannot be based on the interpretation of data and experience alone, but increasingly upon intuition. This requires a different sort of organisational culture and a manager who does not rely upon logical analysis but on intuition and judgement. In these circumstances it is not only the control systems but the entire process of strategic management that must be adapted, and this is considered in Chapter 12.

Finally, in some circumstances, particularly in the not-for-profit, public and political sectors, control is a matter of negotiation, persuasion, manipulation and the use – or abuse – of position, influence and power. Machiavelli's Prince might be a suitable manager in this type of environment. In these circumstances, greater emphasis must be placed on *manager–management* systems, i.e. selection, reward and punishment systems for controlling the behaviour of key personnel. However, whichever of the above systems is the most appropriate, the motivating effect of the control system cannot be overestimated: individuals or groups will attempt to maximise whatever criteria are used to judge their performance and targets should be chosen and set with this in mind.

The motivating effect of targets is applied in the system of *Management by Objectives* (MBO). This is a formal procedure under which individual managers agree their objectives for the coming year, usually in discussion with their immediate boss. Progress is sometimes monitored during the year, with a formal review at the year's end. This is customarily the basis for reward systems, management development and for setting next year's objectives.

The objectives concern the manager's area of responsibility, and should in turn contribute to achievement of the department's objectives, so that the procedure is a form of manager–management system. There are several other procedures similar to MBO.

As often happens, these stereotypical situations blend into each other so that hybrid situations will arise. Furthermore – as is also often the case – different circumstances requiring different approaches will occur in different parts of the organisation. Control systems and management styles appropriate to the production line of a car manufacturer are not suitable for the design department and vice versa. This is frequently a major problem when a well-established organisation in a mature industry decides to diversify into an emerging market by acquiring a young, vigorous and entrepreneurial firm with a successful track record in that area. The degree of tolerance required of the parent to accept the completely different ways of its acquisition, and the willingness of the stepchild to conform to the expectations of its new parent, parallel the problems such an addition causes in human families.

MEANS OF CONTROL

In a sense, the *mission* acts as a form of control of the organisation as a whole by defining the nature of its activities, and so too, in this sense, do *objectives* and *strategies* at both the corporate and lower levels.

At a level lower than strategy, but still a means of influencing decisions at all levels from strategic to operational, are stated *policies*. It is a policy of the John Lewis Partnership never to be knowingly undersold, which influences their pricing strategy. It also prevents them from offering goods on which they cannot obtain a target level of profit because of the low prices charged by other retailers. Policies may apply to all areas of an organisation's activities, and act as guidelines to thinking.

Somewhat tighter control is exercised by *procedures*, which are guidelines to action, that is, they give broad guidance as to what should be done in certain circumstances, while *rules* actually prescribe exactly what should be done. Rules can be laid done when the circumstances can be predicted and defined; they enable decision making to be delegated to low levels of management if appropriate.

While *strategy* implies guidelines to action on a relatively long-term time-scale, a *programme* offers guidelines in the short term, the time-scale usually being defined. If the programme has not only a time-scale but is quantified, particularly with financial values, it becomes a *budget* – a rigid framework within which to operate. This is a very common means of control, and so-called plans are often no more than a reactive update of last year's figures.

EXERCISES

1 **(a)** What are the factors that might allow RTZ to control a larger and wider-spread organisation than ASDA with fewer staff?

(b) What are the advantages and disadvantages?

2 In what circumstances might head office prefer to appoint an outsider as the CEO of a subsidiary when there appears to be a suitable internal candidate?

3 Discuss the issues that should be taken into account when deciding the control systems for:

(a) a research laboratory;

(b) an advertising agency;

(c) a medical practice.

FURTHER READING

Mintzberg, H. and Quinn, J. B., *The Strategy Process*, Prentice Hall, 1983. Chapter 14 contains several interesting readings. Mintzberg, H., *Power In and Around Organisations*, Prentice Hall, 1983, although out of print, is also highly recommended.

Moss Kanter, R., *The Change Masters*, Centrepoint, 1983. This text contains very readable case studies. Moss Kanter, R., *When Giants Learn to Dance*, Unwin, 1989. This text covers a wider range of relevant topics.

Stacey, R. D., *Strategic Management and Organisational Dynamics*, Pitman Publishing, 1993. This book adopts a dynamic systems approach and is 'Structured around the implications of different types of feedback'. and strongly recommended as an important alternative view to the above titles. Chapters 1, 7 and 10 give the main argument.

REFERENCES

1 *Unilever Magazine*, January 1994.
2 *Marks & Spencer Annual Report*, 1994.
3 *Sunday Times*, 4 December 1994.
4 Goold, M. and Campbell, A., *Strategies and Styles*, Blackwell, 1987.
5 *Long Range Planning*, 20/5, p.46.
6 *Telegraph*, 5 November 1994.

CHAPTER 12

The turbulent environment

The reputation of forecasters, like that of astrologers, may depend on their public having short memories.

In 1986, the consultancy firm of John Naisbitt, whose book *Megatrends* had sold seven million copies and had been translated into 22 languages, was commissioned to forecast future trends for the leisure industry. They predicted that 'One of the most far-reaching changes in leisure life style that will occur over the next ten years is . . . a shift in values to conservatism that is . . . environmentally unconcerned and less inclined to worry about health and fitness.'[1]

The authors of a book on strategic management published in 1990 – on which much of this chapter is based[2] – wrote of our present society, which they described as the post-industrial era: 'The post-industrial era is the arrival of affluence . . . The arrival of affluence casts doubt on economic growth as the main instrument of social progress.'

Strategic planning is generally seen as the core of strategic management, and strategies drawn up in the late 1980s – based on the expectation of an affluent, hedonistic society in the early/mid-1990s – are now probably shredded and forgotten, while the importance of economic growth as the main driver of social progress is now painfully obvious. This chapter considers some of the problems of strategic management when the environment is unpredictable, and in particular when the organisation is complex.

Strategic plans must be based on many assumptions about the future: the economic or social climate; technological developments; the price and availability of raw materials and components; the rate of market growth; the nature and extent of competition; the introduction of substitutes or alternatives; and the cost of capital – to name but a few. These assumptions are based on forecasts which are in turn derived from extrapolations and analyses of historic data; the past is used as a guide to the future, and advocates of strategic planning and statisticians have devised a multitude of matrices, frameworks, models, and techniques to assist the process. All of the assumptions will nevertheless be inaccurate to a greater or lesser degree, but whether this matters depends less on the magnitude of the error than on:

(1) the consequences of a decision based on incorrect forecasts; and
(2) the ability to remedy or recover from the situation.

At one extreme, a sales forecast that turned out to be pessimistic may merely mean that the sales force, in overshooting its target, has exceeded its budget of allocated costs – a notional sum. At the other extreme, a manufacturer, having invested in a factory costing scores of millions of pounds and then finding that demand is below forecast, could be in a very difficult financial position.

But what if, by the nature of the situation, the future cannot be predicted with acceptable certainty? The orthodox view is that plans must nevertheless be made – how can you possibly run an organisation without planning ahead?

In some circumstances of course, feeling one's way – which reduces the need for detailed preplanning – may be both a possible and appropriate way to move into the future. For example, if the demand for an innovative new product is difficult to judge, it may be possible to invest in limited production facilities and undertake test marketing in one area of the country. Should it fail, then the loss is minimised. If it succeeds, production lines can be added and the geographical coverage extended at whatever rate resources permit and test results suggest, a strategy of *logical incrementalism*. However, this may not always be possible; the nature of the product or market may be such that small-scale production or marketing is not feasible; for example the Channel Tunnel required total and continuous commitment despite the actual costs being twice those forecast, while a national delivery service requires national coverage, even if it is necessary to subcontract third parties in order to provide it.

Another difficulty could be that small-scale manufacture is prohibitively expensive when compared with large-scale operation (as is the case with most mass-market products such as cars). Alternatively, the problem could lie in marketing the product; an example of this is the perfumery industry where the cost of publicising a new fragrance worldwide has been put at £35 million. Despite this cost, global marketing is essential for the major companies if they are to maintain their international status and obtain an adequate financial return.

In late 1993 Yves Saint-Laurent (YS-L) launched a new perfume, Champagne, throughout much of the world. Three champagne houses objected to the name, and a French court ruled that they must drop it in France. Because of the global nature of the market, YS-L had seriously to consider renaming the product rather than market it under two different names, even though this meant losing the £12 million it had invested in the launch. (In the event, the publicity resulted in French sales of the product – renamed Yves Saint-Laurent – being vastly above estimate.)

ENVIRONMENTAL PREDICTABILITY

The outcome of the launch of a new scent is very uncertain, and a major characteristic of the environment of the industry is its *unpredictability*. For example, about 75 new fragrances were launched in the USA in 1993; only about 15 were expected to recover their launch costs within three years – although those that succeed are highly profitable. The examples of the Channel Tunnel and Champagne illustrate the importance of adequate resources and appropriate scale of operations in these circumstances.

The predictability of the environment depends not only on the rapidity of change, but also on the extent to which the future can be seen – the *adequacy* and *timeliness* of information about the future. In the case of perfumes, both are unfavourable, and this feature of the environment has to be reflected in the overall corporate strategy and the nature of the organisation itself. The relatively short time-horizon, together with rapid changes in taste, demand appropriate information-gathering and processing systems, with the capability of rapid response, which has important implications concerning the organisational culture and structure.

ENVIRONMENTAL COMPLEXITY

Yves Saint-Laurent is a fashion house as well as a perfumery manufacturer, so they are accustomed to operating in a fast-changing world – YS-L is in fact owned by a pharmaceuticals company which, as previously mentioned, itself operates in a turbulent environment. However, the environment is not only unpredictable, it has a high level of *complexity*: firms in the fashion, beauty and pharmaceutical industries operate in many different countries with different prices, different markets, and different cultures. The local characteristics must be borne in mind when deciding objectives and strategy, but these must nevertheless be consistent with the overall corporate needs.

ENVIRONMENTAL NOVELTY

The unexpected court case brought against YS-L by the champagne houses is an example of the third aspect of environmental turbulence: *novelty*.

In some environments, whatever the degree of complexity, events will be largely familiar – 'That's happened before, we know how to deal with it.' In other environments one must expect the unexpected, even when the environment is not particularly complex. It may also arise when the firm diversifies into new ventures beyond its previous experience, and is particularly problematic when the organisation is pioneering innovative technologies or products. This demands a culture and management style that are at ease with novelty, for example, the vast and complex Chinese market is beginning to open up to the West. The market for fabric detergents alone is worth US$1 billion, and is growing, but the head of Unilever Shanghai Co Ltd said, 'In some respects I can tear up my previous experience because it is so different here . . . I imagine it is similar to the east coast of the US a hundred years ago.'

The three sections that follow outline some of the approaches that may be used to cope with the different levels and mixes of *predictability*, *complexity* and *novelty* that comprise environmental turbulence.

PREDICTABILITY

'Win some, lose some' is an accepted fact of life in many industries where the probability of the outcome of frequently repeated events or decisions is known to a greater or lesser degree. It is, of course, basically gambling – and, like bookmakers, management's strategy must be to maximise long-term overall gain.

Bookmakers, however, are fortunate: they can adjust the odds at any time as a result of environmental changes – the weather, the bets placed, etc., whereas the punter, in order to win in the long run, must study form in order to identify likely winners. Both collect and interpret data in order to calculate probabilities, outcomes, pay-offs and expected values. For organisations that repeatedly make similar decisions, and so have a wealth of data: banks offering – or refusing – loans, insurance companies setting premiums, oil companies drilling for oil, firms tendering for contracts, as well as professional gamblers, a number of statistical techniques are available as powerful aids to decision making. In some cases they can be encapsulated in computer expert systems or neural network applications, making the process available to non-experts within the organisation, for example, Barclays Bank use a knowledge-based system, Lending Adviser, to vet loan applications. In these circumstances, even important decisions involving the investment of very large sums of money become almost *operational* rather than *strategic*. However, we are here concerned with strategic management decisions.

Decision trees

Drawing a decision tree and considering each branch in turn is one way of methodically analysing the possible alternatives of a situation when there is a wide range of choices. If the probabilities and outcomes of each branch can be estimated, this will provide a quantified basis for comparing them. This helpful approach to coping with a situation involving both complexity and uncertainty is illustrated in Fig 12.1.

For the organisation faced with an infrequently occurring major decision for which there are few or no precedents from which to predict outcomes, it might appear that this technique is of limited value in providing an answer: having no data from which to calculate the probabilities of alternative outcomes it must rely on subjective estimates which are likely to reflect the attitude of the estimator. Nevertheless, the principles underlying techniques and concepts such as decision trees, pay-off matrices, alternative criteria and

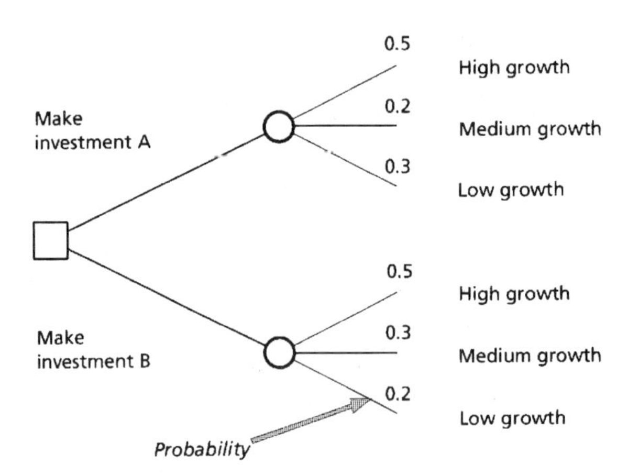

Fig 12.1 A decision tree

so on, are simple, easily understood, and are often relatively easily applied by employing user-friendly computer software. Furthermore, their value lies not only in the answers they provide, but in the methodology itself, considering in a systematic way the implications of the alternative outcomes of a decision.

Alternative scenarios (1)

Where the situation is less complex, a simpler approach is to consider a number of different courses of events or scenarios where the differences are differences of *degree*, for example, adopting an optimistic estimate of demand, a pessimistic one and one in the middle – the most likely one.

Consider the example of building a factory. For a given size and level of investment, there will be an optimum level of production at which unit costs will be minimised: above that level it will be necessary to pay overtime to meet higher demand, while below that level, fixed costs per unit of production will rise. In addition to this, there will probably be economies of scale and other factors that will vary according to the plant installed.

If the data are known, or can be estimated, the implications of building say a large, a medium-sized and a small factory, the financial implications of low, medium and high demand, or different rates of growth, costs or prices can be calculated for each combination, and a decision reached.

Although Benson Crisps is the fourth largest quoted savoury snack maker in the UK, in 1993 they had only a five per cent market share. Their bigger rivals were all multinationals: Pepsico and UB each claimed 40 per cent, while Dalgety had 13 per cent. Benson's costs were therefore proportionately greater than those of their competitors, and analysis of their situation showed that there were only two alternatives: either to sell up, or to make a major investment. They decided to stake nearly £10 million on a new factory which they calculated would reduce costs by about 12 per cent and enable them to match their competitors. The increased capacity would also enable them to change the focus of their sales strategy by supplying large chains which they had previously been unable to do.

However, the most efficient snack producer in Europe has its factory only 40 miles away, and they had invested more than a third as much again . . .[3] The effect of this on *their* costs was not reported, but questions such as: 'What would be the result if we did this . . .?' are ideal applications for spreadsheets, since quite complex situations can be examined.

Delphi technique

When in doubt, ask an expert; better still, ask several. That is the essence of what is now a well-established method of trying to foretell the future. A panel of authorities in the particular field are asked for their opinion using one of a number of methodologies, each of which has advantages and disadvantages.

In 1993, only one per cent of consumers used a telephone banking service. A Delphi exercise conducted by Andersen Consulting among 400 top European banking staff predicted that by the year 2000 about 40 per cent of transactions across Europe will be conducted by phone. This clearly has important implications for the financial services industry, and several major banks have commenced offering the service.

Delphi has now been in use for long enough to see how well predictions have actually foretold the future. The results have been mixed, but some were as good as predictions using quantitative methods, particularly when the uncertainty was high. Furthermore, it has been found that results from panels of managers at the operational level have often been as good as those of 'experts', thus encouraging use of the technique within an organisation.

COMPLEXITY

'Effective control in a changing environment requires a controller with a set of responses which can match the variety of the environmental information' (Ashby's law of requisite variety). Put rather more simply, this means that even if the environment is predictable, the internal structure of an organisation must reflect the complexity of its environment. Unfortunately, the more complex an organisational structure, the greater will be problems of managing it: problems such as those of communication, control, co-ordination, resolving tension and rivalry between different interests, and acting swiftly when the need arises.

There will always be conflict between the need to match the complexity of the environment and the advantages of keeping the organisation as simple and as flat as possible, and this problem is most acute when the organisation is too big for its present structure, but too small for what appears to be the logical structural development. For example, a manufacturer's sales of two ranges of products may have reached a volume that really warrants splitting into two autonomous divisions. In this way, each will better match the market it serves, but the problems and additional management costs of splitting the organisation could be considerable. This is as true of large as of small firms: ICI had this experience when Zeneca was created as an autonomous organisation.

However, as discussed in Chapter 6, structuring an organisation around its *product* range is only one of a number of approaches; another is on a *geographical* basis, while a third is to match the structure to different *customer groups* or *markets*. Many firms will be divided into divisions based on all three approaches, and in this way will match their strategic business units to the complexity of the markets in which they are operating – the strategic business areas. In principle, this is the way – based upon Ashby's law of requisite variety – of coping with complexity, but the larger and more fragmented the organisation, the greater the problems of management. The international electronics giant Philips foundered because it had such a multiplicity of products in so many markets that overall strategic control was not merely difficult but impossible.

Countering Ashby's law of requisite variety is the fact (formally stated as Simon's concept of bounded rationality) that individuals and organisations cannot manage complexity above a certain level. Over and above that level, the practical problems are too great for effective management, and this can result in pressure to 'get back to basics', to oversimplify complex problems. As a result, we have the paradoxical situation that most organisations seek growth, but may then be driven to split into smaller, autonomous, more manageable businesses – a force they will nevertheless tend to resist.

NOVELTY

Novelty – circumstances never previously encountered – may be experienced as the result of environment changes or as the result of the organisation diversifying into new areas. Here, we are concerned with the first case. An organisation that constantly operates in such an environment is likely to have developed most of the necessary characteristics in order to survive but, to be successful, *all* of the 7-S framework must be matched to this environment:

(1) it will need *information systems* – possibly very sensitive ones – to detect, monitor, interpret and report weak signals from the environment;
(2) the *strategy* cannot be rigid but must be flexible and adaptable;
(3) the organisational *structure* must facilitate quick decisions and optimum response;

(4) this will require an appropriate managerial *style*, and the recruitment of *staff* who have the requisite *skills* and who enjoy and can cope with these conditions;
(5) finally, the ethos of the organisation – its *superordinate goals* – must be *centred* on the challenge of such an environment.

The more turbulent the environment, the more important are these characteristics. Thus if the rate of change in the environment is high, early detection, rapid decision making and speedy response are essential. If the changes are likely to be of major importance, then contingency plans should be prepared. The problem is to decide the possible eventualities against which to prepare such plans; the use of *alternative scenarios* is such an approach.

Alternative scenarios (2)

While there are many forces at work in an organisation's environment, most industries or markets are *significantly* affected by relatively few factors, and these are often easily identified – it was earlier suggested that the list of really important elements in a SWOT analysis will be fairly short. The problem is usually not that of identifying them, but of predicting their behaviour. If for a particular industry or market there were, in fact, relatively few elements, then it would not be too difficult to generate a number of possible plausible future environments based on various combinations of changes in these factors – multiple scenarios – either to see what the future might look like and work back to the present, or to consider possible evolution into the future. These are alternative scenarios which differ in *kind* rather than in *degree*. In some cases there might be one dominant issue around which others should revolve, for example, some industries – such as nuclear energy – are strongly affected by ecological pressures, others – such as the motor industry – by economic growth.

Important issues should have been identified by analyses such as the PEST environmental audit, the KSF industrial audit, or Porter's five-force model. Delphi exercises may identify others, as in the case of telephone banking, but these techniques focus on the expected not the unexpected, and it is usually the unexpected that is the downfall of otherwise well-managed companies.

CROSS-IMPACT ANALYSIS

The impact of one industry upon another is often crucially important: for example, developments in the computer industry are profoundly affected by processor speed and the capacity of memory chips which are currently growing at rates that were unimaginable a few years ago; in other industries the reverse is often true – component manufacturers being dependent upon the sales of their customers.

The furniture industry is very dependent on the housing market – 40 per cent of sales are related to house purchase – and even more so is the estate agency business. In 1985 during the housing boom, Abbey National, which until then had been a building society only, acquired an estate agency chain. Six years later, when the housing bubble had burst, they sold it for less than one-tenth of the price per outlet paid by many buyers in the late 1980s – £23 000 against an average of £250 000 – and made an estimated loss of over £250 million: if only they could have foreseen the future!

Cross-impact analysis of this sort can be a useful source for scenario building. However, no development occurs in isolation: changes in the coal industry were shown to be the result of a host of environmental forces – as was the decline in the housing market – and this is a feature of cross-impact analysis: the need to consider interactions between a number of relevant factors, not merely industries, although the number must be kept low or the analysis becomes too unwieldy.

The DIY market is equally dependent upon the housing market, and yet the Homebase chain was extremely successful, showing a profit of £24 million on sales of £328 million, while market leader B&Q also performed satisfactorily. Do It All, however, was obliged to sell up to 100 stores, and Texas, whose 1994 sales were more than twice those of Homebase, showed a profit of less than a third. The reasons for these differences are complex.

STRATEGIC ISSUE MANAGEMENT

The problems of strategic management that emerge from this discussion expose the shortcomings in a turbulent environment of the conventional means–ends strategic planning system that has been the model for the first part of this book. That model is appropriate for a stable environment, for example, commodity markets that are not susceptible to influences such as the weather, and low-technology industries which are relatively stable and predictable. In these circumstances, strategic planning, if conducted periodically – say every three to five years – sets the pattern for the intermediate period, with only minor alterations to corporate strategy being necessary as a result of evaluation and feedback, usually on the basis of an annual review. Subsidiaries or divisions will, of course, be fine-tuned within that corporate strategy. However, some industries such as the distributive trades and retailing are facing rates of change which impose strains on such an approach, although it may well still be appropriate when strategy is reviewed frequently and environmental monitoring is more intensive, and when there is also an acceptance of flexibility within the organisation and a willingness to adapt.

For other firms, often those in high-technology industries, and particularly those connected with or heavily reliant upon information and information technology – in other words, when major changes to strategy and/or objectives are likely to be both necessary and frequent because of environmental turbulence – strategic management based on conventional strategic planning cannot cope. An approach which is more flexible, responsive, and action oriented is required.

Typical of several approaches to this problem is *strategic issue management*. The most important characteristic of this is the absence of those most basic foundations of conventional strategic management: objectives and strategic planning. Strategic issue management has the following characteristics:

- continuous monitoring of the environment
- identification of issues likely to be of strategic importance
- frequent assessment of the relative importance and possible impact of issues
- planning or adapting strategy according to priorities in terms of urgency and importance
- implemention of tactics and activities speedily
- constant reviewing of the general situation.

Advocates of this approach say that the process should be continuous rather than periodic, the responses being carried out in parallel rather than sequentially, and that it is intrinsically reactive rather than proactive, focusing on events as they happen rather than depending on the timing of a predetermined plan. It is also without the constraints of objectives that could become inappropriate.

It is basically a return to the nature of a dynamic, entrepreneurial small firm, but with the resources of a large organisation. In a discontinuous and hostile environment where early identification of significant issues could result in substantial competitive advantage, such an approach to strategic management could clearly be of enormous benefit, but it demands appropriate organisational characteristics which are alien to conventional firms, most of which in this situation will probably adopt an approach closer to that of logical incrementalism.

CRISIS MANAGEMENT

Despite sensitive environmental-scanning systems and contingency plans and the use of multiple scenarios – or even strategic issue management – an organisation may nevertheless be hit by a crisis, particularly if they had been looking in the wrong direction and made the wrong contingency plans – like the Maginot Line, built to defend France against a possible attack from the Germans, who swept down through Belgium instead.

In retrospect, and with hindsight, a crisis is often seen to have been predictable or even avoidable: when the temperature reaches a certain level a thermostat will suddenly snap from one state to another; a thermometer would have shown that the temperature had been rising.

Frequently, however, an organisation will recognise that something is wrong but treats symptoms rather than underlying causes – particularly if its basic ideology or mission is at the root of the problem. The emphasis is usually on taking action rather than identifying and solving the problem: for example, saying, 'We must increase sales' rather than asking, 'Sales are down, why?' Information has to pass through the filter of the minds of management, and the more successful they have been in the past, the less likely are they to perceive that times have changed.

Many organisations have contingency plans prepared for crises such as failure of a computer system, but cases will occur of sudden, unexpected environmental change. What, then, of the organisation that suddenly realises it is in a crisis situation when it had previously been operating in a comfortable stable environment? An example of this was the way in which Johnson and Johnson (J&J) handled the Tylenol crisis – although at the time they had no crisis plan as such.

Tylenol was one of the most successful consumer products in the USA with more than 35 per cent share of the analgesic market – until someone contaminated bottles with cyanide and caused seven deaths, with predictable results on public demand.

A strategy committee of seven top executives met twice daily for six weeks. Executives gave nationwide TV interviews and press briefings while volunteers manned free telephone hot-lines to handle nearly half a million calls. Nearly half a million mailgrams were sent to the medical community and over 2000 sales staff were drafted from other J&J companies to call on them, while, to monitor public reaction, 150 000 press clippings costing nearly $100 000 were analysed.

At the same time, however, in the very first week while all of this was going on, a tamper-proof pack was being designed, and a strategic plan was being prepared. In less than three months the product was back on the shelves, and within a year their market share had returned to nearly 30 per cent.

Crises such as these are fortunately rare, although there is one view of the world that all futurologists are agreed upon: that the rate of change in the environment is itself increasing. Nevertheless, almost all writers on management topics would claim that the environment of most organisations is at present still sufficiently predictable to enable approaches which are founded on conventional strategic planning-based management systems to cope – but then they would, wouldn't they?

A contrary view[4] is that the environment has always been uncomfortably turbulent and unpredictable; that not only is the track record of strategic planning poor, but that it is inevitably so – although the conventional model is not so much wrong as misapplied, and that 'there is a conflict that cannot be resolved between the need to institutionalise and formalise management processes, and the ability to be flexible, to bin previous agreed intentions and think again.'

EXERCISE

In 1941, when the future of the world was as uncertain as it could be, Pelican Books published *The Managerial Revolution* by James Burnham. It evoked reviewers' comments such as 'extraordinarily impressive'. The publishers condensed his argument into the sentence: 'The control of the world is passing into the hands of the managers.'

Discuss Burnham's argument.

FURTHER READING

Ansoff, I. and McDonnell, E., *Implanting Strategic Management*, Prentice Hall, 1990. This text is the main recommendation and is a *must* for anyone interested in the many problems of coping with a turbulent environment.

Stacey, R. D., *Strategic Management and Organisational Dynamics*, Pitman Publishing, 1993. This recommendation closely follows behind Ansoff and McDonnell's *Implanting Strategic Management*.

Facing the Future: Mastering the Probable and Managing the Unpredictable, OECD, 1979. An impressive, if dated, example of the application of alternative scenarios and was based on a three-year project by an international team of 19 authorities. It is particularly interesting because it was an attempt to predict the possible worlds that we now inhabit, a generation later. The methodology, layout and structure of the report, and their forecasts are worth looking at.

REFERENCES

1 *Financial Times*, 9 October 1986.
2 Ansoff I. and Mcdonnell E. *Implanting Strategic Management*, Prentice-Hall, 1990.
3 *Financial Times*, 14 July 1993.
4 Mintzberg, H., *The Rise and Fall of Strategic Planning*, Prentice-Hall, 1994.

CHAPTER 13

Strategic planning

Earlier chapters have looked at influences on strategic management in general, and a distinction was made between maintaining an existing strategy and undertaking a major review – a strategic planning exercise. This chapter draws on earlier parts of the book in order to develop a basic model of the process of strategic planning, and then provides a framework for doing so in Chapter 14, with the steps of this framework described in worksheets which are referred to in this chapter. These steps are also illustrated here in a series of figures.

By *strategic planning* is meant a deliberate, systematic, formal process of analysing the present and probable future situation of an organisation in order to review corporate strategy, possibly revising it and, as a result, deciding what should be done and how it should be done in the future. Note that, unlike some definitions, this description does not include the actual operationalisation or implementation of any strategic plan that results, nor how the organisation or the planning process itself should be managed and controlled. That is because they are features of strategic *management*, not of the *planning process* which is only one of the many aspects of strategic management.

Applying the basic model described here must therefore take into account the context of the organisation, for example, internally, a participative approach or alternatively a top-downwards model may best suit the particular circumstances; externally, the degree of turbulence of the environment is clearly relevant not only to the choice of strategy, but also to management style, and so on. In practice, therefore, the process of strategic planning – the formulation of strategy – is inextricably interwoven in the fabric of strategic management, and any attempt to impose a plan that does not take this into account is likely to fail.

Finally, as was pointed out in Chapter 1, there are a number of ways in which strategies actually do develop, of which formal strategic planning is only one, and there is no conclusive evidence that in practice, the process of formal strategic planning has a higher success rate than other ways of deciding the future direction of an organisation. Many successful firms did not adopt it, many unsuccessful firms did – although advocates of the approach would probably argue that failure was the result of not doing so correctly. Furthermore, even when organisations claim to plan, they often – like many of us – first decide what they want to do, and then work back to justify the choice.

Chapter 3 started with the statement: 'While strategic decisions are made in order to achieve objectives, both objectives and strategy are themselves constrained by the organisation's mission.' It is therefore logical to start the model by first defining or redefining the mission (Worksheet 1) and then considering objectives (Worksheet 2). This is illustrated in Fig 13.1.

Chapter 2 pointed out that it may be necessary to change not only the strategy but the objectives and mission as a result of the analysis, because of present or anticipated changes in the environment. The next stage should therefore be an environmental analysis, possibly feeding back to the objectives and mission as well as forwards towards strategy (Worksheets 3, 4, 5, 6, 7, 8) as shown in Fig 13.2.

Chapter 2 also stressed that 'Adapting an organisation to its environment is an essential aspect of strategic management', and hence requires an internal audit. Chapter 4 advises that the internal audit should follow rather than precede the environmental analysis, and this is also necessary in order to make the comparisons advocated in Chapter 5 (Worksheets 9, 10, 11, 12), shown in Fig 13.3.

Chapter 8 suggests that a SWOT analysis, and other approaches based on the findings of the internal and external audits, will identify the key issues which strategic decisions should address (Worksheet 13), shown in Fig 13.4, and that the next stage should be to generate strategic options that are possible responses to these key issues. Some of these options may require further analysis of the organisation and/or the environment before a choice is made, including a full financial evaluation (*see* Fig 13.5).

Which strategies are 'best' will depend upon the criteria used to evaluate them. Some of these will stem from the mission and objectives, others from the audits (*see* Fig 13.6).

Strategic decisions are reached by matching strategic options against the criteria and choosing those that fit best. It should, however, be noted that one result could be a restatement of mission and/or objectives, as shown in Fig 13.7.

The next step would then be to implement these, possibly revising the objectives and or mission in the light of experience. The final model is given in Fig 13.8.

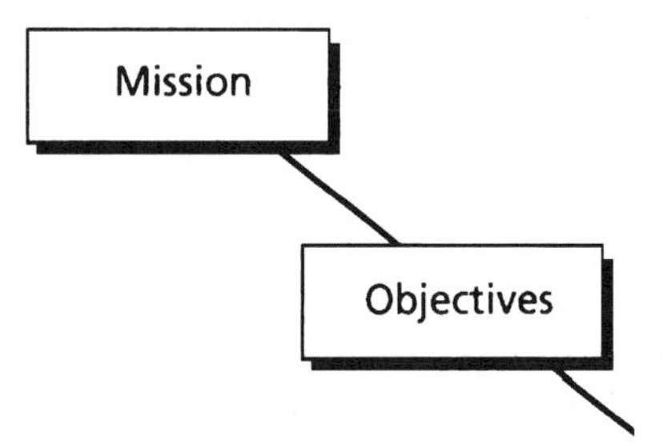

Fig 13.1

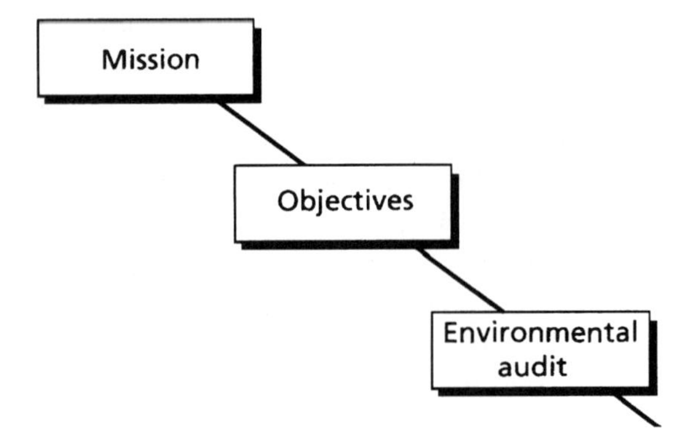

Fig 13.2

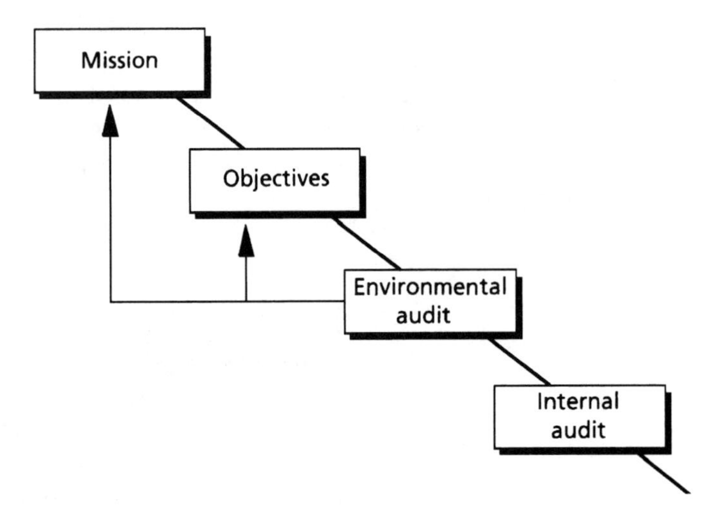

Fig 13.3

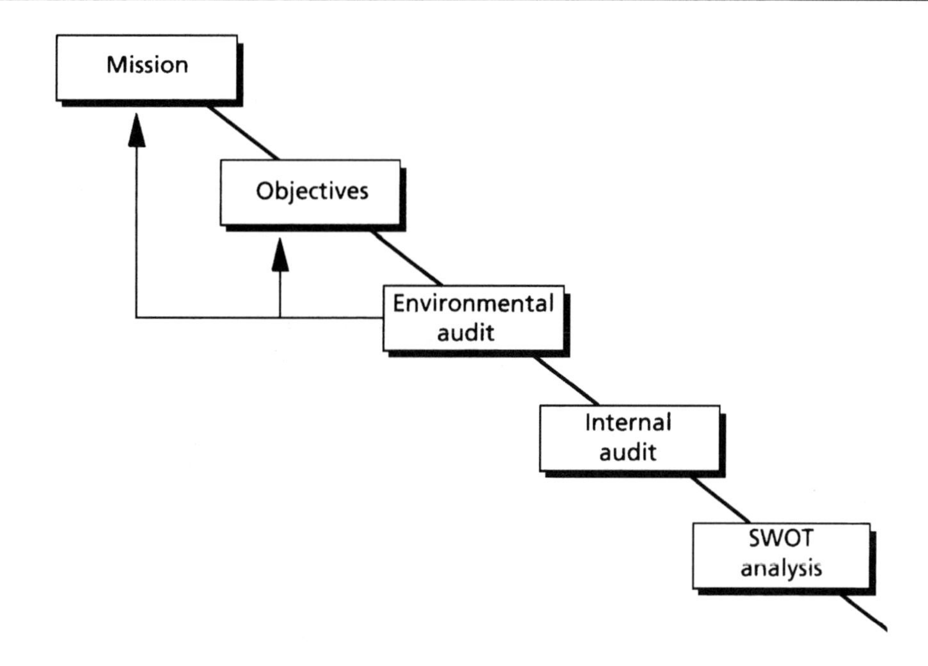

Fig 13.4

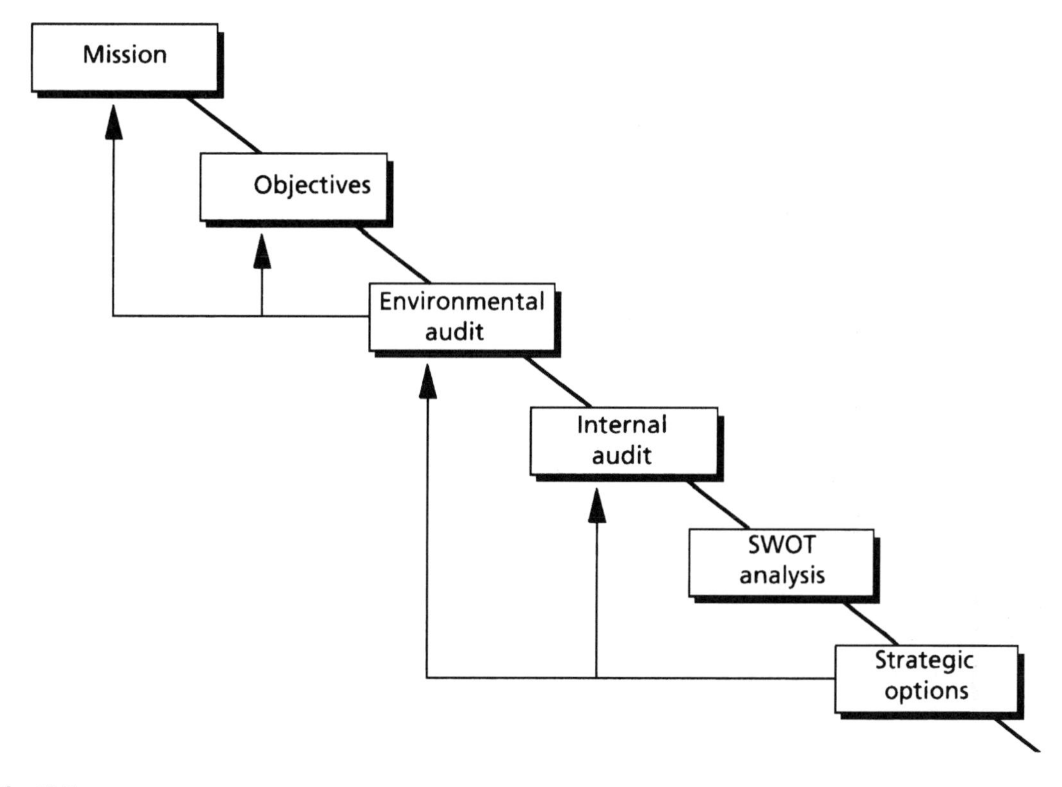

Fig 13.5

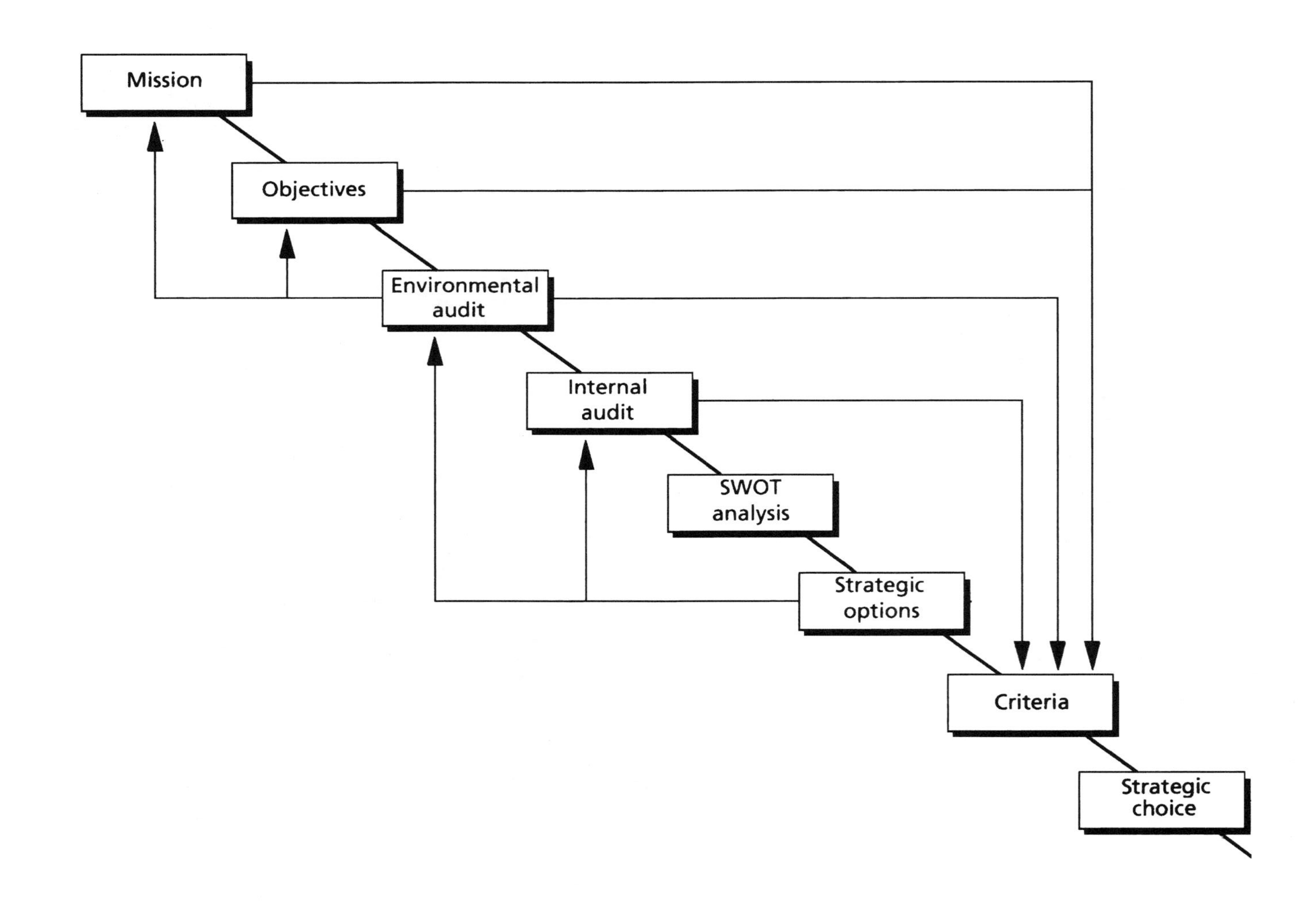
Mission
Objectives
Environmental audit
Internal audit
SWOT analysis
Strategic options
Criteria
Strategic choice

Fig 13.6

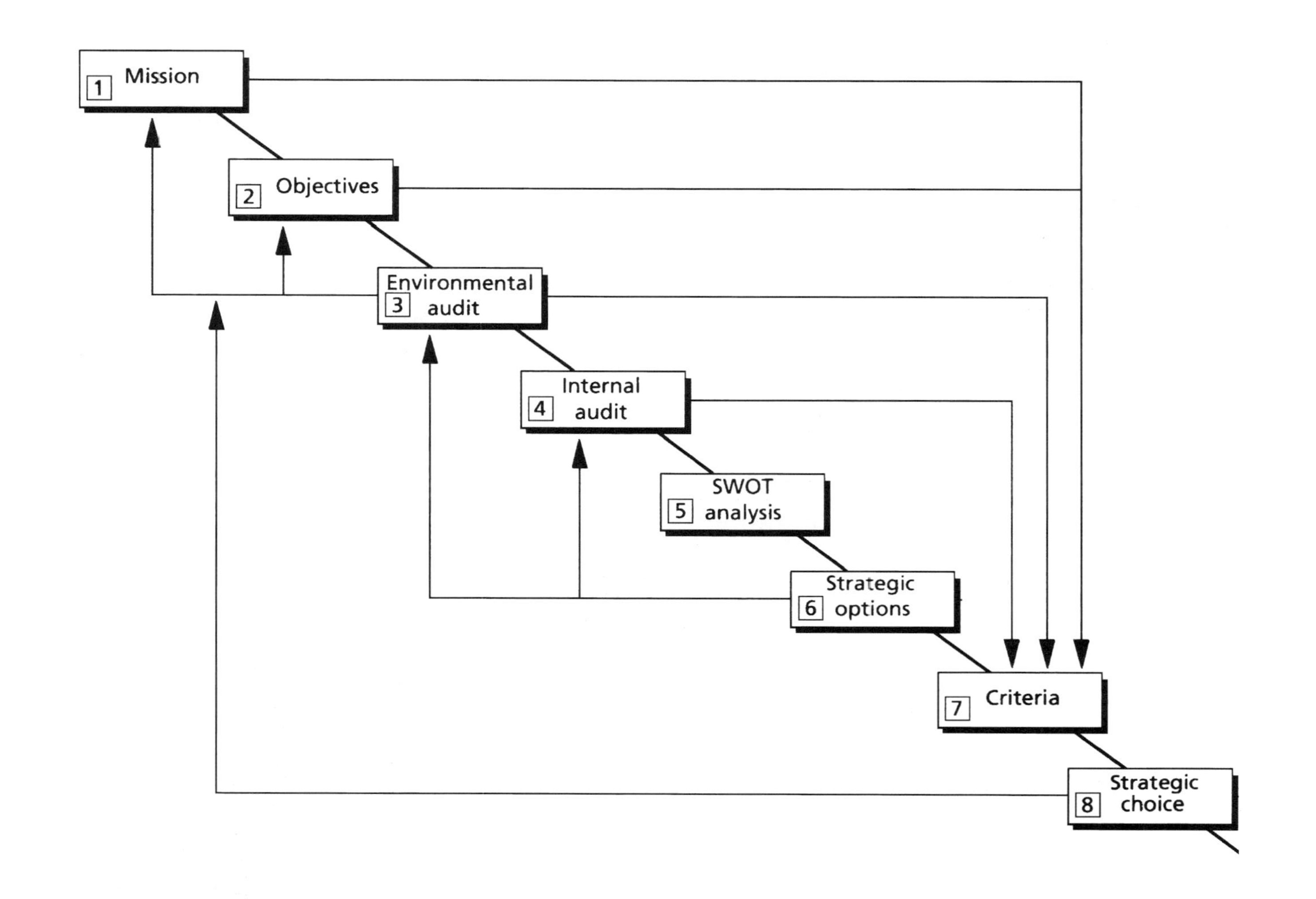
1 Mission
2 Objectives
3 Environmental audit
4 Internal audit
5 SWOT analysis
6 Strategic options
7 Criteria
8 Strategic choice

Fig 13.7

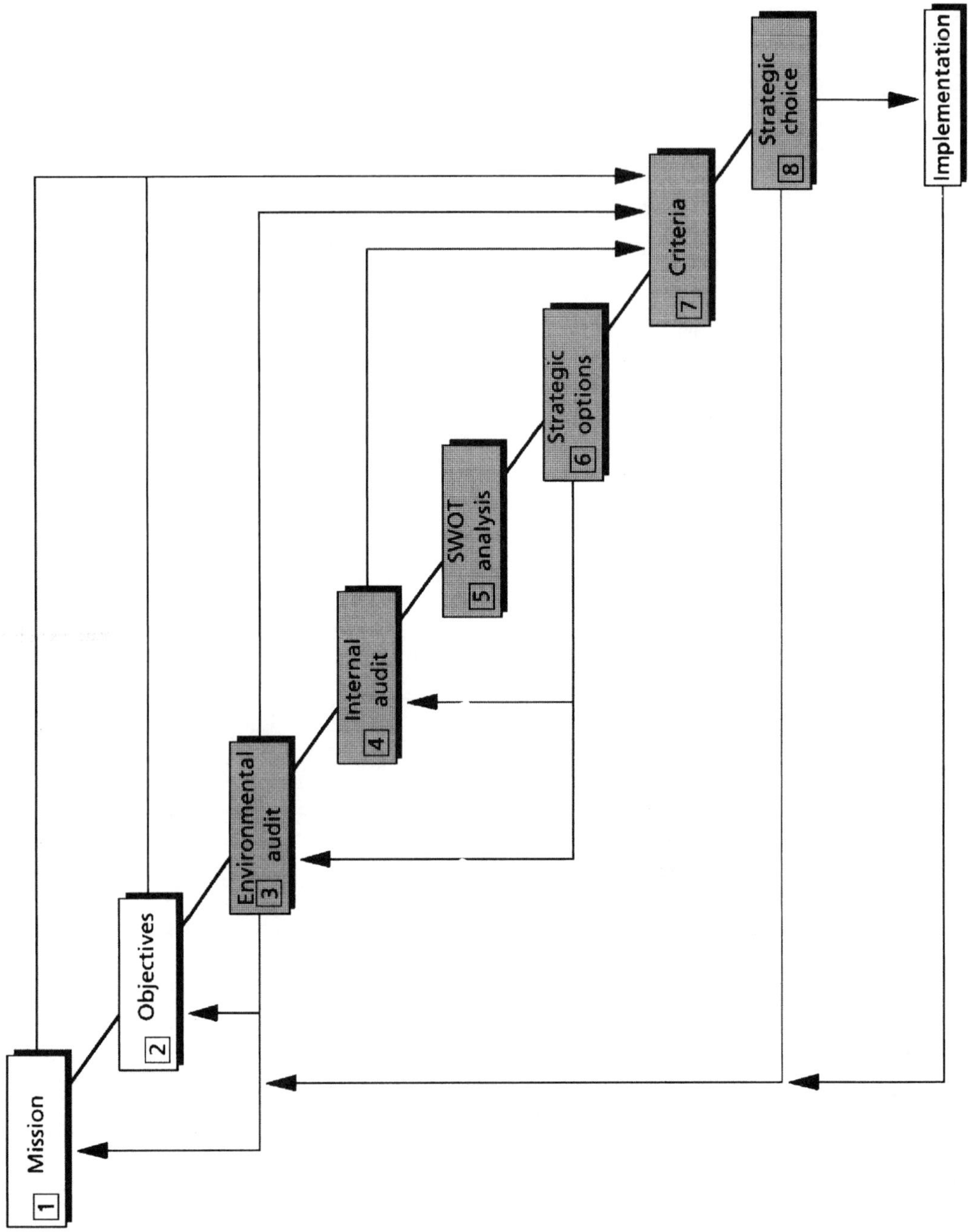

1 Mission

2 Objectives

3 Environmental audit

4 Internal audit

5 SWOT analysis

6 Strategic options

7 Criteria

8 Strategic choice

Implementation

Fig 13.8

EXERCISE

Use the worksheets in Chapter 14 to produce a list of key issues for an organisation of your choice or for a published case study, explaining their importance.

FURTHER READING

Mintzberg, H., *The Rise and Fall of Strategic Planning,* Prentice Hall, 1994. This text gives a detailed and provocative examination of strategic planning.

CHAPTER 14

Strategic planning worksheets

Because the purpose of the exercise is to reappraise the firm's strategic posture rather than merely to improve operations, the analysis should concentrate upon those issues that could be of strategic importance rather than on fine detail – although other issues warranting attention should be noted for later investigation. There can be no universal pattern to the analysis since much will depend upon the findings themselves. Nevertheless, the worksheets that follow provide a general framework, although their importance will depend upon the particular circumstances.

In some cases, adequate data will not be available, but that reflects the business world where decisions must nevertheless be made in the absence of perfect information. Where the issue is crucial, make an informed guess – recording that fact. It may also be helpful to compare the consequences of optimistic and pessimistic views of the particular situation, and if an important decision depends very heavily upon which is correct, then offer appropriate alternative strategies together with the recommendation that the data *are* obtained if they are available.

Summarise your conclusions at the completion of each worksheet, noting any factors which, at first sight, appear to be of strategic importance. List them as internal strengths or weaknesses (or both), and as environmental opportunities or threats, recording their urgency and importance.

Where a factor is identified on one worksheet but relates to another, a cross-reference should be made so that the implications are not overlooked, for example, the PEST analysis may expose a threat that is particularly relevant to production costs. This may relate to the internal audit, and to key success factors. Another may interact with the competition, with a market segment, with distributors, or with other stakeholders. These interactions should be considered before conducting the SWOT analysis itself as they may affect the importance and urgency of the factors recorded.

Worksheet	*Page*	*Worksheet*	*Page*
1 The mission	139	**9** Gap analysis	161
2 Corporate objectives	140	**10** Value chain analysis	163
3 PEST analysis	143	**11** The internal audit	165
4 The industry	146	**12** Portfolio analysis	167
5 The marketplace	149	**13** SWOT analysis	172
6 Key Success Factors	153	**14** Opportunity analysis	174
7 Competitor analysis	156	**15** Strategic choice	177
8 Stakeholder analysis	159		

WORKSHEET 1 THE MISSION

We are here concerned with the *mission*, not with a mission statement. The mission statement should be completed *after* the strategy has been decided. The mission defines the company's purpose – its *raison d'être*. It provides a sense of strategic direction, influences the corporate culture and management style, and is a back-stop for the organisational objectives.

The following questions refer to the *present* mission based on the current situation, and the answers should describe the actual not a desirable or future state; that should be derived from the study. However, if you have second thoughts or wish to revise your answers during the analysis you should do so.

You may also wish to recommend a different mission at the end of the exercise because you will be critically examining your answers later in the analysis, and may decide that they reveal a less than satisfactory situation.

1 How does (or would) the organisation respond to the question: 'what business are we in?'

2 Who are the *main* customers the organisation attempts to serve at present?

3 What are the particular needs and wants that the organisation attempts to satisfy?

4 What skills and technologies are presently used to satisfy them?

5 What is the nature of the product or service that is offered to satisfy them?

WORKSHEET 2 CORPORATE OBJECTIVES

The most important corporate objective of any business is to obtain a *satisfactory* return on capital employed (ROCE). This may have been published as a stated objective, otherwise an attempt should be made to assess it if at all possible. Note, however, that an objective such as: 'To maximise profit' is meaningless since there is no way of knowing whether this was achieved, and that to include objectives that merely describe effort or the good management practices that all organisations should adopt only dilutes the effectiveness of objective setting.

An approach to deriving a target value of ROCE is described below, but cannot be completed until after the environmental audit has been undertaken, but an alternative or additional method is to use not the book value of capital, but the value of shares. This reflects the interests of the major stakeholders – investors – and should, in particular, be considered if the past financial performance is a cause for concern. In this case 'return' should be based on changes in the total of the value of shares plus dividend payments. This can be found in the financial press for major public companies.

Whichever you use, derive the trend of ROCE by plotting values for, say, the last five years on a graph. You will then need to consider whether this was satisfactory bearing in mind the economic environment in general, inflation in particular, changes and trends in the industry and market-place, the performance of comparable direct competitors and, in particular, the reactions of the stock market as revealed by trends in the price of the shares compared with similar companies.

Base the future objective upon your assessment, and project the trend for a time-horizon of, say, five years. You may also wish to set intermediate targets. These can then be used to identify any planning gap as described in Chapter 5 and Worksheet 9.

Other quantified objectives

Many quantified objectives will be influenced by the expectations of stakeholders, and are usually based on the following factors or ratios between them:

Volume Value Costs Time Quality

However, unless there are policy or other overriding reasons, great care should be taken in quantifying objectives which are relative, such as profit margin as a percentage of sales, unless and until they have been established as actually being optimal. Thus although a firm may set as a target a particular level of profit as a percentage of sales, a lower margin might in fact be a better strategy. This could be the case if it resulted in increased volume and achieved lower costs as a result of economies of scale and the experience effect, or if the greater revenue more than compensated for the lower margin.

Similarly, setting over-ambitious targets for return on investment (ROI) may exclude otherwise attractive projects, while ROCE can be improved by buying in components rather than producing them in-house, although this might increase costs.

These are strategic decisions that should *result* from the study when all of the factors have been considered. In other words, they are means, not ends, and should not be constraints on strategic choice before evaluating otherwise suitable strategic options – when they may well be rejected.

Non-quantified objectives

Other objectives may not be quantified or quantifiable, but nevertheless exert an influence on the way resources are deployed. These could include references to technological leadership, commitment to R&D, innovation, investment or quality – if these really are forces that drive strategy and not merely platitudes.

However, since it is not possible to drive in several different directions at once, the number of such should be strictly limited, others being referred to in a mission statement.

1 If possible, derive the historic trends for quantified objectives.

2 Compare these with:

- **(a)** the industry as a whole;
- **(b)** competitors who are closest in size and products.

3 Set appropriate target values to be achieved at stated time(s) in Table 14.1.

Table 14.1

Objective	Priority	How measured	Target value	Target time

WORKSHEET 3 PEST ANALYSIS

The PEST analysis should identify and evaluate:

1 environmental factors that should or do influence strategy;

2 trends and possible/probable environmental developments, opportunities or threats that could be of strategic significance in the future.

Note:

(a) The *urgency* and *importance* of each factor.
(b) When an event is likely to occur and its probability.
(c) When aspects of the environment interact with each other and thereby amplify the impact.

The analysis should consider the implications for:

- The organisation
- Customers
- The industry/marketplace
- Intermediaries
- Competitors
- Other stakeholders

Briefly record noteworthy factors in Table 14.3, using the suggestions in Table 14.2 as a guide, including others that are relevant. Adopt a global perspective where appropriate, and do not clutter up the list with relatively trivial or very obvious items. Once completed, your conclusions should be transferred to the appropriate analysis sheets, e.g.: industry analysis, competitive analysis, SWOT analysis, etc. to be considered together with other findings.

Table 14.2 PEST analysis

Political/legal	Economic
Specific legislation Taxation Foreign trade regulations Governmental attitudes and policies Stability of government Special allowances/incentives Government involvement/intervention Public expenditure International relationships	EEC, Pacific basin, USA, E. European OPEC, China Trade cycles Inflation/exchange rates Economic growth/GNP trends Interest rates Money/credit supply Unemployment/labour availability Disposable/discretionary income Energy availability/cost
Social/cultural	**Technological**
Environmentalism Consumerism Life styles New needs and wants Attitudes to work/leisure Propensity to buy Wealth/income distribution Demographic/age distribution Birth rate/life expectancy Training and education Socio-economic changes Ethical pressures	IT New materials Energy sources/availability Alternative/new technologies Sources/costs/availability of inputs Expenditure on R&D by government/ industry/university Ecological factors Technological transfer Infrastructure technologies

Table 14.3

	Parties affected					
	Organisation	Industry	Competitors	Customers	Intermediaries	Others
Urgent and Important (Transfer to SWOT analysis sheet)						
Important but not Urgent (Transfer to appropriate analysis sheets)						
Noteworthy (Use as background for report/transfer to analysis sheets)						
Urgent but not Important (Don't wait, delegate)						

WORKSHEET 4 THE INDUSTRY

This stage of the analysis is primarily concerned with the supply side of the market; the demand side is considered next. By 'industry' is meant those firms using similar technologies and raw materials to produce similar products that are used for similar purposes. Thus although in the same market, railways and coach-lines are different industries. (Use SICs if appropriate.)

1 Define your industry.

Growth

2 At what stage of its life-cycle is the industry *as a whole*? Forecast the pattern of change.

3 Are sectors of the industry changing at different rates? By how much?

4 How does/will the production capacity compare with demand for:

(a) the industry as a whole;

(b) different sectors of the industry.

5 What issues does this raise concerning present and future activities such as:

(a) investment;

(b) profitability;

(c) likely entry or exit of competitors.

Relate your reply to Question 11.

Technology and product

6 At what stage of its life-cycle is the basic production technology, and what are the implications for the industry and the firm?

7 What threats/developments are there to this technology within or from outside the industry?

8 Are the costs, availability, quality and reliability of inputs such as raw materials, components or skilled labour likely to change?

9 List other industries, or products from other industries, that are substitutes or alternatives, and evaluate their present and future importance and significance.

10 Are the products/services of firms in the industry broadly similar, somewhat diverse or highly differentiated? Relate your reply to Question 11.

Structure

11 Which of the following descriptions best fit the industry at present; what are future trends? (This list is based on the Boston Consulting Group's Advantage Matrix.)

- **(a)** *Volume*: fixed costs are high, economies of scale and experience reduce costs. Success depends on low costs/high volume.
- **(b)** *Stalemated*: economies of scale do not lead to benefits. (Unless, for example, production is in countries with low labour costs, or different sales or distribution channels are adopted.)
- **(c)** *Specialised*: divided into several segments, each offering benefits of scale and experience, particularly to the market leaders in each segment.
- **(d)** *Fragmented*: profitability not related to size or segmentation but to added value, innovation, efficiency.
- **(e)** *Mixed*: dominated by relatively few large firms, but also containing a significant number of smaller companies.

12 **(a)** What are the implications for the firm of your answer to Question 11?

- **(b)** Does the firm occupy a particular sector, serve several, or serve the entire industry?

13 **(a)** Is demand derived from another industry?

- **(b)** Is this industry highly dependent on inputs from another industry?

14 Summarise your conclusions, giving reasons and assumptions:

- **(a)** For the industry as defined.
- **(b)** For each sector occupied by the firm.
- **(c)** For sectors that the firm may consider entering.

Deal in particular with:

(i) prices;
(ii) profits;
(iii) demand;
(iv) potential/need for product development;
(v) advisability of withdrawal;
(vi) advisability or need for further investment;
(vii) competition.

15 Transfer conclusions of strategic importance to the SWOT analysis.

WORKSHEET 5 THE MARKETPLACE

In order to avoid unnecessary complexity, the analysis now assumes a single-business, single-market situation. If this is not so, then each SBU should be considered individually.

By 'market' is meant the arena in which the firm or SBU competes with its rivals for the custom of buyers seeking solutions to their problems. It should be very carefully defined, particularly where aspects of it – such as size – are quantified. The focus of this analysis is on the future attractiveness and profitability of the market so that possible and probable developments should be included.

Record the following, together with your comments:

1 *Definition of the market* (relate your definition to that of the industry).

2 *Size*:

- **(a)** quantity
- **(b)** value
- **(c)** profitability

3 *Growth rates*:

- **(a)** current
- **(b)** possible future trend
- **(c)** stage in life-cycle (if different from that of 'industry')

4 *Geographical scope of market* (e.g. global, continental, national, local).

If the factors above are favourable, the market could attract new competitors or encourage further investment unless there are barriers to entry.

5 *Barriers to entry*. Will any of the following or other forces restrict new entrants to the market?

- Economies of scale necessary in order to compete
- Access to expertise, patents, technology

- Lack of experience-curve benefits compared to incumbents
- Access to distribution channels already occupied or unwilling to stock new products
- Brand preferences and loyalty to existing brands; the time and resources needed to switch customers' purchases
- Capital requirements: manufacturing, working capital, promotion
- Other cost disadvantages in location, procurement, labour, capital, technical know-how
- Regulatory factors: permits, licences, regulations
- Tariffs, trade restrictions, quotas

What is, and will be, the effect of any such constraints or lack of them on the nature and extent of competition, on customer–supplier relationships, and on profit?

6 *Structure*. Which of the cells in the matrix in Table 14.4 best fits the structure of the market as defined earlier?

Table 14.4

Suppliers (firms not products)	**Buyers**			
	one large buyer	a few large buyers	mixed buyers	many small buyers
one large supplier				
a few large suppliers				
mixed suppliers				
many small suppliers				

Depending upon the relative power relationships between the firm, competitors and the firm's customers, the market structure may influence the particular supplier–customer and segmentation strategies adopted by the firm. The examples in Fig 14.1 illustrate the point, but size is not the only relationship.

7 *Power of customers.* Can important customers easily switch suppliers? Does their buying power give them negotiating strength which they use? Are less powerful segments available?

8 *Power of suppliers.* Is the firm restricted to powerful suppliers or is it possible to switch easily to alternative and satisfactory inputs or suppliers? Could the firm integrate backwards and produce the input itself?

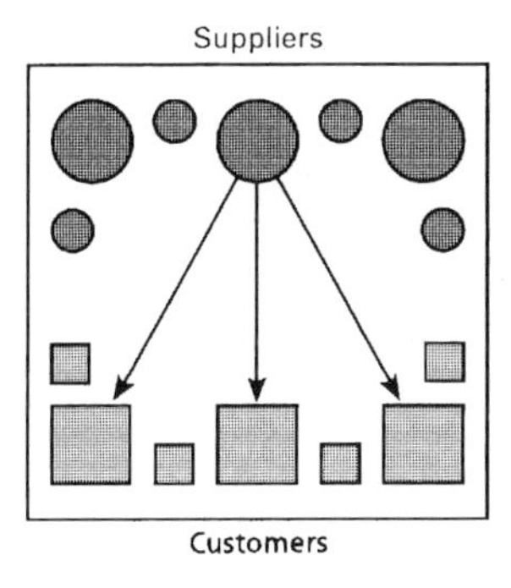

(a) A large supplier serving large customers only

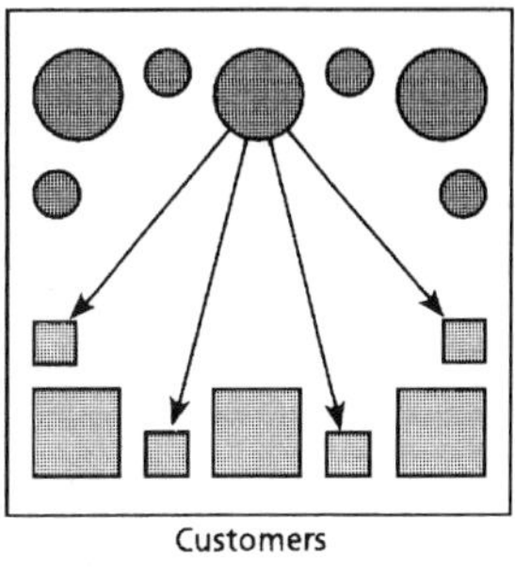

(b) A large supplier serving small customers only

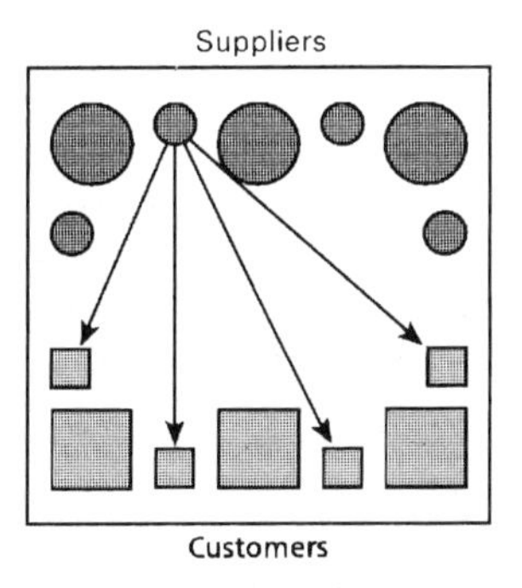

(c) A small supplier serving small customers only

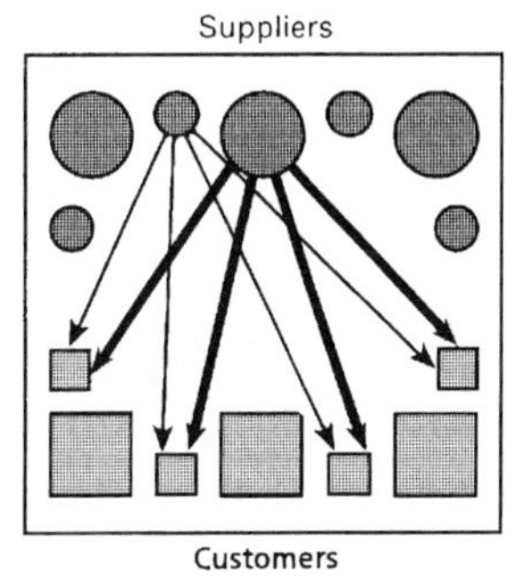

(d) Large and small firms in direct competition

Fig 14.1 Power relationships

Do suppliers use their power in negotiating price or quantity?

Do customers or suppliers strongly influence the attractiveness or profitability of the market? How? Can it be countered? Is there a trend towards concentration?

9 *Products*. Evaluate the strengths and weaknesses – current and future – of any alternatives and substitutes previously identified in the industry analysis or present in the market-place:

  (a) From the perspective of the customer. How attractive are they and why? What are any differential advantages?

  (b) From the perspective of the firm. How much of a future threat? When?

  Alternatives with a differential advantage must be countered in some way, frequently by lowering the price and hence profit; by product modification; or by adding value. Summarise the strategic implications for the future.

10 *Competitive rivalry*. The following factors may influence the intensity of competition, and hence strategy and profitability:

  (a) *stage of product life-cycle and rate of growth of demand*. Competition is less intense in earlier stages, when demand is growing;

  (b) *costs to customers of switching suppliers*. Low costs encourage switching or threatening to do so as a negotiating ploy;

  (c) *industry production capacity near or greater than demand*. This inevitably forces prices down as suppliers seek orders;

  (d) *difficulty in quitting the market*. If the market is unattractive but the exit barriers are high, competition will intensify;

  (e) *very aggressive competitor(s) or new entrants seeking to dominate the market*, especially if they are increasing production capacity;

  (f) *number of rivals*. The greater the number of direct competitors, the stronger the competition. ('Direct' implying similar size and product aimed at the same customers.)

11 Transfer your findings to *Worksheet* 6 – *Key Success Factors*, *Worksheet* 7 – *Competitor analysis*, and *Worksheet* 8 – *Stakeholder analysis*, as appropriate.

WORKSHEET 6 KEY SUCCESS FACTORS

A Key Success Factor (KSF) is not necessarily the means whereby a firm differentiates itself from its competitors, but is a feature essential for success in the marketplace, i.e. without it, the firm is seriously disadvantaged.

Using Table 14.5, identify the key factors *essential* for success in the segment(s) the firm occupies by a tick in the first column, adding any additional KSFs not listed. Then, in the second column, number those you ticked in descending order of importance.

Table 14.6 enables a comparison to be made between the extent to which the firm meets the KSFs and up to four competitors. If the firm occupies a number of segments, each should be considered separately, as should any that the firm might consider entering as a result of subsequent study.

1. List competitors at the top of columns A to D. Add a continuation sheet if necessary.

2. List the Key Success Factors in the first column and allocate 100 points between them in the next column, according to their relative weight.

3. Enter a score (S) from 1 (low) to 5 (high) according to how well the firms match each KSF in the left-hand column below their names.

4. Multiply the weight (W) by the score (S); enter the product in the $W \times S$ column.

5. Sum each $W \times S$ column to compare the total scores.

6. Identify the most successful rivals and the factors that account for their success. Do the totals accord with your assessment? If not, review both the weightings and the scores; also consider whether you have overlooked an important KSF.

7. If a rival has an exceptionally high value of $W \times S$ for a particular KSF which accounts for its success in the market-place, this should be noted in your conclusions.

8. If the firm has a value of $W \times S$ for a KSF which is significantly lower than that of rivals, this may be a weakness that should be recorded in the conclusions. A significantly higher value might be a strength.

Table 14.5 Key success factors

Production/product					
Skilled labour			High tech products		
Low material costs			Design capability		
Low labour costs			High quality		
Low production costs			Product range		
Low-cost product design			Product R&D capability		
Process R&D capability			Fast product development		
Flexible production			Purchasing power		
High tech systems/skills					
Marketing					
Quality sales force			Speedy delivery		
Large sales force			Low-cost distribution		
After-sales service			Reliability		
Technical advice			Extensive advertising		
Wide distribution			Competitive pricing		
Customer finance/credit			Market share		
Customer relations					
Organisation					
Patents			Management ability		
Information systems			Location		
Financial strength			Size		
Speedy responses to change			Local autonomy		
Image/reputation			Large corporate resources		

Table 14.6 Competitor comparison

Key Success Factors (KSFs)	Weight W	Firm		A		B		C		D	
		Score	W × S	Score	W × S	Score	W × S	Score	W × S	Score	W × S
1											
2											
3											
4											
5											
6											
7											
Totals	**100**										

9 A KSF may have a high weighting but relatively low score. This may be because it is underexploited and might provide the firm with a differential advantage. Note any such for later study.

10 Note whether particular KSFs are the focus of a competitor's positioning strategy or differential advantage.

11 Divide the KSFs into three groups:

(a) Vital – *must* influence strategy;

(b) Important – *could* influence strategy if consistent with other elements;

(c) Noteworthy – *should* be monitored in future.

12 Summarise your conclusions. Groups (a) and (b) should be noted in the SWOT analysis.

WORKSHEET 7 COMPETITOR ANALYSIS

The purpose of this step is formally to assess those existing and potential competitors who are or who might become sufficiently important to be taken into account when determining strategy.

The magnitude of the *existing* threat from a competitor depends upon a combination of factors (*see* Table 14.7). However, a high rating for one factor may – at present – be compensated for by a low rating for another. The possibility of a future change which would result in a threat intensifying must therefore be considered. If this is likely, the strategy should include either contingency plans or pre-emptive action. For example, a powerful competitor aiming at the same market through the same channels of distribution, but with a different product providing different benefits, may not be a serious threat at present, but if they decided upon a direct challenge to the firm . . .

The intensity of competition will depend not only upon competitors themselves, but also upon the competitive environment (*see* Worksheets 5 and 7) and this too must be taken into account. For example, in mature markets where opportunities for growth are declining, competition is likely to be fiercer as the only way to grow is at a competitor's expense.

Finally, competition occurs at the operational, SBU or product level, and this must be the basis of the analysis, rather than at the corporate level, although the availability of corporate resources or back-up may be important.

Stage 1

Use Table 14.7 to evaluate each of the main competitors in turn. This will enable you to identify those which warrant closer subsequent investigation. To use the table, follow either 1 or 2 below:

1 **(a)** place a tick in the appropriate column numbered 1 (low) to 5 (high) according to your assessment of the importance of each factor and the extent to which the competitor meets the description, i.e. the magnitude of that particular threat;

(b) total the ticks in each column;

(c) multiply the number of ticks by the number at the head of the column; and

(d) add these values to find the overall score for each competitor.

Table 14.7 Factors in competitor analysis

Competitor : .... Weighting:	X	Low 1	2	3	4	High 5
1 Power relative to the firm: market share, size, financial resources, distribution						
2 Extent to which they aim at the same market segments						
3 Use of similar channels of distribution						
4 Similarity of their product characteristics: physical attributes, price, features, packaging, size						
5 Similarity of their marketing strategy: promotions, advertising, terms of trade, credit, service						
6 The perceived relative importance to the *firm's* target market of the competitor product's benefits						
7 The similarity of the positioning of their product or service; that is to say, the differential advantage that the competitor is trying to communicate to *their* target customers						
8 Their relative costs/technological advantage						
9 Their employment of the Key Success Factors						
10 Other:						
Totals:	**100**					

You may wish to weight each factor more sensitively than on a scale of 1 to 5 – according to how seriously you perceive that factor to be a threat – and independently to assess how well the competitor exploits the factor. (Refer to Table 14.6.)

2 (a) Give a weighting to each factor (which should sum to 100) in column X.

(b) Score each competitor on a scale of 1 to 5 according to the extent to which they meet the description of the factor, ignoring the numbers at the heads of the columns.

(c) Multiply the score by the weighting you have given.

(d) Find the total as before.

Stage 2

Having identified the significant competitors, the next stage is to:

1. identify the objectives which drive their strategies;
2. analyse the strategies whereby they hope to achieve their objectives;
3. evaluate their resources, capabilities, and competencies; if not done under Worksheet 6 above, plot their locations on perceptual maps as described under opportunity analysis, Worksheet 14.

Your conclusions should be considered in developing strategies to counter their strengths and exploit their weaknesses.

WORKSHEET 8 STAKEHOLDER ANALYSIS

A stakeholder is any person or organisation that influences or is influenced by actions of the firm, either directly or indirectly. This means that one stakeholder may act in a particular way as the result of the response of another stakeholder to an action of the firm. For this reason, a stakeholder 'map' which shows relationships between stakeholders may be helpful when these are important, but the main purpose of the analysis is to identify interested parties whose responses to proposed activities should be taken into account.

Stakeholders and their importance will depend on the particular circumstances, but the following list is a starting point:

- Customers and clients
- Competitors
- Employees
- Senior management
- Local community
- National government
- Regulatory bodies
- Suppliers
- Shareholders and owners
- Sources of finance
- Media
- Trade unions and professional bodies
- Local authorities
- Religious, political and other interest groups

Stakeholder maps can show:

(a) relationships between stakeholders by means of a line joining them;
(b) the directions of influence by arrow-heads on the lines;
(c) the strength of influence by the thickness of the lines.

Stage 1

This is undertaken at the start of the study:

1 Identify current stakeholders.

2 Using the map, predict how they will be affected by and respond to:

   (a) trends identified in the environmental audits;

   (b) continued implementation of the firm's existing strategies.

3 Evaluate the strategic significance of these predictions concerning:

   (a) important stakeholders;

   (b) the reactions – favourable or unfavourable – of other stakeholders.

4 Include your conclusions in the SWOT analysis as opportunities or threats and, in the case of internal stakeholders, as strengths or weaknesses.

Stage 2

When strategic options are being evaluated, the probable reactions of not only the previously identified stakeholders to a proposed new situation should be considered, but also those of previously uninvolved stakeholders.

1 Identify any individuals or organisations that would become stakeholders as a result of the new strategy, and add them to the list from Stage 1.

2 Repeat steps 2 and 3 of Stage 1 for the proposed strategy.

3 Include the results of your analysis in the evaluation of the options, or modify these appropriately.

4 Consider the value chains of the options in the light of your conclusions.

WORKSHEET 9 GAP ANALYSIS

The purpose of gap analysis is to identify, at the corporate or at the SBU level, any difference between what is likely to happen in the future unless new decisions are made, and what management wishes to happen – their targets or objectives. This provides a measure of the gap that must be filled by changes to the strategy. (*See* the section on The organisation in relation to the environment in Chapter 5.) The parameters measured could be revenue, sales volume, profit, return on capital, market share or any other important quantifiable objective.

Note, however, that the analysis depends very heavily on the ability to make reasonably accurate forecasts, and is a perfect example of the principle: garbage in – garbage out; although the theory is sound, in practice there are considerable difficulties in obtaining a reliable result.

Because the components of a firm's portfolio are likely to perform in different ways, the analysis should, if possible, be conducted separately for each SBU, division, product line or product which makes a significant contribution to the parameter measured (say more than five per cent). The remainder can be aggregated into one or more groups, depending upon their size and homogeneity.

The stages of the analysis are as follows:

1 Plot a trend for the past performance of the parameter and extrapolate it into the future to an appropriate planning time-horizon, say five years. You may wish to take a cautious or slightly pessimistic view but, if so, this fact should be recorded.

2 Identify the reasons for the nature of the trend: is the slope declining because the product is reaching the maturity stage of the product life-cycle? Was it the result of strong new competition or the economic climate? Did production costs increase? Is it cyclical? Will the effect increase or diminish? Modify the projection according to your evaluation of the future effect of these causes if they continue to apply.

3 List assumptions concerning *future* events and their probable effect on the parameter measured. *Do not anticipate any likely strategic response. That must come* ***out*** *of the analysis, not be built into it.*

   For example: 'Raw material costs will rise by 15 per cent next year and that will reduce gross margins by . . .' or 'A major competitor will launch their new model in 18 months' time and the effect of that on the sales of our existing product over the next two years will be . . .'

4 Build these future events into the projection which thus becomes a *forecast* of what will happen unless new decisions are made.

5 To determine the gap at the corporate level:

(a) find the year-by-year totals by combining the individual forecasts, correcting for inflation or other effects if appropriate;

(b) compare the resulting aggregate forecast with the target performance in order to measure any gap and to determine when it is likely to occur.

Note that the target used may be higher than that actually required in order to provide a safety margin for the target, to motivate greater effort within the organisation, or to allow for errors in forecasting.

WORKSHEET 10 VALUE CHAIN ANALYSIS

Value chain analysis is one of the most fundamental approaches to achieving success (*see* Chapter 5). This aspect of it considers the question:

> *What do our existing and potential customers most value, and how can we best provide it profitably?*

However, the analysis should not be a general review of the organisation; do not become too involved in detail.

Organisations can be considered as systems having inputs which are processed within the organisation. This process or its output must be stored, marketed and delivered to clients or customers. These primary activities must in turn be supported by others such as ordering raw materials and components, training staff in particular skills, processing paperwork, making financial, legal or other decisions, answering customer enquiries, repairing or replacing faulty goods, doing so speedily, courteously and so on. These support activities may play a vital role in the system, contributing to any or all of the benefits sought, and adding to customer satisfaction and perceived value.

Note that the analysis should focus on the *activities* required, not on the departments responsible for them.

1 Define the particular strategic business area or market segment considered.

2 Draw a conventional process chart for the individual organisation being studied by tracing activities and relationships between them involved in adding value to the product or service.

3 List the Key Success Factors and competitive or differential advantages offered by the firm – such as quality, cost, helpfulness, speedy design, production or delivery – which relate to the particular benefits sought by that market segment.

4 Trace the process of meeting these requirements throughout the organisation. Start at the *end* of the process, rather than the beginning. This may reveal the importance of certain preceding activities.

5 Identify:

(a) those *specific* activities which could and should contribute significantly to providing this perceived value and which must therefore be preserved or intensified, particularly when related to the most important benefits;

(b) those activities which the internal audit has shown fail to do so, or which this analysis shows to be deficient – an actual impediment – or where an improvement in performance will enhance perceived value;

(c) those activities which appear to contribute less to perceived value than their cost or the resources they employ, or whose costs could be reduced without detracting from perceived value or other important attributes – in other words, examine the *cost chain*;

(d) linkages and interrelationships between activities which must be borne in mind if changes are made as the result of the analysis.

Linkages between activities should be considered very carefully: very often it is possible to modify one activity at additional cost, but gain the benefit elsewhere in the system; for example, quality control during production can eliminate rejects – or even detailed final inspection – while higher quality can minimise servicing costs as well as adding perceived value among other benefits.

Note that many activities may lend themselves to being conducted simultaneously rather than sequentially, particularly with the aid of information technology, while concurrent engineering both reduces costs and saves time. Speedy response is frequently the means of obtaining a major competitive advantage and adding value.

6 Summarise your conclusions concerning the activities to be modified, then relate them to the particular department or functions concerned, which may be affected by recommendations originating from other aspects of the exercise.

WORKSHEET 11 THE INTERNAL AUDIT

The internal audit is a review of each and every department and function of the firm in order to identify strengths and weaknesses that could be acted upon to improve performance, and these four principles should inform the analysis:

1. The strategy and success of many firms depend upon particular specific competencies or attributes, and these must be identified for reinforcement and possible further exploitation as strengths, or weaknesses, as appropriate.

2. Whether a certain feature is a strength or a weakness – and it may be both – depends upon existing or future environmental characteristics and forces; they are situational.

3. A weakness may not necessarily expose the firm to a threat, but may prevent an existing or potential opportunity to be exploited. This should be noted.

4. The terms *strengths* and *weaknesses* may be misleading. Some characteristics which could be defined as strengths, weaknesses or both, might also be defined as *unexploited assets*. For example, spare production capacity, large cash reserves earning a low return, an expensive and sophisticated data-processing facility, or under-utilised skills may well be defined as weaknesses. These could be of strategic significance by identifying *new* ways in which they could be utilised, rather than attempting to match them against previously identified opportunities or threats as above.

Most quantifiable characteristics should be evaluated by making comparisons. These should, if possible, include past trends, current performance, and future forecasts, and they should also be compared with the performance of the industry as a whole, with the firm's closest competitors, and with the best performers in the industry. The reasons for any differences should then be identified for further action. This is particularly important for costs if a firm is to remain competitive.

Performance is frequently best evaluated by ratios which measure the use made of resources – return on investment is perhaps the most important example, but how the capital is actually invested should also be considered. For example, in the case of a chain of stores, capital is invested in a number of branches, in selling space, in different commodity groups, and in stock for each. The return on all of these investments should be measured.

Examples of characteristics that *may* be important are:

Financial
Gearing
Rate of stock-turn
Value of stock-holding
ROI, ROCE
Sales volume
Value of average transaction
Profit
Resources, access to capital
Liquidity, available internal funds
Investment

Operations
Productivity/efficiency
Age of plant/facilities
Technology and skills
Cost advantages
Production capacity
Reject rate
Flexibility
Patents and licences
Location
R&D expenditure, capability
Quality, quality control
Inventory control

Marketing
Corporate image, reputation
Brand names
Use of market intelligence
Effectiveness of promotion
Promotional expenditure/sales
Relationship with distributors
Market share
Loyal customer base
Distribution network
Review of the Four Ps: Product, Price, Promotion, Place
Average order delivery time
Ratio of complaints to sales
Product range – wide/narrow

Managerial
Culture and style
Analytical and planning ability
Responsiveness, adaptability
Attitude to risk
General competence and skills
Influence in environment
Negotiating skills
Use of management information systems

Human resources
Employee turnover
Skills and capabilities
Morale
Training and development
Staffing levels
Capital investment/employee

WORKSHEET 12 PORTFOLIO ANALYSIS

The purposes of portfolio analysis are to:

1 provide an overview of the portfolio as a whole;

2 identify those SBUs, divisions or products that warrant particular attention because of their strategic significance or their unsatisfactory performance;

3 suggest a strategy for individual units in the portfolio.

Although a single product may well be described as, for example, a 'cash cow', portfolio analysis is really only appropriate when a firm has a sizeable range of different strategic business units (SBUs) operating in different markets or market segments.

The portfolio analysis may be conducted in two stages; the first stage uses the BCG matrix to identify those units warranting particular attention. If the number of SBUs thus identified is large, a second stage could be based on the GE matrix, otherwise consider each SBU individually.

The original Boston Consulting Group (BCG) Matrix

The matrix is a tool not a theory; it shows, for each activity, product, country, division or other SBU:

- Its relative market share – on the horizontal axis
- The rate of growth of the *market* – on the vertical axis
- Its contribution to company turnover – by the size of the circle representing it on the chart

To prepare the chart, for each SBU in the portfolio:

Step 1 Define the particular market in which the SBU competes with other brands satisfying the same needs, and determine its share of that market.

Step 2 Identify the largest competitor in that market and determine their market share.

Step 3 Calculate the relative market share (RMS) of the SBU by obtaining the ratio of the firm's market share to that of the largest competitor and dividing the former by the latter, as in the example in Table 14.8.

Table 14.8 Calculating relative market share

Firm	Market share (%)	Biggest competitor and share (%)	Ratio	Relative market share
A	30	B: 20	30/20	= **1.50**
B	20	A: 30	20/30	= **0.66**
C	15	A: 30	15/30	= **0.50**
D	10	A: 30	10/30	= **0.33**

Step 4 Calculate the *market* rate of growth. This is the difference between the current total market sales figure and that of the previous year, expressed as a percentage of the previous year's sales. It will be positive if sales have increased, but negative if sales have decreased over the period. (Note this application refers to total market sales, not merely those of the SBU.)

Step 5 Decide on that rate of growth which divides 'high' from 'low' growth according to the characteristics of the market(s), the macro-environment, and the investment policy of the firm. Some authorities suggest a value of 10 per cent, others use the average growth rate of the industry as a whole.

This 'dividing value' should be plotted at the middle of the vertical scale on the BCG matrix. The bottom value on the vertical scale (the origin) is usually zero unless there are negative rates of growth in the portfolio (*see* Fig 14.2).

Step 6 The horizontal axis should ideally be on a logarithmic scale, but if this graph paper is not available, an adequate approximation is to have equal divisions between the following values, starting with 10 at the origin, and ending with 0.1 on the extreme right of the axis:

10.0 4.0 2.0 1.0 0.5 0.3 0.1

Step 7 **(a)** Draw a heavy horizontal line across the chart at the value separating 'high' from 'low' growth.

(b) Draw a heavy vertical line at the RMS value of 1.0, i.e. the line which separates SBUs with competitors larger than themselves from those with the highest share of their market. (Note that

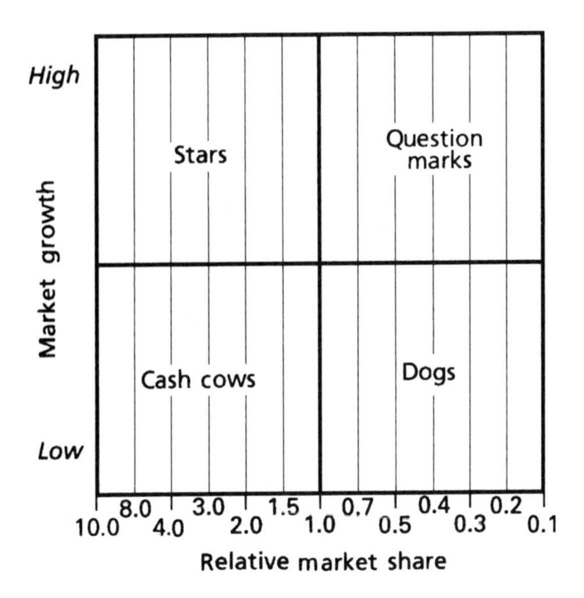

Fig 14.2 BCG matrix

some authorities suggest drawing this at a value of 1.5 as a brand cannot be said to *dominate* the market if it is an equal brand leader.)

Step 8 Plot the position of each component of the portfolio with a point according to its relative market share and its rate of growth.

Step 9 Show the relative contribution to sales of each SBU as follows:

(a) calculate the percentage contribution to total sales made by each product;

(b) calculate the square root of that value;

(c) draw a circle with radius proportional to this, centred at the plotted point. (The area of the circle is then proportional to its contribution since Area = πr^2.)

In Table 14.9, the radius of a circle in millimetres is twice the square root of the percentage of sales. The BCG matrix for this example is shown in Fig 14.3. In Fig 14.3, Product 1 is a star, with high relative market share and in a market with the highest rate of growth in the portfolio; Product 2 is a question mark, but despite having the lowest relative market share, is making the greatest contribution to sales; Product 3 is a dog; still making a useful contribution, but in a declining market; Product 4 is a star, the market leader in its field, but has at least one close competitor (RMS $\approx$ 1). The market is growing at a

Table 14.9 Calculating the relative contribution of sales

Product	Sales £ × 000	% of sales	Square root of % sales	Radius (mm)	RMS	Growth rate (%)
1	3 000	10	3.2	6	3.0	+15
2	12 000	40	6.3	13	0.3	+8
3	6 000	20	4.5	9	0.9	–5
4	9 000	30	5.5	11	1.2	+10
Total	30 000	100				

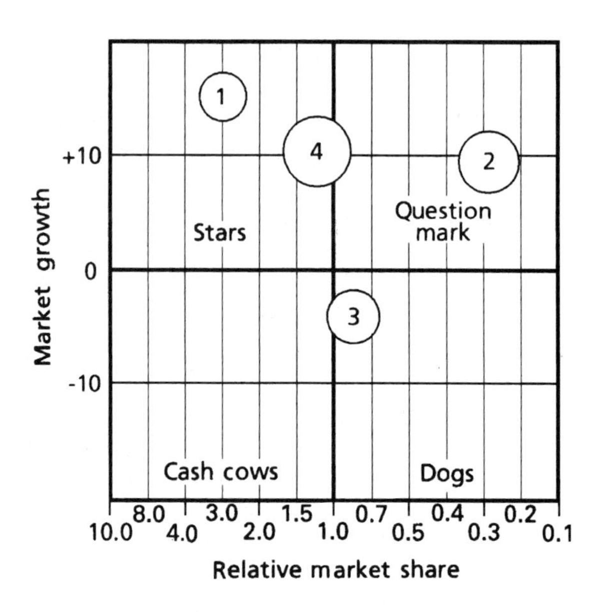

Fig 14.3 BCG matrix (from figures in Table 14.9)

healthy rate, but an equally sized major competitor suggests a bitter fight if growth declines.

The main questions to be addressed in analysing the portfolio are:

1 *Is the portfolio balanced?* Are there too many question marks or stars competing for managerial and financial resources? Alternatively, is there an adequate supply for the next generation? Does the portfolio contain cash cows to fund their development and the growth of stars?

2 *Are individual SBUs performing satisfactorily?* Are they gaining share in a growing market? Does it matter if an SBU is losing share in a market that is declining? Has a star failed to develop as anticipated?

3 *How should available funds be allocated among the portfolio?* Would it be a good use of funds to support an SBU which is losing share? Could the resources devoted to a dog be better employed? Should support be trimmed for a star that is now in a market that has slowed down? Does it warrant support to improve market share?

4 *Are there links between SBUs which must be considered?* Are they completely independent or will a decision concerning one affect the performance of another?

5 *Are there dangers from lesser competitors?* Only the largest one is considered in the matrix.

6 *What are the implications concerning profit contribution?* There is often a trade-off between sales and profit, reflected in the pricing strategy. The matrix does not address this issue.

WORKSHEET 13 SWOT ANALYSIS

Chapter 8 describes the SWOT analysis and the matching process in some detail; you may wish to re-read Chapter 8 before proceeding.

The analysis is conducted in three stages. The first two of these were outlined in the introduction to this chapter, and should have been completed. They consisted of:

1 identifying, from the various environmental and internal audits, those factors which, at first sight, could be of strategic significance, i.e. excluding any which are judged to be neither important nor urgent. These should be summarised under the headings Strengths, Weaknesses, Opportunities, Threats, together with a note of their degree of urgency, importance and probability if applicable; and

2 a preliminary evaluation of interactions between worksheets; for example, the particular effect that a macro-environmental factor could have on stakeholders or on the firm. This may have resulted in a re-assessment of the urgency and/or importance of the strengths, weaknesses, opportunities or threats.

The next stage is to identify those factors that *must* be included in future strategy. The question should therefore be asked 'Is this factor likely to be of strategic significance?' Each group should be considered in turn. Questions to ask include:

1 *Threats*

(a) Are there any threats which *must* be countered in the strategy?

(b) If so, are the strengths adequate to meet them?

(c) Are there weaknesses which increase vulnerability to a threat?

(d) How is the situation to be met?

Other threats should be evaluated according to their urgency, importance, probability, and the pay-off and cost-effectiveness in terms of resources needed to meet them.

2 *Strengths*

(a) Are there any strengths which are under-exploited in existing strategies?

(b) If so, what is their further potential, how can they be capitalised upon?

3 *Weaknesses*

(a) Are there any weaknesses which, if remedied, would improve results from existing strategies?

(b) Do any weaknesses prevent a desirable strategy from being followed, or an attractive opportunity being pursued?

4 *Opportunities*

This is the most problematic group. In theory the number of opportunities is infinite (e.g. the local baker may think there is an opportunity for selling do-it-yourself brain-surgery kits). An important point is to seek synergy between an environmental opportunity and internal strengths. The findings of Worksheet 14 – Opportunity analysis should be included.

This list comprises the Key Issues referred to in the text.

WORKSHEET 14 OPPORTUNITY ANALYSIS

In addition to other audits already undertaken, opportunities may be revealed by:

1 *Inspiration*. Unfortunately beyond the scope of this analysis.

2 By identifying *a trend* that others have not spotted or fully exploited. This could concern, for example: a growing market segment, a growing need or benefit sought, a growing demand for a product or service, a new or modified channel of distribution or technology, or synergy between complementary products and technologies such as is developing in multi-media applications. It is for this reason that the environmental audit should be conducted imaginatively rather than merely mechanically.

3 By spotting a *gap* in the market. This could be:

   (a) an existing attractive market segment whose needs are not being met;
   (b) one which the firm could serve better than current providers;
   (c) one currently being served by the firm but which could be better served.

These may be identified by the approach outlined below, although it is unlikely that the necessary data will be available; the purpose is to illustrate two important components of a successful strategy. Having identified a worthwhile market segment, the aim is to:

(a) satisfy their needs and wants better than competitors;
(b) differentiate the firm and/or its product or service from competitors.

Perceptual mapping

The factors mentioned above are:

(a) *Attractive market segments*. There are many ways of segmenting markets, and whether a segment is attractive will depend upon a number of features such as size, accessibility, the extent of competition, propensity to buy and so on. The market analysis should include a study of the market structure and the attractiveness of the different segments within it.

(b) *Needs, wants and benefits sought by segments*. Products and services invariably possess a number of attributes, the relative importance of which will vary from segment to segment. For example, in the case of a car these could include low price, image, acceleration, comfort, speed, safety, size, economy, insurance group and so on. The Competitor analysis and the Key Success Factor analysis should have identified the most important of these, together with an assessment of the extent to which existing suppliers satisfy them.

(c) *The ability of the firm to meet these needs and wants.* The internal audit may have evaluated strengths and weaknesses related to these abilities, but further specific analysis will probably be necessary.

The attributes can be used, two at a time, as the axes of a chart, and the positions of market segments plotted according to how important those particular attributes are to each segment. For example, Fig 14.4 represents two characteristics of a market for spare parts: price and ready availability. Customers in segment A value the ready availability of spare parts very highly and are less concerned with low price, unlike segment B. Furthermore, each segment can be represented by a circle, the size of which indicates its attractiveness. Thus segment A is more attractive than segment B.

The positioning of existing suppliers, together with an indication of their market strength, can also be plotted on Fig 14.4. It will be seen that most competitors (numbered 1 to 4) concentrate on low price, competitor 3 not only being the biggest, but also almost exactly matching the needs of segment B. This suggests that segment A offers a market opportunity, provided that the firm can both provide readily available spare parts and communicate the fact to that segment.

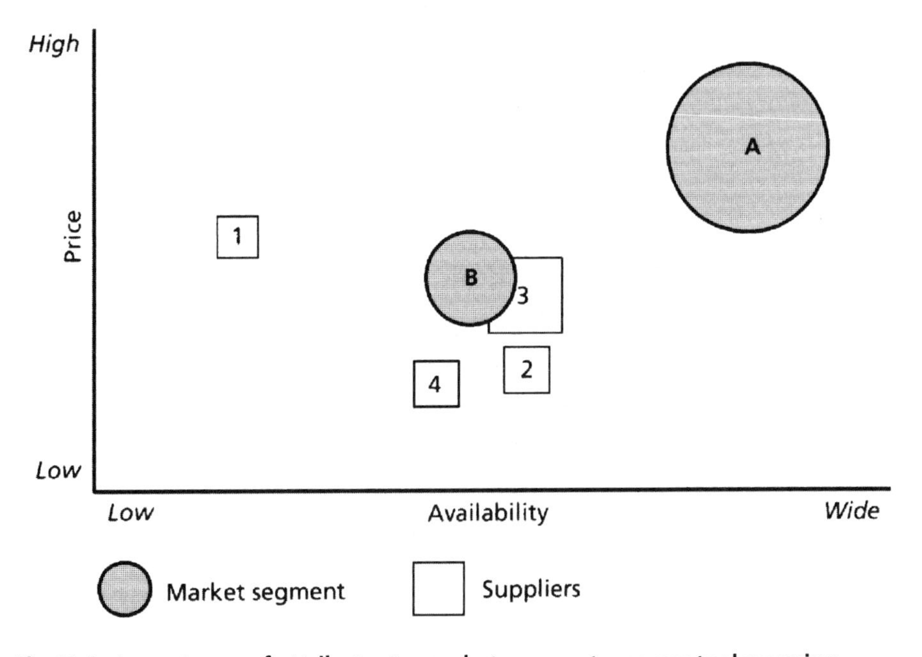

Fig 14.4 Importance of attributes to market segment – perceptual mapping

It may be necessary to take a number of pairs of attributes in turn in order to identify a practical market opportunity, but the technique may also be used to reposition a product closer to the needs of a segment, or to distance it – obtain a differential advantage – from competitors.

Any opportunities and relevant strategies identified by this approach should be evaluated alongside other strategic options.

WORKSHEET 15 STRATEGIC CHOICE

Chapter 10 outlines an approach for making strategic choice, and lists criteria repeated below. A number of these may require further analysis to be undertaken, for example, the consequences of the strategy failing or the consequences of stakeholders' reactions. The following suggested approach may also influence the relative importance of the criteria:

1 Strategies that minimise organisational or strategic change are preferable to those requiring greater changes – provided that the resulting strategic choice will meet corporate objectives.
2 In general, the simpler the overall approach the better; e.g. one straightforward strategic thrust is better than a combination of two or more different strategies.

In order to minimise change, the first issue is whether continuing with the present strategy will achieve the firm's objectives.

Case 1

If the present strategy does appear to still be appropriate, then the next step is to ensure that the firm will have, or can acquire, the resources necessary either to maintain or to achieve success. If the analysis then reveals that not only is the current strategy still appropriate but that the firm is capable of any necessary adaptations, then a major review of strategy is not urgent, and attention can turn to improving performance further as a result of the SWOT findings. It may, however, be desirable to set more ambitious targets and improve performance accordingly, or perhaps to modify the firm's mission in the light of the findings.

Case 2

If the strategy either:

(a) *will not* work in the future because environmental changes have made it inappropriate; or
(b) *cannot* work because, internally, the firm is incapable of adapting to the requirements of the strategy, i.e. the internal weaknesses cannot be overcome,

then a new or modified strategy is clearly necessary and, preferably, should be based on existing strengths, since this will minimise major internal changes.

If, however, the analysis suggests that:

(a) existing strengths are inadequate to meet the situation, cannot fully take advantage of an opportunity, or meet a threat that jeopardises success; or
(b) existing weaknesses, which are the reason for the lack of success, cannot be overcome,

then a more fundamental change may be needed. This implies that either:

(a) some resources must be sold or exchanged for others, or additional resources otherwise acquired (by purchase); or
(b) it will be necessary to go outside the firm to find appropriate resources, for example, by a bank loan, or by forming a joint venture with another firm.

This general approach is not a cookery book recipe, and will certainly need adaptation to the particular circumstances of a given situation.

Criteria

(a) How well does it contribute to meeting corporate objectives?

(b) Is the project consistent with the organisation's policies/culture?

(c) Does the strategy overcome strategic weaknesses and counter serious environmental threats?

(d) What would be the consequences of the strategy failing or of only partial success?

(e) Is the strategy based on a *sustainable* competitive advantage?

(f) Is the strategy feasible?

(g) What will be stakeholders' reactions?

(h) What are the potential rewards?

1 Making use of Table 14.10, list and number the strategic options to be evaluated:

Option 1 . . . .

Option 2 . . . .

Option 3 . . . . , etc.

2 Enter the numbers or an abbreviation at the column headings on the worksheet.

3 In descending order of importance, list the criteria to be applied, and then divide 100 points among them to give a relative weighting:

Weighting

Criterion A . . . . ☐

Criterion B . . . . ☐ etc.

4 Enter the weightings in the first column of Table 14.10.

5 For each option, enter a score from 0 to 5 according to how well the option meets that criterion.

6 Multiply the score (S) by the weighting (W) and enter under S × W.

7 Find the total score for each option.

8 Review the weightings and/or the score if the result is questionable.

Table 14.10 Analysing strategic choice

Weighting	**Option 1**		**Option 2**		**Option 3**	
	Score	S × W	Score	S × W	Score	S × W
A						
B						
C						
D						
E						
F						
G						
H						
I						
J						
Total: 100	Total:		Total:		Total:	

GLOSSARY

acid test (Also known as **quick ratio**.) The ratio of liquid assets to current liabilities. Liquid assets are those that are cash or nearly cash, and the ratio therefore shows the ability of the firm to pay its immediate debts. Normally about 1:1 (*see also* **current ratio**).

added value Inputs to a product or service go through many stages and possibly several hands before the finished product reaches the end-user. Each time, costs are added but the value to the consumer increases – ideally more than the cost of that stage, e.g. Value Added Resellers (VARs) are retailers who customise standard computer packages for their clients.

adhocracy An organisation which has very little formal structure, but usually consists of a variety of highly trained experts who form teams to solve specific problems. The emphasis is on creativity and innovation rather than formal planning – an emergent strategy approach.[1]

attractiveness/strength matrix *See* **directional policy matrix**.

backward integration When a firm gains ownership of its inputs or suppliers; e.g. a chain of shoe shops acquiring a shoe manufacturer. This is one form of **vertical integration** and is also **related diversification** since it is in the same industry. It is 'upstream' since the move is towards the source.

BCG matrix (Also known as **growth/share matrix**.) A 2 × 2 cell chart for displaying a portfolio of several products or **SBUs**. The horizontal axis depicts market share relative to that of the biggest competitor, the vertical axis measures the rate of market growth. Components are described as **fledglings**, **question marks** or **problem children**; **stars**; **cash cows**; and **dogs**. A broad strategy is recommended for each while the portfolio should be balanced overall.

break-even analysis A chart which shows the sales volume at which sales revenue just equals the total of fixed and variable costs. Above this level the activity is profitable; below, it makes a loss. The profit or loss at any level of sales can be read off the chart.

business strategy This emphasises that the strategy is at the **SBU** – the market-place level – rather than at the corporate level, with which it must nevertheless be consistent.

buy in To acquire inputs by purchase rather than by manufacturing them. This *may* possibly cost more per unit (thus reducing gross profit) and does not ensure supply, but avoids investing in plant so that **Return On Investment** (ROI) is higher, and enables resources to better match demand.

cash cow A product, division or other **SBU** with high relative market share although the market is not growing. Because of this it does not need investment in growth, and is generating high positive net cash flow. This can then be allocated to components of the portfolio which do require funding. (It may nevertheless still need support to maintain its strong competitive position.)

competitive advantage In the context of strategic management this refers not merely to having an edge over competitors in the market-place, but to achieving above-average profitability so that funds are available for the marketing, R&D, capital investment and so on that will maintain that position.

concentration A characteristic of many markets, often in or approaching the maturity stage of their life-cycle, which are dominated by relatively few giants who grow by acquisition. Smaller firms, unable to compete, usually seek niches or fail.

concentric diversification A strategy of adding new but related products or activities to a firm's portfolio.

conglomerate A large firm with a portfolio of unrelated activities or subsidiaries to which it applies its skills of overall management.

consolidation A strategy, often adopted after a major acquisition or other internal change, in which the firm digests the change and adapts to the new conditions rather than being more dynamic. May also be appropriate in a recession or other environmentally unfavourable circumstances.

consumer orientation An organisational attitude which recognises that success ultimately depends upon meeting customer needs.

corporate objectives Objectives for the organisation as a whole, defined mainly in financial terms such as **ROI**, sales and profit; but sometimes including references to such as R&D, innovation and social responsibility.

corporate planning An unfashionable term, don't use it.

corporate strategy Read Chapter 1.

cost/benefit analysis When comparing alternative strategies, the total costs of each are compared with an assessment of the benefits, expressed in financial terms. For example, an increase in market share could be evaluated in terms of extra sales, lower unit costs, etc.

cost leadership One of Porter's three 'Generic Strategies',[2] consisting of obtaining competitive advantage through having *the* lowest costs in the industry.

critical mass Some outcomes cannot be achieved below a certain level of size, effort or market share. Thus, a national retail chain may not buy from a supplier who cannot ensure nationwide delivery or a given market share; a conventional insurance company must have a minimum number of agents to be viable.

current ratio The ratio of current assets to current liabilities. 'current' means payable within 12 months. Current assets include items such as finished goods that can be turned into cash at fairly short notice.

customer orientation *See* **consumer orientation**.

debtors' ratio A measurement of how quickly a firm is collecting money it is owed:

$$\frac{\text{Debtors}}{\text{Average daily credit sales}}$$

decentralisation A policy of allowing major decisions to be made at lower levels of the organisation.

decision tree A technique for analysing problems which are multi-stage, that is, when the result of one decision affects future decisions, and each has a number of possible outcomes. Every outcome of each decision therefore has a number of alternative branches, each of which has a number of branches and so on.

decline stage The final stage of the product (or other) **life-cycle**, following that of maturity, when demand decreases.

delphi technique A method of predicting the future based on the opinions of experts in the particular field.

demographics Population characteristics such as age, sex, socio-economic group, marital and family situation which influence demand.

differentiation A strategy of distinguishing your product or service from those of competitors in order to obtain a differential advantage.

directional policy matrix (Also known as **General Electric business screen**, or **attractiveness/strength matrix**.) A 3 × 3 cell matrix used to display a product portfolio in which the horizontal axis denotes a strong, average or weak competitive position, and the vertical axis low, medium or high industry attractiveness.

discounted cash flow (DCF) A way of comparing strategic alternatives which have different future patterns of cash flow. By discounting each future year's flow to a present value and finding the total, the **net present value** of each project can be obtained and compared.

diversification Adding new products to the range. *See* **related** or **unrelated diversification**.

divestment, divestiture Selling or disposing part of the business.

divisionalisation A stage in organisational growth when complexity and size warrant dividing the business into different groups. These could be geographical, market, production or product related, or a combination of two or more of these. *See* **multidivisional structure**.

dog A product or unit of a portfolio with low relative market share in a declining market. It is a serious candidate for discontinuation unless there are reasons for retention.

economies of scale The lower-cost benefits that result from operating on a large scale, such as more efficient plant and greater buying power.

effectiveness The results of the *ends* to which resources are deployed; would they be better deployed on a different task?

efficiency For a given task, the relationship between the output of a process and its maximum capacity.

efficiency ratios (Also known as **operating ratios**.) Financial ratios which measure the efficiency of management in running the organisation; e.g. how long to collect debts, how much capital is tied up in stock, costs in relation to results, etc.

emergent strategy A strategy which resulted, not from formal strategic planning, but from a development that had not necessarily been foreseen.

entrepreneurship A management style which actively seeks growth, searches for opportunities, and is prepared to take risks.

entry barrier Barriers to entry prevent easy access to markets. For example, lack of expertise, raw materials, or channels of distribution, high capital or other costs, legislation, location, customer loyalty to existing brands.

equity That share of a business that belongs to the owners when all other parties have been paid; shareholders' investment.

exit barrier It may be difficult for a firm to quit an unattractive industry or market due to: no alternative available; high level of investment; long-term commitments, contracts or obligations.

experience curve A graph which shows how costs decline as a firm gains experience in an industry. This is typically at a rate of a 15–30 per cent decline every time that the cumulative total of units produced is doubled.

expert system A computer package which encapsulates the expertise and wisdom of specialists. Lesser mortals can then input data and receive an expert opinion or diagnosis. It reduces reliance on experienced managers and may improve the quality of decisions.

fledgling *See* **question mark**.

forward integration Gaining ownership of a 'downstream' stage of the chain from raw material to the end-user, e.g. a manufacturer acquiring retail outlets. Confusingly described as a form of **vertical integration** and is **related diversification**.

franchising A relatively low-risk way for the inexperienced to enter an established market, usually in retailing or a service. The franchisee pays an initial fee and then buys supplies from the franchiser who provides training and other support. The franchiser gains rapid growth with little capital expenditure.

functional structure An organisational structure in which separate departments each deal with a specialised aspect of the management of the enterprise: marketing, operations, finance, R&D, etc.

gap analysis A method of determining any difference between a firm's objectives, and what it will achieve in the future if it makes no changes to its strategy. This reveals the *planning gap*.

gearing The relationship between share capital and loan capital. Shareholders will receive dividends in good years and the value of their shares may rise – or fall. The interest on a loan, however *must* be paid regardless, and the capital must eventually be repaid.

General Electric business screen *See* **directional policy matrix**.

generic strategy This usually refers specifically to one of Porter's[3] three generic strategies: **cost leadership, differentiation** and focus, which he claims lead to sustainable **competitive advantage**. It is also used in a more general sense to describe the overriding strategy that drives the firm.

goal This is an ambiguous term; some writers use it as a synonym for objective, some only as a quantified objective, and some as a distant aim that is never actually reached – lying between **mission** and objective. Avoid its use.

gross margin The difference between sales revenue and the cost of goods sold.

growth/share matrix *See* **BCG matrix**.

holding company A company owning a portfolio, usually a **conglomerate** of unrelated subsidiaries.

horizontal integration A strategy of acquiring control over direct competitors or over very closely related activities.

incrementalism The process of deliberately evolving in a particular desired direction, rather than following the stages of a plan is **logical incrementalism**.[4] Deciding strategy by a process of 'successive limited comparisons' – repeatedly comparing the outcomes and the practicality of strategic options – is **incrementalism**, 'The science of muddling through'.[5]

integration *See* **forward, backward, horizontal, vertical integration**.

intrapreneurship The attempt by a large organisation to obtain the benefits of *entrepreneurship* by setting up an autonomous task force or group with its own independent resources.

joint venture A company or project set up by two or more organisations that themselves remain independent but to which they contribute resources, expertise, rights, production capacity, etc.

just-in-time (JIT) A manufacturing system which relies on supplies being made available by frequent delivery just as they are needed, rather than by holding larger quantities of stock.

key issues Major strategic decisions usually revolve around a very few key issues. Identifying these enables the wood to be seen despite the trees.

key success factors (KSFs) Every market demands certain attributes without which a business cannot hope to succeed. They will differ according to the market: a *haute couture* fashion house and a double-glazing firm have different essential requirements that each must identify.

life-cycle The concept that products and industries, like life-forms, go through the stages: Introduction, Growth, Maturity and **Decline**. Each stage will require a different strategic approach, and understanding which stage a product has reached provides strategic insight.

liquidation The sale of a company or part thereof to obtain its worth.

liquidity The ability of a firm to pay its way. An enterprise may have the potential to be highly profitable but fail through lack of liquidity.

liquidity ratios Ratios measuring the ability of the firm to pay its bills as they fall due. *See* **current ratio, acid test**.

logical incrementalism *See* **incrementalism**.

logistics Inbound logistics are activities concerned with the reception, storage and distribution of inputs to an enterprise; outbound logistics relate to the distribution and delivery of the goods or services. These are two of the five primary activities of Porter's model of the **value chain**.

machine bureaucracy One of five configurations into which Mintzberg divided organisations. It is typified by the stereotypical mass-production enterprise.

market development A strategy based on selling existing products to new geographical or other market segments, or to new users.

market penetration A strategy based on continuing to sell the existing products in the same market, but gaining market share.

marketing mix Everything a firm can do to influence the market, classified under the four Ps: Product, Price, Place, Promotion.

matrix structure An organisational structure in which the individual operational units are each responsible to two authorities. These are usually responsible for different geographical areas, different products or different market segments.

mission The reason for the existence of the organisation; the nature of the business it is in.

multidivisional structure An organisation divided at the operational level into different units or divisions on a basis such as products, market segments or geographical areas. The division may occur at two levels, e.g. first into geographical regions, each of which is further divided into different product ranges – or vice versa.

multinational corporation A firm operating in more than one country, and where overall control is exerted from outside countries in which goods or services are offered.

net present value (NPV) The total present worth of a future cash flow, obtained by discounting at a given rate per annum.

niche strategy The strategy of confining a firm's activities to a relatively small market segment and concentrating on serving its needs and wants particularly well, rather than the market as a whole.

oligopoly A market dominated by a few giant firms.

optimise To maximise the achievement of an objective, for example, to minimise costs or to maximise profit.

P/E (price to earnings) ratio A measurement of considerable interest to investors. It shows the ratio of the share price to net dividends. A high ratio suggests a well-managed firm with high hopes of the future.

PIMS An acronym for the Profit Impact of Market Strategy.[6] This is a computer model which analyses data from a large panel of firms, mainly in the USA and western Europe, in order to explore relationships between performance (primarily **ROI**) and up to 100 data headings such as market share, relative quality and plant newness.

PLC (product life-cycle) *See* **life-cycle**.

portfolio analysis When a firm has a variety of products or **SBUs** in different markets, at different stages of their life-cycle, with different needs and demands on resources, the **product portfolio** can be viewed and analysed methodically using matrices such as: **BCG**, **directional policy** and/or several others.

problem child Also known as **fledgling**. *See* **question mark**.

product development A strategy based on increasing sales in an existing market through new or improved products rather than by finding new markets.

product life-cycle *See* **life-cycle**.

product portfolio *See* **portfolio analysis**.

professional bureaucracy One of five configurations into which Mintzberg divided organisations. It is typified by a university or hospital.

profitability ratios Ratios which measure profitability. The 'primary ratio' is Profit/Capital; some others are: Earnings per Share, Profit on sales, **P/E ratio**, Dividend cover.

question mark A product or unit in a portfolio with low relative market share, but in an industry with a high rate of growth. To develop further may require considerable resources.

quick ratio — *See* **acid test**.

ratio analysis — Interpreting financial data in order to measure performance. *See* **profitability ratios, liquidity ratios, solvency ratios, efficiency ratios**.

related diversification — The strategy of remaining within an industry, but extending operations beyond the present products and markets. *See* **forward integration** and **backward integration**.

relative market share — The market share of an **SBU** expressed as a fraction of the market share of its biggest competitor, thus indicating relative power in the marketplace.

retrenchment — A strategy of contraction: cutting costs, reducing activities, disposing of peripheral ventures.

ROCE (return on capital employed) — A simple measure of how well the enterprise is using the total capital employed. (Profit before interest and tax/total capital.)

satisfice — To perform at a level which is just satisfactory – i.e. to achieve minimum standards, rather than to strive for maximum performance.

SBU (strategic business unit) — A unit within the organisation which is sufficiently autonomous for it to have a strategy which could be distinct from that of other units if this were desirable. Ideally, it should be matched to a strategic business *area* in the environment.

scenario — A possible future situation, the strategic implications of which can then be explored. (E.g. What should be done if *this* were to happen in five years time?)

segmentation — The division of a market into homogeneous and different sections having different needs or wants. One or more of these may then be targeted more precisely and effectively than in aiming at the market as a whole.

seven-s framework — The view of an organisation as a system that has seven interacting elements; change one, and the others may well be affected.[7]

simple structure — One of five configurations into which Mintzberg divided organisations. Typically a small, entrepreneurial business with no specialist functions.

solvency ratios — Financial ratios which indicate how vulnerable the firm is to environmental fluctuations (interest rates and market conditions) in the longer term, such as capital gearing ratio and times interest earned.

SPACE (strategic position and action evaluation) matrix — A matrix which suggests a strategic posture for a firm depending upon an evaluation of four factors: financial strength, **competitive advantage**, environmental strength, and industry attractiveness.[8]

stakeholder — An individual or organisation that influences or is influenced by the decisions of the firm.

star — A product or unit in a portfolio, with high relative market share and in an industry with a high rate of growth. Nevertheless, to develop further it may still demand considerable resources. A term used in the **BCG matrix**.

suboptimisation — The apparent 'best' performance may not be so when a wider view is taken. Thus, cutting costs by using cheaper raw materials may increase the reject rate. Hence *sub*optimisation in one area may result in a superior overall result.

sustainable competitive advantage *See* **competitive advantage**.

SWOT analysis A list of a firm's internal **S**trengths and **W**eaknesses, and its environmental **O**pportunities and **T**hreats.

synergy Interaction between components of a system so that the combined effect is of greater benefit than the sum of the parts: i.e. 2 + 2 = 5. An opposite *harmful* analogy is taking alcohol with certain drugs.

technostructure A term used by Mintzberg to describe the staff functions which, while not line management, plan and control the work of others – such as production schedulers.

total quality management (TQM) An organisation-wide complete commitment and dedication to the pursuit of the highest quality (zero defects) in *all* that a firm does, to identify and provide total customer satisfaction while lowering costs.

turbulence (environmental) According to Ansoff and McDonnell,[9] a measure of the extent to which a firm's environment is unpredictable, complex and novel.

turnaround strategy A strategy whereby a firm on the edge of failure can by **retrenchment** survive and then recover because the means to do so – such as a new product under development – are available.

unrelated diversification Entering a different market with a product or service not related to previous activities. The strategy of a **conglomerate**.

value chain This usually refers to Porter's model of five primary activities which, together with support activities, generate customer value. The term is, however, of wider significance.

vertical integration Either **backward integration** which is acquiring control over inputs to the firm such as suppliers – going upstream – or **forward integration**, which is gaining control of downstream activities, such as a manufacturer acquiring retail outlets.

Z-score The score obtained from applying a formula to a firm's financial data. A score below a certain level is claimed to be a predictor of financial failure.[10]

zero-based budgeting Budgeting the activities of a firm as though they were to be undertaken for the first time in order to evaluate their cost-effectiveness and priority.

REFERENCES

1. Mintzberg, H., *The Structuring of Organizations*, Prentice Hall, 1979.
2. Porter, M., *Competitive Strategy*, Free Press, 1980.
3. Ibid.
4. Quinn, J. B., *Strategies for Change: Logical Incrementalism*, Irwin, 1980.
5. Lindblom, C. E., 'The Science of Muddling Through', *Public Administration Review*, Vol. 19, 1959.
6. Buzzell, R. D. and Gale, B. T., *The PIMS Principles*, Free Press, 1987.
7. Waterman, R. H., Peters, T. J. and Phillips, J. R., *Structure is not Organization*, Business Horizons, 1980.
8. Rowe, A. J., Mason, R. O., Dickel, K. E. and Snyder, N. H., *Strategic Management: A Methodological Approach*, 4ed, Addison Wesley, 1994.
9. Ansoff, I. and McDonnell, E., *Implanting Strategic Management*, Prentice Hall, 1990.
10. Altman, I. A., 'Why Businesses Fail', *Business Strategy*, 3/4 pp15–21, 1983.

INDEX

acid test 180
added value 37, 89–90, 180
adhocracy 65, 180
administrative objectives 26
administrator 72
Allied Lyons 4
alternative scenarios
  novelty 125
  prediction 122–3
Amstrad 84, 99
analysers 71
analytic management style 72
Ansoff's product/market matrix 81–5
ASDA 13–14, 110–11
Ashby's law of requisite variety 123–4
attractiveness/strength matrix *see* directional policy matrix
attributes 76
audit, environmental 45
authority location 65–6
Automobile Association 22
Avis Rent-a-Car 57

BTR 106, 107
Babycham 5
backward integration 84, 180
Barclays Bank 15
Bass 3
behavioural management style 72
benchmarking 34
beneficiaries of reward 101–2
Benson Crisps 122–3
Bird's Eye 48
Body Shop, The 13
Boots the Chemist 62
borrowing 95
Boston Consulting Group
  experience curve 88, 89
  product portfolio matrix 53–4, 180
Bounded rationality 124
Bovril 6
Branson, Richard 59
  see also Virgin Group
break-even analysis 180
break-even point 93, 94
Bristol-Myers Squibb 16–17
British Home Stores (BhS) 7, 22, 28
Brook Bond 4
Bulmer Holdings 88
bureaucracy
  machine bureaucracy 184
  professional bureaucracy 185
Burton Group 26, 38, 54
business ethics 74
business objectives *see* objectives
business re-engineering 49, 50
business strategy 180
  corporate strategy compared 18, 19
  meaning 18
business unit objectives 26
buy in 180

capital investment
  alternatives to 96–7
  equity capital 96
  loan capital 95
cash cows 52, 53, 94, 180
Cathay Pacific 6
central control 107–8
changes
  lead times 14
  mission and 22–3
  resistance to 112–13
Citibank 49
Club 24 15
Co-operative Bank 67
Coca-Cola 48
Comet 25
Compaq 73, 91
competitive advantage 18–19, 180–81
  strategic choice and 99–100
competitive rivalry 40
competitor analysis 39
  worksheets 156–158

complacency 76–7
complexity 120, 123–4
  Ashby's law of requisite variety 123–4
concentration 181
concentric diversification 181
conceptual management style 72
Confederation of British Industry 34
conglomerate 64, 84, 181
  diversification 84
  planning processes 113
consolidation 16, 181
  Ansoff's product/market matrix 83
consumer
  buying behaviour 67
  marketplace analysis 37–9
  orientation 21, 77, 181
  power 39
  satisfaction 56
consumers, core customers 23
contingency plans 99, 128
contracting out 15
control
  central control 107–8
  financial control style 109
  mission as form of 116–17
  procedures 117
  strategic control style 109
  strategic planning style 109
  structure and 109–11
  styles 108–9
control process
  corrective action 115
  data management control 114–15
  intuition 115
  management by objectives 116
  motivation and 116
  negative feedback loops 114
  negotiation and persuasion 116
core customers 23
corporate objectives *see* objectives
corporate planning *see* planning
corporate strategy
  see also strategy
  business strategy compared 18, 19
  meaning 18
cost/benefit analysis 181
costs
  experience curve 88, 89
  leadership 87, 181, 183
  market share and 88–9
  strategic choice and 101
creativity 80–1
crisis management 127–9
critical mass 181
culture 48, 69–72
  see also management style
  classification 71–2
  environmental warning signals 70
  influence of 13
  life-cycle and 73
  market-oriented 69–70
  mission and 71
  organisational development 71
  positioning and 13
  strategic choice and 98
  strategy and 71
current ratio 181
current strategy 7
customer 56
customers
  buying behaviour 67
  core customers 23
  marketplace analysis 37–9
  orientation 21, 77, 181
  power 39

Dalgety 18
data management control 114–15
day-to-day management 2
debtors' ratio 181
decentralisation 181
decision trees 121–2, 181
defenders 71
Delphi techniques 123, 182
demand elasticity 91
demographics 182
departmental objectives 25
design 80
differentiation 87, 182, 183
  focus strategy 89
  strategy 89
Direct Line insurance 67

directional policy matrix 54–5, 180, 182, 183
directive management style 72
directors 29
discounted cash flow 182
disposals 16, 17
diversification 182
  concentric 181
  conglomerate 84
  horizontal 83
  related 61, 66, 84, 186
  unrelated 16, 62–3, 84, 187
divestiture/divestment 16, 17, 182
  Ansoff's product/market matrix 82–3
divisional objectives 26
divisional structure 60–2, 73, 182
  divisionalisation 182
dogs 52, 53, 54, 94, 182
Dorothy Perkins 38
downstream activities 84

economies of scale 182
effectiveness 182
efficiency 46, 182
efficiency ratios 182
elasticity of demand 91
electronic warehousing systems 107, 108
emergent strategy 8, 9, 182
entrepreneurial structure 59–60, 73
entrepreneurs 9, 62, 72, 182
entry barrier 182
environment 131
  choices overcoming threats 98–9
  complexity 120, 123–4
  customer power 39
  external influences 11–12
  industry analysis 34
  influence of 11–12
  internal influences 13–19
  key issues 45
  life-cycles 34–7
  macro-environment 41–2, 43
  marketplace analysis 37–9
  monitoring 33–4
  novelty 120–1, 124–5
  organisation analysis, in 51
  PEST analysis 42–5
  Porter's five-force model 40–1
  predictability 119–20, 121 3
  reallocation of resources 16–17
  stable 44
  supplier power 40
  turbulence *see* turbulent environment
environmental audit 45
equity capital 96, 182
ethics 74
exit barrier 183
experience curve 88, 89, 183
expert systems 67, 183

feasibility of strategy 100–1
feedback 114
financing *see* sources of funds
five-force model 40–1
Five-Pints 90
fledglings 52, 53, 54, 93–4, 183
focus 183
  cost focus 88
  differentiation focus strategy 89
  market segments 89, 90
Ford, Henry 23
forecasts 118–19
Fortune 500 77
forward integration 84, 183
franchising 183
Friedman, Milton 74
functional structure 60, 61, 73, 183
future prospects, focus of strategic management 3

GEC 2, 23, 95
gap analysis 183
  planning gap 51–2
  worksheets 161–2
gearing 96, 183
General Electric business screen 54–5, 183
generic strategy 90, 183
Generic Strategies (Porter) 90
geographical management structure 63–4

Gillette 100
go-fast stripes 57
goals 183
  superordinate 125
Greenalls 17
gross margin 183
growth share matrix 53–4, 180, 183

Handy, CB 72
Hanson Trust 65
hard systems thinking 1
Heinz 37
Heller, Robert 23
Hewlett-Packard 80–1
holding company 64–5, 183
horizontal diversification 83
horizontal integration 83, 183
human resource planning 113

IBM 13, 16, 22, 23, 76, 110
Imagination group 65
impact analysis 44
implementation 2, 111–12
  incremental 6–7
  resistance to change 112–13
importance, strategic option 27–8
In Search of Excellence (Peters and Waterman) 23
incrementalism 45, 183–4
  implementation 6–7
  logical incrementalism 7
  muddling through 8
industry analysis 34
  worksheets 146–148
information technology 14, 108
  organisation structure and 67
integration 184
  backward 84, 180
  forward 84, 183
  horizontal 83, 183
interest groups, influence 13–14
internal analysis *see* internal audit; Seven-S framework
internal audit 47–9, 131
  worksheets 165–6
intrapreneurship 184
investment companies 64–5
investors 29

John Lewis Partnership 116
Johnson and Johnson 128
joint venture 184
just-in-time management 56, 57, 77, 184

key issues 45, 184
key success factors (KSF) 34, 184
  industrial audit 125
  worksheets 153–5
Kingfisher 25, 50
Kodak 58

Laker Airways 89, 90
lead times 14
leader 72
leadership 72–3
  cost leadership 87–8, 181, 183
Levercrest 16, 17, 28
Levi-Strauss 29, 40
life-cycles 4
  Boston Consulting Group product portfolio matrix 53–4
  break-even point 93, 94
  cash cows 52, 53, 94, 180
  decline stage 182
  dogs 52, 53, 54, 94, 182
  fledglings 52, 53, 54, 93–4, 183
  maturity stage 36–7, 94
  meaning 184
  organisational 34–7, 59–65, 73
  problem children 52
  product 34–7, 36, 89
  production capacity 36–7
  profits and 93–4
  stars 53, 54, 94, 186
  technologies 35
Lindblom, CE 8, 45
liquidation 184
liquidity 184
liquidity ratios 184
  gearing 96, 183
loan capital 96
logical incrementalism 7

logistics 184
London International Group 101
long-term aims 3
Lucas Industries 97

machine bureaucracy 184
macro-environment 41–2
  markets in 43
management *see individual types eg* day-to-day management; strategic management
management by objectives (MBO) 116
management style 72–3
  see also culture
  analytic 72
  behavioural 72
  changes 111
  conceptual 72
  leadership 72–3
  life-cycle and 73
  taxonomies 72
market development 7, 83–4, 85, 184
market-oriented culture 69–70
market penetration 184
market price 93
market share 3–4, 94
  costs and 88–9
  relative 186
marketing expenditure 94
marketing mix 184
marketing strategy 25, 26
marketplace analysis 37–9
  beyond boundaries of activities 38–9
  competitor analysis 39
worksheets 149–152
markets
  consolidation 83
  definition 37–8
  differentiation 89–90
  ease of entry 40
  focus 89, 90
  interactions between segments 38
  niche markets 89, 90, 185
  profitability 40–1
  substitutes and alternatives 40
  test markets 119
Marks & Spencer 7, 22, 23, 24, 50, 67, 108
matrix structure 63–4, 73, 184–5
maturity stage 36–7, 94
Mazda 38
Mazola 53
Megatrends (Naisbitt) 118
Mercury Communications 71
Microsoft 76
Miles, RE 71
mission 21–4, 185
  as control 116–17
  change 22–3, 131
  culture derived from 71
  determination of 27–8
  flexibility 22–3
  worksheets 139
mission statement 21–4
Montague Burton 12
Morgan Motor Company 13, 38, 39
motivation 116
muddling through *see* incrementalism
multidivisional structure 62–3, 73, 185
multinational corporation 185
multiple objectives 24

Naisbitt, John 118
negative feedback loops 114
Nestlé Rowntree 33
net present value 185
neural networks 67
niche markets 89, 90
niche strategy 185
Northern Foods 30
novelty 120–1, 124–5
  alternative scenarios 125
  Seven S framework 124–5
Nutrasweet 58

objectives 3–5, 24–7, 25, 26
  administrative 26
  business unit objectives 26
  change 9, 131
  conflicting 25
  corporate 25, 26, 181
  departmental 25
  determination of 27–8

divisional 26
functional 25–6
hierarchy 25–7
in organisation analysis 51
long and short term 24
measurement 27
multiple 24
of plans 2–3
operational 27
personal 28
prioritising 25–7
strategic choice and 98
unquantifiable 27
worksheets 140–42
obsolete products 47
oligopoly 185
operational objectives 27
opportunities 76
see also SWOT analysis
worksheets 174
optimise 185
options *see* strategic options
ordering 49
organisation
adaptation to environment 12
as a whole 2–3
culture 48
development 71
effectiveness 46–7
efficiency 46
organisation analysis 46–58
department by department 47, 48–9
environment and 51
intangibles 48
internal audit 47–9
objectives and 51
organisation as whole 47–50
organisational structure 47–8
portfolio analysis 51–6
Seven S framework 49–50
value chain 56–8
outsourcing 15, 67
overdraft 95

PIMS (Profit Impact of Marketing Strategy) 89, 185
PA Consulting 104
payback period 101
person, culture classification 72
personal objectives 28
PEST analysis 42–5
worksheets 143–145
Peters, TJ 23
Phileas Fogg, market development 6, 7
planned strategies 6–7
planner 72
planning
based on assumptions 118
corporate 181
gap 51–2
human resource planning 113
objectives 2–3
process 113–14
strategic planning 130–7
policy, meaning 98
political priorities 29
Porter, ME 40, 90
Porter's five-force model 40–1, 55
Porter's three generic strategies 183
portfolio analysis 51–6, 185
BCG product portfolio matrix 53–4
directional policy matrix 54–5
General Electric business screen 54–5
interaction between products 55
worksheets 167–71
positioning 5–6
culture and 13
power
culture classification 72
location of 65–6
positions of 65–6
prediction
alternative scenarios 122–3
decision trees 121–2, 181
Delphi technique 123, 182
price elasticity of demand 91
price to earnings ratio 185
Principles 38
prioritising objectives 25–7
problem child 52, 185
product development 7, 14, 83, 85, 185
Ansoff's product/market matrix 83

product improvement 35–6
product life-cycle *see* life-cycles
product portfolio matrix 53–4, 180
product technologies 35
production capacity life-cycles 36–7
production strategy 26
production technologies 35
professional bureaucracy 185
professionalism 60
profit
  as objective 4
  routes to 87
Profit Impact of Marketing Strategy (PIMS) 89, 185
profit margins 4, 93
  suppliers 58
profitability 19
  ratios 185
profits
  break-event point 93, 94
  increasing 91–3
  product life-cycle and 93–4
programmes, meaning 117
promotional activity 4, 94
prospectors 71
public sector
  contracting out 15
  logical incrementalism 7
  objectives 26
  stakeholders 28–9

quality circles 77
question marks 53, 185

RTZ 106, 111
ratio analysis 186
rationality, bounded 124
re-engineering 49, 50
reactors 72
reallocation of resources 16–17
recruitment planning 113
reductionism 45
related diversification 61, 66, 186
  Ansoff's product/market matrix 84
relative market share 186
repositioning 5
research and development 4
  investment 4
resistance to change 112–13
resources 76
  acquisition 16
  additional 14
  consolidation 16
  contracting out 15
  disposals 17
  divestiture 16, 17
  influence of 14–18
  outsourcing 15, 67
  reallocation 16–17
  strengths 15–16
retrenchment 186
  Ansoff's product/market matrix 83
return on capital employed (ROCE) 186
  strategic choice and 101
return on investment (ROI) 89, 96, 180
  as objective 4
rewards 101–2
rights issues 96
risk, attitudes to 48
role, culture classification 72
Rolls Royce 79

Safeway 5, 66
sale and leaseback 96
sales, control process 115
satisfice 186
segmentation 186
Seven S framework 49–50, 110–11, 186
  novelty 124–5
  shared values 50
Simon's concept of bounded rationality 124
simple structure 59–60, 186
Single Market, acquisition of resources 16
skills, Seven Ss 50
Snow, CC 71
The Social Responsibility of Business is to Make a Profit (Friedman) 74
Solex 35
solvency ratios 186

Sonessons 47
Sony 80
sources of funds
  alternatives to capital investment 96–7
  borrowing 95
  equity capital 96
  loan capital 95
  overdraft 95
  retained earnings 95
  sale and leaseback 96
  third party provision of goods and services 96
SPACE matrix 186
staff, Seven Ss 50
stakeholder analysis 28–30, 41
  coalitions 30
  compromises 30
  conflicts 30
  definition 28–9
  trade-offs 29
  worksheets 159–60
stakeholders 186
  influence of 13–14
  reactions to strategic choice 101
stars 53, 54, 94, 186
strategic business units (SBU) 18, 53
  central control 107
  objectives 26
strategic choice
  competitive advantage 99–100
  consequences 99
  criteria for 98–108
  culture 98
  environmental threats 98–9
  evaluation 102–5
  feasibilities 100–1
  objectives 98
  potential rewards 101–2
  resource implications 104
  stakeholder reactions 101
  weighting 104
  worksheets 177–9
strategic issue management 126–7
strategic management
  future impacts 3
  meaning 1–9
  objectives *see* objectives
  organisation as a whole 2–3
  planning and *see* planning
  positioning 5–6
strategic options 76–86
  Ansoff's product/market matrix 81–5
  creativity 80–1
  importance 77–8
  SWOT analysis 78–80, 98, 131, 186
  urgency 77
strategic planning 130–7
  see also planning
  worksheets *see* worksheets
strategy 3
  see also corporate strategy; *individual types eg* business strategy
  changes to 9
  current 7
  generic 183
  Seven S 50
  willingness to accept 100
strategy formulation 6–9
  current strategy 7
  emergent strategy 8, 9
  logical incrementalism 7
  muddling through (incrementalism) 8
  planned strategies 6–7
  unrealised strategy 8
strategy implementation *see* implementation
strengths 76
  see also SWOT analysis
  as resource 15–16
structure 50
  adhocracy 65, 180
  central control 107–8
  centralisation 62
  centralised and decentralised balance 67
  control and 107–8, 109–11
  divisional 60–2, 73, 182
  dual authority 63–4
  entrepreneurial 59–60, 73
  functional 60, 61, 73, 183

geographical management 63–4
holding company 64–5
information technology and 67
innovative organisation 65
matrix structure 63–4, 73, 184–5
multidivisional 62–3, 73, 185
positions of power 65–6
related diversification 66
simple 59–60, 186
unrelated diversification 62–3
style, Seven Ss 50
suboptimisation 186
subsidiaries, objectives 26
superordinate goals, Seven Ss 50
suppliers' power 40
SWOT analysis 78–80, 98, 131, 186
strategy choice criteria from 98
worksheets 172–3
synergy 187
systems, Seven Ss 50

target market 5–6
identification 6
task, culture classification 72
Taunton Cider 88
technostructure 187
test markets 119
threats 76
see also SWOT analysis
Tibbett & Britten 16
time scale 14
The Times 34
Top Man 38
Top Shop 38
top-down approach 1
Toshiba 5
total quality management 187
Trebor Basset 40
turbulence 187
turbulent environment 12, 44, 118–29
complexity 120, 123–4
crisis management 127–9
novelty 120–1, 124–5
predictability 119–20, 121–3
strategic issue management 126–7
turnaround strategy 187

Unilever 39, 66, 113
United Biscuits 48, 98
unrealised strategy 8
unrelated diversification 16, 62–3, 187
Ansoff's product/market matrix 84
urgency, strategic option 77

value chain 56–8, 187
analysis 77
contribution evaluation 57
customer satisfaction 57
internal links 57
negative aspects 57–8
worksheets 163–4
Van den Bergh 16
Virgin Group
divisional structure 62
holding company 64–5
matrix structure 63–4
multidivisional structure 62–3
related diversification 61
simple structure 59–60
unrelated diversification 62–3
'virtual organisations' 15

warehousing
central 110
electronic systems 107, 108
Waterman, RH 23
weaknesses 76
see also SWOT analysis
weighting 104
Wilkinson Sword 100
willingness to accept strategy 100
Woolworth (FW) 22, 50
worksheets
competitor analysis 156–158
gap analysis 161–2
industry 146–148
internal audit 165–6
key success factors 153–5
marketplace 149–152
mission 139
objectives 140–42
opportunity analysis 174
PEST analysis 143–145

portfolio analysis 167–71
stakeholder analysis 159–60
strategic choice 177–9
SWOT analysis 172–3
value chain analysis 163–4

Yves Saint-Laurent 119–20

Z-score 187
zero-based budgeting 187
zero-defects management 77